U0946190

1918年11月7日，梁漱溟的父亲梁济正准备出门，遇到漱溟，二人谈起关于欧战的一则新闻。

“世界会好吗？”梁济问道。

漱溟回答：“我相信世界是一天一天往好里去的。”

“能好就好啊！”梁济说罢就离开了家。

三天之后，梁济投净业湖自尽。

博雅双语
名家名作
精选集

Has Man a Future?
—Dialogues with the Last Confucian

汉英对照

这个世界会好吗?
——梁漱溟晚年口述

梁漱溟 （美）艾恺 著 （美）艾恺 译

外语教学与研究出版社
FOREIGN LANGUAGE TEACHING AND RESEARCH PRESS
北京 BEIJING

图书在版编目（CIP）数据

这个世界会好吗？：梁漱溟晚年口述：英汉对照 / 梁漱溟，（美）艾恺著；（美）艾恺译. — 北京：外语教学与研究出版社，2010.9（2020.4 重印）
ISBN 978-7-5135-0084-5

Ⅰ. ①这… Ⅱ. ①梁… ②艾… Ⅲ. ①英语－汉语－对照读物②梁漱溟（1893～1988）－访谈录 Ⅳ. ①H319.4：K

中国版本图书馆 CIP 数据核字（2010）第 177121 号

出 版 人　徐建忠
系列策划　吴　浩
责任编辑　赵雅茹　蒲　瑶
装帧设计　视觉共振设计工作室
出版发行　外语教学与研究出版社
社　　址　北京市西三环北路 19 号（100089）
网　　址　http://www.fltrp.com
印　　刷　中农印务有限公司
开　　本　650×980　1/16
印　　张　20
版　　次　2010 年 9 月第 1 版　2020 年 4 月第 10 次印刷
书　　号　ISBN 978-7-5135-0084-5
定　　价　45.00 元

购书咨询：（010）88819926　电子邮箱：club@fltrp.com
外研书店：https://waiyants.tmall.com
凡印刷、装订质量问题，请联系我社印制部
联系电话：（010）61207896　电子邮箱：zhijian@fltrp.com
凡侵权、盗版书籍线索，请联系我社法律事务部
举报电话：（010）88817519　电子邮箱：banquan@fltrp.com
物料号：200840001

记载人类文明
沟通世界文化
www.fltrp.com

“博雅双语名家名作”出版说明

1840 年鸦片战争以降，在深重的民族危机面前，中华民族精英“放眼看世界”，向世界寻求古老中国走向现代、走向世界的灵丹妙药，涌现出一大批中国主题的经典著述。我们今天阅读这些中文著述的时候，仍然深为字里行间所蕴藏的缜密的考据、深刻的学理、世界的视野和济世的情怀所感动，但往往会忽略：这些著述最初是用英文写就，我们耳熟能详的中文文本是原初英文文本的译本，这些英文作品在海外学术界和文化界同样享有崇高的声誉。

比如，林语堂的 *My Country and My People*（《吾国与吾民》）以幽默风趣的笔调和睿智流畅的语言，将中国人的道德精神、生活情趣和中国社会文化的方方面面娓娓道来，在美国引起巨大反响——林语堂也以其中国主题系列作品赢得世界文坛的尊重，并获得诺贝尔文学奖的提名。再比如，梁思成在抗战的烽火中写就的英文版《图像中国建筑史》文稿（*A Pictorial History of Chinese Architecture*），经其挚友费慰梅女士（Wilma C. Fairbank）等人多年的奔走和努力，于 1984 年由麻省理工学院出版社（MIT Press）出版，并获得美国出版联合会颁发的“专业暨学术书籍金奖”。又比如，1939 年，费孝通在伦敦政治经济学院的博士论文以 *Peasant Life in China—A Field Study of Country Life in the Yangtze Valley* 为名在英国劳特利奇书局（Routledge）出版，后以《江村经济》作为中译本书名——《江村经济》使得靠桑蚕为生的“开弦弓村”获得了世界性的声誉，成为国际社会学界研究中国农村的首选之地。

此外，一些中国主题的经典人文社科作品经海外汉学家和中国学者的如椽译笔，在英语世界也深受读者喜爱。比如，艾恺（Guy S. Alitto）将他 1980 年用中文访问梁漱溟的《这个世界会好吗——梁漱溟晚年口述》一书译成英文（*Has Man a Future? —Dialogues with the Last Confucian*），备受海内外读者关注；

此类作品还有徐中约英译的梁启超著作《清代学术概论》(*Intellectual Trends in the Ch'ing Period*)、狄百瑞(W. T. de Bary) 英译的黄宗羲著作《明夷待访录》(*Waiting for the Dawn: A Plan for the Prince*),等等。

有鉴于此,外语教学与研究出版社推出"博雅双语名家名作"系列。

博雅,乃是该系列的出版立意。博雅教育(Liberal Education)早在古希腊时代就得以提倡,旨在培养具有广博知识和优雅气质的人,提高人文素质,培养健康人格,中国儒家六艺"礼、乐、射、御、书、数"亦有此功用。

双语,乃是该系列的出版形式。英汉双语对照的形式,既同时满足了英语学习者和汉语学习者通过阅读中国主题博雅读物提高英语和汉语能力的需求,又以中英双语思维、构架和写作的形式予后世学人以启迪——维特根斯坦有云:"语言的边界,乃是世界的边界",诚哉斯言。

名家,乃是该系列的作者群体。涵盖文学、史学、哲学、政治学、经济学、考古学、人类学、建筑学等领域,皆海内外名家一时之选。

名作,乃是该系列的入选标准。系列中的各部作品都是经过时间的积淀、市场的检验和读者的鉴别而呈现的经典,正如卡尔维诺对"经典"的定义:经典并非你正在读的书,而是你正在重读的书。

胡适在《新思潮的意义》(1919 年 12 月 1 日,《新青年》第 7 卷第 1 号)一文中提出了"研究问题、输入学理、整理国故、再造文明"的范式。秉着"记载人类文明、沟通世界文化"的出版理念,我们推出"博雅双语名家名作"系列,既希望能够在中国人创作的和以中国为主题的博雅英文文献领域"整理国故",亦希望在和平发展、改革开放的新时代为"再造文明"、为"向世界说明中国"略尽绵薄之力。

外语教学与研究出版社

人文社科出版分社

第二章 现实问题和人生问题占据着我的头脑 48

第三章 我对他人、世界和自身的看法 150

Preface

I am honored to be able to write a preface to this volume.

First I want to explain how this dialogue between Mr. Liang Shuming and me came about.

I became interested in Mr. Liang's life and career as a graduate student at Harvard University, and took it as the subject of my Ph.D. dissertation. I gathered materials in Taiwan and Hong Kong, as well as sought out and interviewed many of his old friends and acquaintances. Because of the Sino-American political situation at the time, I never had an opportunity to go to Chinese mainland and meet personally the subject of my research, Mr. Liang.

In the first part of 1973 I had my first opportunity to go to Chinese mainland. For an American to be able to go to Chinese mainland at that time was still extremely unusual. Why was I able to make the trip? After President Nixon visited China, several Chinese delegations visited the United States in succession, and I served as their interpreter, and so became a channel of communication between the two countries. So in 1973, my wife and I had this rare opportunity to visit Chinese mainland. At the time, the first request I made of the Chinese was that I hoped I could meet with Mr. Liang. But because it was the time of the Cultural Revolution, and a very sensitive time, my wishes to pay my respects to Mr. Liang were not answered, so I could only return regretfully to America.

In 1979, at the same time as my study of Liang Shuming *The Last Confucian* was published, the Chinese political situation underwent a tremendous change. This current of reform and openness also changed Mr. Liang's life. He had originally been living with his wife in a small room, but then he was moved by his unit, the People's Political Consultative Conference, into Building Number 22, called the "Ministers' Mansion," where many celebrities such as the writer Ding Ling also lived. Having more comfortable quarters, Mr. Liang felt that it was more appropriate for receiving visitors, and immediately thought of ways of contacting me.

One day I suddenly received a phone call from a stranger; it was from an octogenarian named Shi who had been Mr. Liang's student in the 1920s at Peking University. He had just come from Beijing and was delivering a verbal message to me at Mr. Liang's request. It was that Mr. Liang already knew of the publication of *The Last Confucian*, and hoped that he could meet me. A few months passed, and after class one day,

序

我非常荣幸能为这本小书作序。

我想先说说我与梁漱溟先生两人对谈的因缘。

我在哈佛读书的时候，对梁先生的生平志业产生兴趣，以他作为博士论文的主题，在台湾与香港收集相关资料，寻访他的故友旧交。碍于当时中美政治局势，我始终无法前往中国大陆，亲见我研究的对象梁先生。

1973 年初，我头一次有机会前往中国大陆。在当时，一个美国人能到中国大陆去，仍是极不寻常的异例。为什么我能成行呢？这是因为在尼克松总统访华后，几个中国代表团在 1972 年陆续来美，而我充当中文翻译，起了沟通两国的桥梁作用，所以在 1973 年时，我与内人才有这个难得的机会可以造访中国大陆。当时，我向中方提出的第一个请求，便是希望可以同梁先生见面，但由于正值“文革”，时机敏感，我并没有如愿以偿地拜见到梁先生，只能抱憾返美。

1979 年，在我的梁漱溟研究《最后的儒家》出版成书的同时，中国的政治局势起了巨大的变化。这波改革开放的潮流也改变了梁先生的生活。原本与夫人蜗居在狭小房间的梁先生，被政协安置到有“部长楼”之称的 22 号楼，与文化名流如丁玲等对门而居。有了舒适的房舍，梁先生认为比较适宜见客，便即刻想办法与我联系。

某日我突然接到一通陌生的来电，电话那头是一位八旬高龄的石老先生。他是梁先生 20 世纪 20 年代在北大的学生，刚从北京来美，受梁先生所托，捎来口讯，说是梁老已经知道《最后的儒家》出版了，希望可以与我见面。又过了几个月，

a Chinese student suddenly came to see me. She had just come recently from Beijing to join her father in the United States. She gave me Mr. Liang's address, and told me that she had been a neighbor of "Uncle Liang," and that he very much hoped to be able to see me, and to see the work on him that I had published.

I immediately sent him a copy of the book. Before long I received an amicable reply from Mr. Liang, agreeing to my definitely going to Beijing to visit him the next year.

In 1980, the first day I arrived in Beijing, I immediately contacted Mr. Liang. He told me how he had moved to Building Number 22. The next morning, I went to Mr. Liang's residence to visit him formally. All of Mr. Liang's family members, who took my visit very seriously, were also there. Mr. Liang introduced me to his family. I then presented him with some Harvard University souvenirs. I also gave him works of his father's. After all of those years and experiencing diverse setbacks, I had finally got to meet Mr. Liang. Sitting face to face, with only a small table between us, we began our chats. In the two weeks that followed, I went to the Liang's home every morning to ask questions of Mr. Liang. I put in order the recordings of our dialogues, part of which later was included in Mr. Liang's published collected works.

In our talks, through Mr. Liang I came to understand more fully the trait of traditional Chinese intellectuals. This is most worthy of mentioning.

During the two weeks of intensive conversation, in the first few days Mr. Liang spoke to me a great deal about Buddhism, which perplexed me, and so I asked, "Didn't you abandon Buddhist thought a long time ago?" He answered that he didn't really abandon it. We talked about the title of my book *The Last Confucian*, which fixed him as a Confucian. He said that he could accept the title. Yet sometimes he would express to me that Marxist-Leninist science was very good. When we spoke about traditional Chinese culture, he also praised Daoism. Once, because he had organized the Democratic League, he met with George Marshall. He evaluated Marshall very highly, and thought that he was a good person because he was a pious Christian.

At the time, I didn't quite understand. How could a person be both a Buddhist and a Confucian, and also identify with Marxist-Leninist

一天课后，有个中国学生突然来见我。她不久前才从北京来美与父亲团聚。她拿着梁先生的联络地址，告诉我她旧日的邻居“梁伯伯”十分希望可以见到我，看到我所出版的关于他的著作。

我即刻将拙著寄给他，不久便获得梁先生友善的回应，约定好次年一定到北京去拜访他。

1980 年我到北京第一天，马上便去寻找梁先生，他告诉了我他是如何搬到 22 号楼来的。第二天早上，我到梁家正式拜见，梁先生所有的亲人都出现在那里，对于我的来访相当郑重其事。梁先生将我介绍给他的家人，我则送予他哈佛大学的纪念品以及一幅他父亲的遗作。经过种种波折，在这多年之后，我终于得以与梁先生仅仅隔着一方小几，相对而坐，开始对谈。之后的两周，我天天一早便到梁家拜访，请教梁先生。我将对话的内容录音整理，后来收进梁先生的全集。回顾两人对谈因缘，真是感慨万千。

在我们的对谈中，我透过梁先生理解到中国传统知识分子的一种特质。这是最值得一提的部分。

在我们密集谈话的两周里，头两三天梁先生多与我说关于佛家的想法，让我很感疑惑，便问：“您不是早在多年前便公开放弃佛家思想了吗？”他说他算放弃也算没放弃，谈到拙作的标题《最后的儒家》将他定位为一位儒者，他表示他可以接受。然而有时他也向我表示马列主义的科学很好；当谈到中国传统文化，他亦赞美道教。有次提到他因组织民盟而见到马歇尔，他对马歇尔的评价很高，认为他是个好人，因为他是一个虔诚的基督徒。

那时我相当不解，一个人如何可以既是佛家又是儒家？

thought and approve of Christianity? Later I finally grasped it. This ability to blend mutually contradictory thought is a special characteristic of typical traditional Chinese intellectuals.

Although, during the Spring and Autumn and Warring States Periods, many schools of thought contended and debated with one another, the scholars of the time did not recognize themselves to be a specific school. For example, when we now discuss Mencius and Xunzi, we recognize them as Confucian, even though one said that human nature was good, and the other that human nature was evil. They were followers of Confucius, but at that time, even Confucius did not necessarily recognize himself to be "Confucian." The academic classifications we are used to today—Sima Qian (in "Preface to the *Histories of Sima Qian*") and his father Sima Tan (in "A Summary of the Six Schools")—actually first classified the various pre-Qin thinkers and invented the system that we use today.

I think that Chinese culture is actually an eclectic blend of many kinds of thought that seem to be incompatible, yet at the same time is a culture that likes to classify things. It's easily seen that actually most Chinese intellectuals amalgamated various kinds of thought into one eclectic body. For example, although the Cheng brothers (Cheng Hao and Cheng Yi), Zhu Xi, Lu Xiangshan and Wang Yangming are all Neo-Confucians who focus on the nature of the mind, there are differences among them. There are Buddhist elements in their thought. Although the late Qing Dynasty intellectuals such as Liang Qichao and Zhang Taiyan were at the two opposite extremes politically and on the New Text/Old Text controversy, they both amalgamated Buddhism, Western thought and Confucianism into their individual thought.

So this perhaps explains why I, having been trained in modern academic standards and categories, thought that it was impossible for someone to be simultaneously a believer in Marxism-Leninism and Confucianism. As far as Mr. Liang was concerned, though, this was not in the least a problem. Looked at in this way, Mr. Liang was still quite a traditional Chinese intellectual.

In my opinion, the various pre-Qin philosophers were each on different paths, but they all assumed the same cosmology, that the universe was an organic whole, with each element in that whole interconnected. So, in such a cosmology, there are no absolute dichotomies and contradictions, only relative ones. This worldview was the underlying bedrock of the thought of all Chinese intellectuals, and so various different elements of thought could coexist in an individual's thought without the currents conflicting.

既认同马列思想又赞许基督教？后来终于想通了，这种可以融合多种相互矛盾的思想，正是典型的中国传统知识分子的特质。

春秋战国百家争鸣时，虽有许多辩论，但百家学者并不认为自己是特定的一家，比方说现在我们讨论孟子与荀子，认为他们虽然一言性善，一言性恶，但都是儒家，是孔子的信徒，然而在当时，即便是孔子也未必认为自己是儒家。我们今日习以为常的学术分类，其实是司马迁在《太史公自序》中论及其父司马谈的《论六家要旨》，为诸子百家分门别派而发明出来的体系。

我认为中国文化本就是个融合许多看似不相容的思想于一体、却同时又喜欢分门别类的文化。只需留心便会发现，其实大部分的中国知识分子都是融合各类思想于一身。比方程朱陆王，同为新儒家，虽然讲义理心性，歧异很大，但他们的思想中都含有许多佛家的成分。晚清的知识分子，如梁启超、章太炎，固然在政治立场与今古文经学上分踞两极，但同样都将佛家、西方思想及儒家融入他们个人的学思中。

这解释了为什么对于受现代学术规范训练的我而言，一个人不可能同时是儒家，又是马列信徒，但对梁先生来说，这完全不是问题。从这点看来，梁先生仍是一个相当传统的中国知识分子。

依我浅见，先秦诸子虽然路线不同，但他们都共享一个宇宙观，认为宇宙是一体而有机的，天地间的每个成分跟其他的成分相互关联，所以在这样的宇宙观里，没有绝对的矛盾，只有相对的矛盾。这种宇宙观，经历数千年，仍深植在中国知识分子思想的底层，是以各种不同的思想成分，可以共存在一个人的思想里，运行不悖。

The greater part of the content of our talks was Mr. Liang's responding to my questions about historical figures in the early twentieth century. Instead of asking him about his contacts and associations in the past, why didn't I just quietly listen to Mr. Liang expostulate his thinking? I study history, and naturally want to preserve much of the historical materials. As far as I know, Mr. Liang was the last person who had personally participated in those several decades of violent cultural change and who was still healthy and clear-headed, and who, moreover knew and had contact with so many important intellectuals. His memories were of great value, so I went well beyond my role of interviewer in guiding the conversation in hopes that these unique experiences of his could be recorded for posterity.

This special case of the biographer finally meeting the biographee only after publication of the biography is unprecedented in modern Chinese history. After having had these talks with Mr. Liang, I added a final chapter to *The Last Confucian* to supplement and revise the original, especially the section on his suffering during the Cultural Revolution. Because I had not been able to contact him before the book was finished, and because there was no other relevant documentation available, I did not know the details, and so couldn't include them in the book. Only after we talked did I know the real situation and added it in this last chapter. On the whole, I did not revise the structure or content of the book after meeting Mr. Liang. After our talks I discovered Mr. Liang's "unity of inner feelings and outer action." His writings had honestly reflected his impressions. He never disguised his true feelings and thoughts in order to be in tune with the times or the situation, so the Mr. Liang that I had seen through his writings and the real-life Mr. Liang with whom I talked were identical. So although I was fated not to meet him before the book was completed, I was still able, through his writings, to know Mr. Liang's real personality and ways of thinking.

Speaking as an historian, I think that a hundred years from now, Mr. Liang will still occupy an important position in history, not only because of the uniqueness of his thought, but because of his truthful character—his unvaring consistency between thought and deed. Compared to many other 20th century Confucians, he is closest to the traditional in that he put his ideas into actual practice in real life, rather than just talk about Confucianism within the academy. Mr. Liang's life embodied the ideals of Confucianism and of Chinese culture. In this respect, he will always have a singular position in history.

Guy S. Alitto

梁先生与我谈话的内容，有一大部分是我向他请教 20 世纪初的人事。为何我不静静听梁先生抒发他的想法，而要询问他许多过去的交往呢？我是历史研究者，自然会希望多多保存历史资料，而梁先生是我所知最后一个健在且头脑清明的人，曾经亲身经历、参与过这几十年中国文化剧变，并且和许多重要知识分子相知相交过。他的回忆是宝贵的，所以我才僭越地主导谈话，希望可以将这些独一无二的经验记录下来。

像我这样，等到传记完成出书之后，作者才终于见到传主，在中国近代史学界可能是前所未有的特例。与梁先生谈话之后，我在《最后的儒家》一书最后加上一章，增补修订了原书的一些未竟之处，特别是他在“文革”期间受苦一节，由于我未能在书成前与他见面，也没有相关记录流通，所以不知悉细节，也无法载入书中，后来与他谈话后才知道实情，补充在这最后一章里。大体来说，我并没有在亲见梁先生之后，修改拙作的结构与内容。与他谈话之后，我发现梁先生表里如一，他的文章诚实地反映出他的观感，未曾因为要顺应时局而掩饰真心，所以我透过文字所见到的梁先生，与我后来实际上对谈的梁先生是一致的。是以我虽无缘在书成前见到他，但透过他的文章，我仍然深刻地认识到梁先生的真实的性格与想法。

从一个历史研究者的角度看来，我认为就算再过 100 年，梁先生仍会在历史上占有重要的地位，不单单是因为他独特的思想，也因为他表里如一的人格。与许多 20 世纪的儒家信徒相比较起来，他更逼近传统的儒者——确实地在生活中实践他的思想，而非仅仅在学院中高谈。梁先生以自己的生命去体现对儒家和中国文化的理想，就这点而言，他永远都是独一无二的。

艾　恺

I'm not a scholar;

我不是学问家，而是一个思想家

I'm a thinker.

我完全不够一个学问家。
我承认自己是一个有思想的人，
并且是本着自己思想而去实行、实践的人，
独立思考，表里如一。

I am completely unqualified to be a man of learning.

I do admit that I'm someone who has his own ideas,

who acts according to his own ideas and puts them into practice.

I am someone of independent thought.

I have consistency between my thoughts and my actions.

Confucianism and Buddhism are my basis.

Liang: I mean, in talking with you, I hope that you will understand the sources of my thought. The basis of my thought is Confucianism and Buddhism. This is the most important thing. That is more important than understanding my past. I hope you can know more about Confucianism and Buddhism. I want to tell you all about my Confucianism and Buddhism. I mean, I will put the emphasis in our conversations on this, rather than on my personal affairs or my opinions. Because Confucianism and Buddhism are my basis, if you can understand the basis, that would be best of all, the most important thing. Not only do I hope this for you but also I hope that Europeans and Americans can better understand these two schools of thought: Confucianism and Buddhism.

Alitto: Mr. Liang, has your interest in Buddhism and Buddhist studies been rekindled, or increased, as you have grown older? At the time of the May Fourth Movement, you publicly abandoned Buddhism and converted to Confucianism.

Liang: That is not relevant. You may say I abandoned Buddhism, but I really didn't abandon it. Originally I did want to leave the secular world and become a monk. What I abandoned was my plan for leaving the secular world and becoming a monk. But in my thought, on the philosophical level, I did not abandon Buddhism.

Alitto: Oh, I now understand a bit better. Actually, I also wrote about the same thing in the book [*The Last Confucian: Liang Shu-ming and the Chinese Dilemma of Modernity,* called *The Last Confucian* for short hereafter], that is, you hadn't completely abandoned Buddhism, but you felt that the problems of the time didn't need Buddhism as much as Confucianism. So because of this, you began to study Confucianism.

Liang: Let me explain myself. When I was young, around sixteen or seventeen, I wanted to become a monk. I didn't give up this ambition until I reached the age of twenty-nine. If I wanted to become a monk, I could not get married. But a person is not only composed of a brain. He is more than just thought. He cannot leave his corporal body. If I had really followed my ambition early on and had gone to a monastery, there probably would have been no problem, and [my life] would probably have been most congenial, and I would have lived out my life quietly.

 我的思想的根本就是儒家跟佛家

梁：我的意思啊，我们彼此谈话，我还是希望你了解我的思想的根本，我的思想的根本就是儒家跟佛家。我的意思就是，如果能够对我的根本的思想——就是对佛家跟儒家多了解，比什么都好，比了解我的过去的一些事情都重要。我希望于你的，就是多了解儒家，多了解佛家，我愿意把我所懂得的儒家跟佛家说给你听。我的意思是把我们的谈话重点放在这个地方，而不是重在我个人的事情。因为佛家的跟儒家的是我的根本，所以如果了解这个根本，是最好，最要紧。不但是我期望于你，并且我是期望欧美人能够多了解这两家，一个儒家，一个佛家。

艾：梁先生，您现在年纪很大了，就是说，对佛教、佛学的兴趣有没有好像恢复了或者增加了？就是说，这个五四时代，您就好像是放弃了佛学而转入儒学。

梁：那个都不大相干，说放弃，也没有放弃，不过是，原来想出家做和尚，把这个“出家做和尚”放弃了，在思想上还是那样。

艾：啊，现在明白一点。其实我书里也是这么写的（指《最后的儒家——梁漱溟与中国现代化的两难》，以下简称为《最后的儒家》），就是说您不是完全放弃，不过觉得目前的问题不太需要佛学，比较需要儒学。因为这个关系，您就开始研究儒家。

梁：我说明我自己啊，我是年纪很小，比如说十六七岁就想出家为僧。那么这个志愿到了 29 岁才放弃这个念头，不出家了。出家当和尚不能娶妻子，可是一个人呢，他不单是一个有头脑、有思想的，他还脱离不开身体。假定啊，如果真是从自己的当初的那个志愿，很早就出家到庙里去了，大概也没有什么问题，也可能很相安，可能没有什么问题。

But before I could leave the secular world and enter a monastery, I was drawn into Peking University to teach philosophy by Mr. Cai Yuanpei. Because of this, my life underwent a change. What change was this? I didn't go off to a monastery, but instead I scurried off into the world of learning and the company of intellectuals. It is difficult to avoid having a spirit of competition. This desire to excel over others arises from the corporeal. If I had been as I first wanted, very early leaving secular life for a monastery, that could have been peaceful and stable, walking a calm path. But when I got to the university and into the company of a lot of intellectuals, debates developed easily, and created a desire to excel over others. This desire to excel over others arises from the corporeal. The problem of sex easily arises from the corporeal. A monk does not need to get married; he is able to live in a monastery and can completely forget [sex], and can completely want no part of taking a wife. But when I got to the university, and was together with intellectuals, often I had this desire to excel over others. This was a corporeal problem. Once it arose, I also wanted to marry.

不过没有很早地出家，就被蔡元培先生拉去，在北京大学要我讲哲学。走上这样一步，就起了变化。走上这一步就是什么样子呢？就是不是去到庙里当和尚，而跑到知识界，跟知识分子在一起。同知识分子在一起，他难免就有知识分子对知识分子这种好胜，就是彼此较量，这个好胜的心是从身体来的。如果是像当初想的，很早出家到庙里去，那个可以也很相安，很平稳，走一种很冷静的路子吧。可是一到大学里头，同许多知识分子在一起，彼此容易有辩论，就引起了好胜之心。这个好胜之心是身体的，是身体的他就容易有那个两性的问题。和尚是不要娶妻的，他在庙里头能够住下去，可以完全忘掉，可以完全不想娶妻。可（我）到了大学，同知识分子在一起，常常有这种好胜之心，这个是身体问题，身体问题来了，这个时候也就想结婚了。

Buddhism

● The Buddhist attitude toward life

Liang: A person is not just of this one life. A person's real substance is transmitted from the distant past down through time. He has a very long and distant past. So his so-called "fate" is none other than his past and his background. A man's life and destiny is decided by his past.

Alitto: Is this related to Buddhism?

Liang: Yes. Buddhism is... "Life, divided into endless instants, is at best similar and continuous; the meaning of life is neither interrupted nor persistent." It is linked, part of a continuous process. The me of today is like the me of the past, but isn't identical. Strictly speaking, the me of a previous period and the me of the present are different entities. So a person, from the time he is a small child growing up to old age—like me, I'm over 80 years old—is changing every instant, different every instant. As for this difference, simply speaking, in one aspect, the body is different; the brain is different; the influence from outside has long been different. So all is different, but within the differences is some similarity. So we call it "similar and continuous." In the phrase "neither interrupted nor persistent," "nor persistent" means "not perpetual as before," or you could say "not permanent." So "neither interrupted nor persistent" does not mean permanent, but it is still uninterrupted. This is to say that the present me is not the me of just now, they are not the same thing, but there is no interruption either—it still continues on. That life is "similar and continuous" not only means that there is similarity and continuity between the me of one year old and the me of two years old, and the me of three years old; it also means that after death this similarity and continuity is not broken. This is the Buddhist attitude toward life.

There are three realms (*trailokya*) talked about in the Buddhist scriptures. This is the Buddhist attitude toward life. The first is called "the realm of sensuous desire" (*kāmadhātu*)—the primal wants for food, drink and sex. This is all desire. The second is called "the realm of form" (*rūpadhātu*). The third realm is called "the formless realm of pure spirit" (*arūpadhātu*). The Buddhist scriptures have it this way, but it seems that this is not a theory created by the Buddhist scriptures. Rather, it seems that this is a common belief in India; it is commonly held that there are

贰 佛家

• 佛家对生命的一个看法

梁： 人不是就是这一生，人是从很远的流传下来的，他的过去很长、很远。所谓定力，不是别的，就是他的过去、他的背景，他总是要受过去的背景的决定。

艾： 那这是跟佛教有关系的观念啊?

梁： 对。佛教它叫做"相似相续，非断非常"。"相似相续"——它是连续的，相似就是了，今天的我和昨天的我很相似，已经不同了，只是相似。严格地讲，前一个时间的我跟现在时间的我已经不同了，一个人从一个小孩长大，像我八十多岁，时时刻刻在变化，时时刻刻在不同。这个不同一方面简单地讲，他自己身体就不同了嘛，头脑不同了，外面给他的影响也早已不同了，所以都是在不同之中，但不同之中也有一定的相似，所以叫"相似相续"。"非断非常"——"非常"，就是不是常恒如故，中国人本来是"常"跟"恒"连着的，也可以说"恒常"，也可以说"常恒"。"非断非常"，不是常恒的，可又不断，"非常"就是现在的我跟刚才的我不是一回事了，可是也没有断，仍然还是相续的。"相似相续"不单是说我一岁的时候跟我两岁的时候还是相似相续、三岁的时候相似相续，不单是如此，是说死后也没有完。这个是佛家的对生命的一个看法。

佛典里头有三界——"界"就是"世界"的"界"：第一个叫欲界，欲就是有欲望，想要饮食男女，这个都是欲望；第二个是色界——"颜色"的"色"；第三个是无色界。佛典里这样说，好像不是佛典创立的说法，而是印度好像普遍有这个信仰，

these three realms. The primal desires exist only in the realm of sensuous desire. It does not exist in the realm of form. In the realm of form there is still gender difference, but no food or drink, no intercourse between male and female. In the formless realm of pure spirit, there is nothing at all. The Buddhist scriptures contain such a theory.

● Hinayana is leaving the secular world.

Liang: We were just talking about my desire, when I was young, to become a monk, so I can be considered a Buddhist in certain respects. But a Buddhist must be viewed from two aspects and, you could say, must be discussed in two parts. Primitive Buddhism, which we can call Hinayana, emphasized leaving the secular world. What does "leaving the secular world" mean? "To leave the secular world" means to leave "Production and Annihilation" (or Birth and Death; *utpàdanirodha*). What do we mean by the "world" (the finite, impermanent world)? That is, the endless cycle of birth and death. In Buddhist terminology this is called the "Wheel of Transmigration" (*samsara*), meaning that this life is all similar and continuous.

The Hinayana school laid down three conditions. The first condition is all phenomena (*sarva dharma*) are impermanent (*anitya*). That is, there are no permanent, constant things. Everything is in constant flux. The second point is that all dharmas are non-self; they have no ego. All phenomena and all dharmas are different. The first point is—"Whatever is phenomenal is impermanent." All are flowing, in flux. That is, the cycle of life is like flowing water, in continuous flux. So, they say, "Whatever is phenomenal is impermanent." The second is that no dharma has an ego. There are two kinds of dharma. One is effective or phenomenal dharma (*Samskrta Dharma*). The other is dharma not subject to causation, condition or dependence (*Asamskrta Dharma*). The first is the dharma of birth and death (*utpàdanirodha*). The second is the eternal, supramundane dharma, "immortal—neither dying nor being reborn" (*anirodhānupāda*). Some people ask, "Can the finite impermanent world have something permanent and eternal in it?" The Buddhist answer is that if there are the birth/death cycle there would be something that neither is born nor dies. Birth-Death and No-Birth No-Death are a single thing, not two separate entities. That is to say, the dharma of birth and death and the dharma of the eternal are reducible to each other.

普遍地说有这个三界。饮食男女，在欲界才有，到了色界没有了，色界还有男女，没有饮食，没有男女的相交，到了无色界那就是什么都没有。佛典里头有这个说法。

- **小乘佛教主要是出世**

梁：……我刚才提到过了，从小的时候就想出家当和尚，所以我可以说是一个佛教徒。佛教徒得从两面看，也可以说从两层上来看。佛教，原始佛教普通管它叫小乘教，小乘教主要是出世。什么叫做出世呢？出世就是要出生灭，（出）世间。怎么样叫世间呢？就是生生灭灭，生灭不已。那么在佛家，它就说是轮回。轮回，它是说生命是"相似相续"。

这个小乘自己规定下来三个条件，一个条件就是"诸行无常"——"常恒"的"常"——没有常恒的东西，都是在变化流行中，这是头一个。第二点是"诸法无我"。头一句话是"诸行无常"，第二句话是"诸法无我"。"诸法"跟"诸行"不一样了，头一句是"诸行"，第二句换作"诸法"。因为"诸行"是流行，就是说生灭，生灭不已。生灭不已好像是水流一样，流行变化。第一点是讲流行变化，所以叫"诸行无常"。第二句话是"诸法无我"。"诸法无我"说有两种法，所以加一个"诸"，"诸法"不是一种法。"诸法"是哪两种呢？一种叫做"有为法"，一种叫做"无为法"。"有为法"就是生灭法，"无为法"就是不生不灭。那么有人问：这个世间还有不生不灭的吗？佛家回答：有生灭，就有不生不灭。生灭、不生不灭是一回事，不是两回事。这是说"有为法"和"无为法"是一而二、二而一。

The first condition is all phenomena (*sarva dharma*) are impermanent (*anitya*). The second point is that all dharmas are non-self. No matter which of the two is concerned, there is no ego. Man is one of "all living beings" (*sattva*). From the lowest organism—the most primitive amoeba—to man, all develop from having "egos." All must eat. All must take from the environment. All organisms, from the most primitive right up to man (as the highest), all share something. What is it? They all seek satisfaction from the external, from the environment. In the Buddhist view, this is a mistake, a loss of their basic nature. What is the basic nature? That is "satisfied and content with their own nature, with no dissatisfactions." This is Buddha. Don't regard Buddha as a god or a ruler. It's not like that. So what is Buddha? Buddha is the thing-in-itself of the universe. The nomenon of the universe can be said to have all inside. All things are inside. The phenomena are all inclusive. Since everything is inside, it has nothing. Nothingness. According to Buddhist doctrines, there are two aspects. One is embracing all phenomena in the cosmos; but all the same it is ultimate nothingness. These are two aspects of the same thing. The Buddha is to leave the world. The mundane world is an endless cycle of birth and death, and this, together with the eternal, perpetual aspect of the world, although seemingly two entities, in reality is the same thing. Didn't I just mention the Hinayana Primitive Buddhist doctrine, the doctrine that "all phenomena are impermanent" and that "nothing has an ego"? The third doctrine is Nirvana—calm and quiet, free from temptation and distress. This is Hinayana. The three Hinayana principles are the only complete Buddhadharma (the law preached by the Buddha).

● Mahayana—why I am both a Buddhist and a Confucian

Liang: The Mahayana school, building on the foundation of the Hinayana, had a great reversal, a major revision. The Hinayana is the Way of the Arhat (the perfect man of Hinayana). The Mahayana is the Way of Bodhisattva. The Mahayana does not escape from the mundane world.

The Mahayana doctrine are these two principles: "non-abandonment of sentient beings" and "non-residence in Nirvana." What does this call for? The doctrine is that the Buddha will return to the mundane world. The Hinayana wants to avoid the trouble of endless cycle of birth and death. The Mahayana has already transcended the endless cycle of birth and

第一条是"诸行无常"，第二条是"诸法无我"。无论"有为法"或者"无为法"，都没有"我"。众生——人也是众生，从那个最低等的生物——原始生物阿米巴，都是从有"我"来的，它都要吃东西，都要向外取。一切生物，从原始生物起一直到人——人是最高的啦，都有一个相同的一点，哪一点相同呢？就是向外取足——足是满足，向外边来满足自己。向外取足，都是错误，在佛家看都是错误，都是丧失了本性。本性是什么呢？本性是自性圆满，无所不足。这个自性圆满，无所不足，就是"佛"。这个"佛"，不要把它看作是一种什么神啊，或者是什么上帝啊、主宰啊，不是那回事。"佛"是什么呢？"佛"是宇宙本体，这个宇宙本体也可以说是什么都在内了，万事万物都在内了，五颜六色很复杂的都在内，可是都在内了，它也就是什么都没有了。按佛家的道理说，就是这两面，一面是森罗万象，一面是空无所有，这个两面是一回事。"佛"就是出世，世间就是生灭，所以出世间，就是不生不灭，而生灭跟不生不灭好像是两面，好像是两个东西，不是，是一回事。原始佛教第一是"诸行无常"，第二是"诸法无我"，第三呢，它叫"涅槃寂静"。这个是小乘，小乘具备这三点，才是佛法，缺一样不是佛法。

- **大乘佛教——我为什么既是一个佛教徒，又是一个儒教徒**

梁： 大乘佛法、大乘佛教是在小乘的基础上，基础就是刚才说的那三句话，在小乘的基础上来一个大翻案。小乘是罗汉道，大乘是菩萨道。大乘道是在小乘道的基础上来个大翻案，就是它不出世，它的话是这么两句话，叫做"不舍众生，不住涅槃"。"不舍众生，不住涅槃"，它要怎样呢？它要回到世间来，它不舍开众生。小乘好像是躲避开生死的麻烦，大乘呢，它也已经超出生死了，可以到了不生不灭。但是呢，引用一句儒家的

death, and so could enter the eternal realm. But that seems, to quote a Confucian saying, "to attend to one's own virtue in solitude—to protect oneself, but alone." The Bodhisattva and the Arhat are different. The Arhat solves the problem for himself, and strives for purity and salvation for himself. The Bodhisattva does not abandon the rest of living things. The Bodhisattva wants to return to the mundane world and already has the possibility of not being born nor dying. But the Bodhisattva still wants to return to the world. Why? Because of non-abandonment of living things... That is to say, the Hinayana rule is to go beyond this world; the Mahayana, given a choice, still returns to this world. This is the Mahayana Way.

So, in my own case, I admit to being a follower of Buddhism; I would not deny being a follower of Confucius either. Why? Why don't I deny it? Because this Way of the Mahayana Bodhisattva—I want to follow the Way of the Bodhisattva—is "not to abandon sentient beings" and "not to reside in Nirvana." So I want to go into the world. Because of this, all through my life, for example, everyone knows that I worked in rural reconstruction, or rural movement, and that I worked in politics as a mediator between the two parties (that is, national affairs), especially when Japan invaded China, so would this be considered "leaving the mundane world" or not? This [activity] does not in the slightest go against "leaving the mundane world." Because this is what? It is the Way of the Bodhisattva.[1] This is not Hinayana. Hinayana wants to go into the mountains, to some monastery and not emerge. Mahayana is "non-abandonment of sentient beings" and "non-residence in Nirvana." You can say that I am a Confucian, a follower of Confucius, and you can say that I am a follower of Siddhartha, because there is no conflict or contradiction [between the two].

Alitto: No conflict between the two. This is a relatively new way of putting it. For example, during the Tang Dynasty, or before then when Buddhism had just reached China, there was conflict between the two. So you are saying...

Liang: Insufficient understanding. The enlightened person has no problem. So, it seems that the Song Confucians had rejected Buddhism and Daoism. I think that it was a question of insufficient understanding. For the wise, enlightened person, there is no obstruction to understand; he sees everything clearly. If there is obstruction, it is that you create an obstruction for yourself. But as a matter of fact, it is not necessary. The enlightened person transcends this. Quite a few of the Song Dynasty Confucians like Master Zhu (Zhu Xi) rejected Buddhism and Daoism.

话——“独善其身”，菩萨跟罗汉不同，罗汉好像自己解决了问题，求得清静，菩萨是不舍众生，他要回到世间来。他已经具备了不生不死的那个可能了，但是，他还要回到世间来，为什么？因为他不舍众生。……这个就是说，小乘以出世为规矩，大乘则出而不出，不出而出，仍回到世间来，大乘是这个样子。

那么就说到我自己，我自己承认我是个佛教徒，如果说我是一个儒教徒我也不否认。为什么呢？为什么也不否认呢？就是因为这个大乘菩萨。我是要行菩萨道，行菩萨道嘛，就“不舍众生，不住涅槃”，所以我就是要到世间来。因此我的一生，譬如大家都知道我搞乡村建设、乡村运动，我在政治上也奔走，奔走于两大党之间，就是为国家的事情，特别是在日本人侵略中国的时候，所以这个算是出世不算是出世呢？这个与出世一点不违背，因为这是什么呢，这是菩萨道，这不是小乘佛法，小乘佛法就要到山里头去了，到庙里头去了，不出来了，大乘佛法就是“不舍众生，不住涅槃”。说我是儒家、是孔子之徒也可以，说我是释迦之徒也可以，因为这个没有冲突，没有相反。

艾： 没有冲突，这个说法是比较新的。比如唐朝的时候，唐朝以前佛教刚到中国的时候，是有冲突啊，那您说……

梁： 不够通达，高明的人通达无碍。所以像是宋儒吧，就有点排佛，排斥道家，在我看就是不够通达。通达的人呢，无碍，没有滞碍，什么事情都看得很通。有碍，是你自己在那里给自己设了妨碍，原来是可以不必的，高明人他就超出来了。宋儒像朱子他们，朱熹他们，有不少儒者都排佛呀，排道家呀。

● Discipline, meditation, wisdom & the stories of "Stick" and "Shout" in Chan School

Alitto: Yesterday you said that you were a Buddhist all along.[2]

Liang: Because very early when I was quite young, a teenager, I wanted to become a monk.

Alitto: Thereupon to the present you have preserved your original...

Liang: It's still that way, but now I don't have to become a monk. In fact, I still want to. If I would be allowed to go live in a mountain monastery, I would be quite happy.

Alitto: Yes. Do you still meditate or do Buddhist cultivation...?

Liang: The basic way involves three words (Liang writes out the words for Alitto to see): discipline (*sila*), meditation (*dhyāna*) and wisdom (*prajñā*). These are disciplines that must be maintained. There are many rules of discipline. For example, one cannot marry. If you have already married, you must leave home and become a monk. Killing is forbidden, eating meat is forbidden, and so on. There are many prohibitions. Only after observing these prohibitions can you achieve meditation (referring to the trance state that we just mentioned). So only after you have observed the prohibitions can you achieve Samadhi. Only through this can you achieve wisdom. Buddhism does not hold what we commonly regard as intelligence and wisdom to be "wisdom." Buddhism regards that kind of intelligence as merely a kind cleverness and perceptiveness, not genuine wisdom, not the Great Wisdom. Great Wisdom comes only through Samadhi, and through it one has a breakthrough in consciousness.

Of course, everyone knows that in the past there were thirteen different schools of Buddhism in China; an important and well-developed one was Chan.[3] In Chan Buddhism there is a saying that expresses its special feature or characteristic. What was the Chan school's special feature? It's "not relying upon language for explanation." So, language and writing are not needed; it is not based upon language and writing. The Chan school was quite well-developed. There was a book called *Jingde Records of the Transmission of the Lamp*. Later there were many more *Sequels to Records of the Transmission of the Lamp*. Altogether there were five books combined to constitute the *Five Lamps Combined*. All tell Chan school stories. Laymen can't understand these stories.

• “戒、定、慧”与禅宗故事中的“棒喝”

艾： 您昨天说，您一直都是佛教徒。

梁： 因为我很早、很年青的时候，十几岁的时候，就想出家。

艾： 于是到现在您还是保存原来的……

梁： 还是那样，不过现在是不必出家了。其实还是想出家，假如说是让我去住到一个山上庙里头去，那我很高兴。

艾： 是。那梁先生还打坐啊，修佛的……

梁： 本来按佛家它有三个字，叫做“戒、定、慧”，这三个字——“戒、定、慧”，就是一定要守戒律。戒律有好几条，比如说是不能娶妻，如果娶了妻之后也要离开家，出家为僧嘛。还有不杀生、不吃肉等等。戒有好几条，从“戒”才能生“定”，“定”就是刚才说的入定。一定要守戒才能够入定。由“定”才能够生“慧”，“慧”是智慧。普通我们的这种聪明智慧，在佛家不认为是智慧，这个算是一种智巧，不是真正的智慧，不是大智。大智一定要从“定”才有，从“定”才能够破悟。

当然在佛家，大家都知道，在中国过去曾经有十三宗，宗派有十三宗，很重要的、很发达的是禅宗。禅宗有那个话，讲出禅宗的特色、特点。禅宗的特点是什么呢？叫做“不立语言文字”——立是“建立”的“立”——不立语言文字，言语、文字都不要，不建立在语言文字上。禅宗在中国很发达，有一个书叫做《景德传灯录》，后来比这个《景德传灯录》还多，《续传灯录》，一共陆续出有五本，合起来叫《五灯会元》，都是讲禅宗的故事。在那里头的故事，外行人不懂。

For example, a famous successful Chan master is called "Most Virtuous" (*Bhadanta*). So one Chan Buddhist went to see the "Most Virtuous." As soon as he saw him, the Most Virtuous struck him with a stick, and he understood. The man understood. Other people don't understand this matter. This is a Chan story. This is called the "Stick." There is another called the "Shout." A pilgrim went to the Chan Most Virtuous for instruction. He didn't say a word, but gave a great shout. The pilgrim also understood. These kinds of stories are in the ***Records of the Transmission of the Lamp***.... The Chan school does not rely upon language or writing, and two sides can influence each other. An old successful monk who has achieved enlightenment can have influence on a newly arrived person, and make him able to achieve enlightenment, but he does not use language. An enlightenment of language is still on the conscious level. Only [an enlightenment] that is life-changing in a fundamental way can be considered true enlightenment.

- **The supreme liberation is becoming Buddha.**

Liang: The learning of the ancient India was not really something you could talk about, or something the brain could comprehend, or something that resides in consciousness. The basic nature of their learning was to fundamentally transform one's life. It is not a kind of idle talk for the mouth and brain. They have something called "yoga," in Chinese called *yujia*. Each school's yoga, although on the surface similar, is different. What is the similarity? It is to achieve liberation or release from the life of this mundane world. It causes one to undergo a basic transformation so that one is no longer an ordinary person. This is called *zhengguo*—the fruits or rewards of each stage of attainment. Each school has its own *zhengguo*. Each is similar in form, but different in actual content.

So, as for my own view, as a Buddhist, I would say that Buddhism, in terms of the fruits or attainments, has never gone astray, and has always reached the supreme liberation. What is the supreme liberation? Becoming Buddha. So, Buddhist books and sutras are different from the writings in which we ordinarily record our thoughts, our consciousness. They have hard content, practical things, i.e., transformation of one's life. A human is no longer human. There are various stages, the highest being transformation into Buddha, Buddhahood. From the bottom to the top

比如有名的、禅宗很成功的人，叫禅宗大德——“道德”的“德”，另外一个禅宗的，去见那个禅宗的大德，他一来见这个大德，大德就打他一棒，他就明白了，那个来的人就明白了，旁人看不懂怎么回事，这是禅宗的故事，这个叫“棒”。还有“喝”，就是来一个人见这个大德求法，他什么话也不说，大喝一声，那个人也就明白了，如此之类，都是在那个《传灯录》上传说的故事。……禅宗是不立语言文字，彼此可以互相影响。一个老和尚，已经成功的，已经悟道的，他对一个新来的人，可以对他有一种影响，让他也能够开悟，但是他不用语言开悟。语言的开悟，它还在意识之中，而真的开悟，是让你生命起变化，你的生命根本起变化，这才算。

- **最高的解放就是成佛**

梁： 古印度人的学问，不是在口头或是头脑、在人的意识上，不是这样。它的学问的根本，就是要人的生命根本起变化。它不是一种在头脑、口头的一种空谈。这个他们叫做 yoga，中文翻作“瑜伽”。印度各宗派有各宗派的“瑜伽”，相似而不同。不同，可是还是有同的地方，因为相似嘛。就是什么呢？就是他们所说的，要从世俗的生命里头得到解放、解脱，让人根本起变化，不再是一个普通的人，这个他们叫做“证果”——证是证了，果是结果。所以印度各宗都有各宗的证果，很相似而不同。

比如照我说吧，我站在佛家的立场，我认为佛家在证果上，是没有走入偏差，是一直达到最高的解放。最高的解放是什么呢？就是成佛。所以佛家的书、佛典，跟普通我们由自己的思想意识写出来，不一样，它有很实在的东西，实在的东西就是实在的生命变化。那个人不再是人了，那个人已经最高，

there are ten stages. Each of the ten stages is called a *di*.[4] So, of Buddhist scriptures and sutras, there is one very famous and very important: the *Yogācārabhūmi*, a work of more than 100 volumes. The message is, to reach Buddhahood, you must practice yoga. Someone who practices yoga is called a *yujiashi*. Each stage, one after another, advances upward. The eighth stage is a Bodhisattva. The tenth stage is Buddhahood.

Yesterday we talked about the three things: discipline (*sila*), meditation (*dhyāna*), wisdom (*prajñā*). You must first observe the disciplines, for only then is it possible to enter into meditation. Only by doing this can you achieve wisdom. These are only three things. Usually they say there are six *pāramitās* [almsgiving, patience, zealous progress, discipline, meditation, wisdom]. That is, aside from discipline, meditation and wisdom, there are three others. One is *dāna* (almsgiving), which means you can give everything away, not retaining anything. One is called *vīrya* (zealous progress). The sixth is *prajñā* (wisdom, *banruo*). [Mr. Liang was speaking of the six pāramitās, and left out "patience" (*kṣānti*) in the listing: almsgiving, patience, zealous progress, discipline, meditation and wisdom; he repeated wisdom (*hui*), that is, *banruo*.] One must practice the six pāramitās. Afterwards, your life is transformed. So, the important essential significance of all of this is transformation, or elevation of one's life. Complete transformation is, level by level, attained at the eighth stage,[5] which is the eighth stage of the *Yogācārabhūmi*, and at the eighth stage one can become a Bodhisattva. Attaining the tenth stage, one can become Buddha.[6]

What I've been talking about above can be summarized into this: the important thing in Buddhism is to transform one's own life, or elevate one's own life. These are not empty theories.[7]

就是成佛了。这个从低层到最高层，它分为10层，这个一层它叫一地——就是“土地”的“地”，十地就是10个阶层。佛经有“论”——“议论”的“论”，有一部很著名的、很要紧的书，就叫做《瑜伽师地论》，这个书有100卷之多，它就是讲要成佛，要做这个功夫，做瑜伽的功夫。做瑜伽的人，就称瑜伽师，瑜伽师从低到高，一层一层的，地位不同，所以叫《瑜伽师地论》，总共十地。到了八地——一共十地——就算是菩萨，八地菩萨，十地也就是成了佛。

昨天不是说过一下，那个“戒、定、慧”。一定要持戒、守戒，然后才能够入定，由定才能够生慧，这个是三样。通常是说六波罗密，六波罗密就是在这个三样之外，又有三样。这个又有三样里头，有一样叫布施，布施就是什么都可以给人，就是无保留。布施是一样，还有一样叫做精进，第六是般若，这个合起来就是六波罗密（梁先生在这里讲六波罗密，将布施、忍辱、精进、戒、定、慧中的“忍辱”遗漏，而将慧，即“般若”，讲重复了）。一定要修六波罗密，然后你的生命才能起变化，以至于达到一种根本变化。根本变化到了第八层——它一层一层，就是《瑜伽师地论》的八地——可以成菩萨了，十地就成佛了。

以上的话，归结起来就是这样一个意思，就是说佛家要紧的是在自己的生命起变化，或者叫生命的提高吧，不是空理论。

● Confucius' knowledge is a knowledge of life and existence.

Alitto: Will you say a few words about what you have learned and what you have never learned in your life?

Liang: All learning is not simply a copying from others. Learning is a very creative activity, all in one's own subjective area. But, there are others who are different. Some create little, and learn much from others. China has a proverb: "To draw the gourd exactly according to its appearance." Some people just learn by copying, with little creativeness. I am the opposite. I have always studied and learned with creativeness. Although all creation involves learning, it is still different. Some people create a lot while learning. I myself am like that. I take some material from the outside, but when in my hands, I apply it in creating. I am a person of great creative nature.

Take Chinese traditional learning and culture as an example. My foundations are very weak. I already mentioned that I never learned the classics well. But the quintessence of the classics has helped me very much. I can still appreciate and comprehend it. For example, the greatest Chinese scholar, Confucius. I feel that I really understand Confucius, better than Zhu Xi in the Song Dynasty did.

I often say this to people as an example. Confucius says of himself, "At fifteen, I set my heart upon learning; at thirty, I established myself; at forty, I no longer had doubts; at fifty, I knew the decrees of Heaven; at sixty, I heard truth with docile ear; at seventy, I could follow the dictates of my own heart, without overstepping the boundaries of right." Zhu Xi explains every stage. One word difficult to explain is the "*ershun*" (docile ear). Zhu Xi explains this as meaning "As soon as the words of the sage enter the ear, the mind/heart understands." I don't agree with this, I think that the meaning for each one of these stages is difficult to understand, and that the meanings should not be guessed at wildly. "At fifteen, I set my heart upon learning" seems easier to understand. "At thirty, I established myself." What does "establish" mean? "At forty, I no longer had doubts." Doubts? Doubts about what? "At fifty, I knew the decrees of Heaven." What are the "decrees of Heaven"? What does "docile ear" mean?

叁 儒家

• 孔子的学问是生命、生活之学

艾： 请您谈一谈，在您的一生之中，您所学到的是什么和从未学到的又是什么？

梁： 一切的学习，实际上不单是一种因袭，不单是向人家学。一切的学习都有创造，都有自己的一面，不完全是学人家。不过也不相同，有的人就是自己创造少，学得多。有一句中国俗话叫“依样画葫芦”——按着样子画葫芦，有不少是这样的人。不过就我自己说，我不是这样的人，我是创造性多过学习。虽然一切的创造里头都有学习，不过是一个比较的不同，有的人是学旁人的东西，但是在学的里边创造很多。我自己呢也就是这样的，好像我从外边所得的都是一些个资料，资料到我手里头，我把它运用、创造。我是一个比较创造性大的人。

就中国的学问说吧，中国的学问、中国的文化，论底子我是很差的。我已经说过了，我没念古书，可是中国的古书里头好的、精髓的，帮助我很多，我还是能够领会。比如像中国最大的学问家——孔子，我觉得我对孔子的了解、懂得，比那个宋朝的朱子——朱熹懂的要多一些。

我常常给人家这样讲，我举一个例，孔子不是自己说自己：“吾十有五而志于学，三十而立，四十而不惑，五十而知天命，六十而耳顺，七十而从心所欲，不逾矩。”在朱子就每个阶段他都讲了，比如那个很不好讲的，就是“耳顺”——一个“耳”，一个“顺”——什么叫“耳顺”呢？他就讲了，他用了一句话：“声入心通”——声音进去了，心通了。我不赞成。我认为，不但是“耳顺”我们不好懂，实际上每一个阶段我们都不好懂，不要乱猜，不要猜想。“十有五而志于学”，好像还好懂一点。“三十而立”，那个“立”是立什么呢？“四十不惑”，“不惑”又是对什么不惑？“五十而知天命”，那么什么叫天命呢？“耳顺”，什么叫耳顺？

I think that when Confucius was forty he didn't know what kind of progress—what stage—he would have reached at fifty. He hadn't achieved it yet. So if even he didn't know, how would we be able to know? When you don't know, don't say, don't talk. So I don't agree with people like Zhu Xi. He had to express an opinion. I don't agree with this explanation. We don't dare explain randomly or guess wildly. If you don't know, then say you don't know. We should admit what we don't know. So, on the one hand, we should admit that we don't know. On the other hand, what we do know is what it isn't. That is, we can eliminate possibilities. We know that Confucius wasn't talking about the natural world, or about social science, or politics or economics. We know that he wasn't talking about all these other matters. He was speaking of his own life, his own existence, not anything external. His kind of knowledge was a knowledge of life and existence, not other kinds of knowledge.

Wasn't his favorite disciple Yan Hui (Yan Yuan)? ... In the *Book of Changes*, there is one section that discusses Yan Hui: "He knows immediately after he made a mistake that he had made one. After he knows, he won't repeat it." So, it is somewhat similar to "not repeating the same mistake." Confucius always spoke from the perspective of the continuous changes and transformation of life. So, when someone asked who loved learning, he praised Yan Hui. Now what was Yan Hui's strong point? Just these two things [not taking anger out on others and not repeating the same mistake], which we cannot truly know. That we can't truly know, however, is only one aspect. Another aspect is that he didn't talk about odd things, didn't speak of natural phenomena or social science.[8] He concentrated on one's own life. So, no matter student or teacher, their efforts were directed toward their own lives. Of those who passed Confucianism along, I recognize the elder Cheng, Cheng Hao, of the Song and Wang Yangming of the Ming Dynasty.

● I can be considered as belonging to the Lu-Wang school.

Alitto: In 1922, when your published *Eastern and Western Cultures and Their Philosophies,* you also said that some of Wang Yangming's followers, Wang Gen (Wang Xinzhai) and the others, also understood

我以为，孔子四十的时候，他也还不知道他五十岁的进步，他还没有那个进步，他那个时候也还不知道。他不知道，我们旁人怎么知道？旁人不知道，不知道你就不要说，不要讲，所以像朱子那样讲，我不同意。所以说，这一些话我们是不敢乱讲、乱猜，知道就是知道，不知道就是不知道，我们应当承认自己不知道。承认不知道是一面，还有一面我们知道，知道什么呢？知道他没有说旁的事情，他没有说到对自然界的知识，也没有说到社会科学，也没有说到政治、经济，他都没有说。他所说的就是他自己的生命，就是他自己的生命、生活在说话，没有说到外头去，因为他本人的学问是这个样子的一种学问：是生命、生活之学，不是旁的学问。

所以他最好的徒弟，不是颜渊吗？颜回吗？……古书的《易经》——《周易》，里边就讲到颜子，它说："颜氏之子其殆庶几乎？有不善未尝不知，知之未尝复行（也）。"他一有点不对、错误、不善，他马上就知道，知道后不再行、不再做，所以"不贰过"是这个样子，他始终是从生命的流行变化来说的。所以人家问孔子谁好学，他就称赞颜子——称赞颜渊、颜回，颜回的长处是什么？就是那两点（不迁怒，不贰过）。那两点我们不能深知，不深知是一面，另外一面是什么呢？他又没有说到旁处去，没有讲到自然现象，没有讲到社会问题，他就是讲自己的生命、生活，所以老师也罢，学生也罢，他们的用功、致力，都是在这个地方。能够传中国的孔门之学，我是承认在宋朝，就是那个大程子——程颢，在明朝就是王阳明，他们是传了这个学问。

• 我算是陆王派

艾： 那您民国十一年（1922 年）出版了《东西文化及其哲学》的时候，也说王阳明的一些门弟子，王艮——王心斋，也是懂孔子

the true way of Confucius. So, you still haven't changed your mind? Your statement now and that [in the book of 60 years ago] are about the same.

Liang: In this respect, my opinions are about the same as before. But in the book of 60 years ago, when explaining Confucius' thought, I used the terms "intuition" and "instinct." In both cases, I didn't use them very well.[9]

Alitto: Yes, but you can still be considered a member of the Wang Yangming school?

Liang: Yes, right. Don't they divide all thinkers into the Lu-Wang [Lu Jiuyuan and Wang Yangming] and the Cheng-Zhu schools? So, I can be considered as belonging to the Lu-Wang school. "Lu" is a Song Dynasty thinker; Wang a Ming Dynasty one. In the Song Dynasty, there were Zhu Xi and the Cheng brothers who I just mentioned. Now, the elder and the younger are different. (The younger brother: Cheng Yichuan; the elder brother: Cheng Hao.) I recognize that Cheng Hao was the correct, or enlightened one. But Zhu Xi didn't understand him. Doesn't Zhu Xi have a book called the *Reflections on Things at Hand*? In that book, he didn't quote Cheng Hao.... It is not that he said Cheng Hao was wrong or no good. Rather, he said that Cheng Hao's thought was too profound, too brilliant! This judgment resulted from Cheng Hao's thought not being suited to his own temperament or disposition. But I think that in the Song, it is Cheng Hao who was the true Confucian, and in the Ming, Wang Yangming. But the thinker I like most of all is the one following Wang Yangming, Wang Xinzhai. Wang was a man from the lower classes, a salt worker. A lot of his followers were workers and peasants, ordinary people. They were not necessarily the highest ranked academic scholars, who were all overly bookish. People from the lower classes were not so learned, and some were illiterate, but they could comprehend and understand their own vital forces, their own lives, and this is what is needed. This sort of approach is in accord with Confucius himself and with the true Confucian school. So, because of this, I have always liked Wang Xinzhai very much, and in my book, *Eastern and Western Cultures and Their Philosophies*, I praised him.[10]

● Wang Yangming's "familiarity with one's disposition"

Liang: But compared to Wang Yangming I am far, far inferior. I can use a term sometimes used in Buddhism—"to attain thorough and complete understanding" (Liang writes the two characters "*chewu*"). "*Che*" means thorough and complete. "*Chewu*" is when our life-being undergoes a great transformation. This kind of understanding is not of the usual "Aha,

之道的。您还没有改变您的主意啊，当年这个结论跟现在差不多啊。

梁： 在这一点上差不多。不过我现在看当初的书，60 年前的书，解释孔子的时候，用那个"直觉"，用那个"本能"，不妥当。

艾： 是，不过您还算是属于王阳明的门派。

梁： 对。不是他们都分程朱派、陆王派（陆九渊、王阳明）吗？我算是陆王派，陆王呢，陆是宋朝了，王是明朝了。在宋朝，刚才提到程朱，大程子，跟二程——程伊川不一样。大程子就是程颢了，程颢我认为是好的、对的、高明的，可是朱子对他不了解。朱子不是有一部著作叫做《近思录》——"远近"的"近"，在这个《近思录》他不引大程子，他对大程子倒不是……虽然他不是说大程子不对、不好，他是说大程子太高明了，他那样一个看法。其实就是，朱子对大程子有点好像不合脾胃，不合他的味道。可是我认为，在宋儒还是大程子，明儒是王阳明。我更喜欢王阳明底下的王心斋——王艮。王艮，在社会里头他是一个下层的人，他是一个工人，他是搞盐的盐场的工人，并且他的门下，王心斋这一派，有许多都是农工，很普通的人，不一定是上级讲学问的人。上层的讲学问的人，容易偏于书本，下层的人呢，他读书不多，或者甚至没有什么文化，可是他的生命、生活他能够自己体会，这个就行了，这个就合于儒家了，合于孔子，所以我喜欢王心斋，《东西文化及其哲学》末了讲到称赞王心斋。

• 王阳明的"明心见性"

梁： 不过比起王阳明来啊，（我）还差得远，还差得远。可以用佛家有时候用的名词"彻悟"，彻就是彻底，彻悟是我们人的生命的一个大变化，不是个普通的事情，不是普通的"噢，我明白了"，

now I understand!" kind. Master Yangming had achieved this kind of enlightenment, and I have not.

There were many important figures among Master Yangming's disciples. He gave them all advice and comments. Of course, because people's natural endowments were unequal—there was a difference in degree of natural intelligence— some were on this end [of the spectrum] and some on that end. Some of his followers achieved more than others. So, a lot of his students were famous and extraordinary. Someone named Qian [Dehong], who was one of his students, later became very famous. He compiled Master Yangming's chronological biography. Originally, he was not a follower of his, and then later studied with him. Mr. Qian would listen to Master Yangming's teachings, and at the same time he would very humbly listen to what his senior fellow students had to say. Mr. Qian was extremely sincere and modest, always looking to progress in his understanding. But he always felt that he was inadequate. He himself said that he had got non-awakening. The so-called non-awakening to the truth meant that he could make neither heads nor tails out of it. He didn't achieve enlightenment. He could not enter the gate. Later, he went into a monastery to study meditation with a monk, "to practice solitude and quieting." Then he cloistered himself, having no contact with the outside world and in the monastery practiced solitude and silence. When he had achieved a profound state of quietude, suddenly [what he experienced] was like seeing the sun from the midst of darkness. This was his "attaining thorough and complete understanding." So he hurriedly ran to ask his teacher Master Yangming about his experience of thorough and complete understanding. Master Yangming nodded his head. He said to Mr. Qian, "Yes, right, [you have attained enlightenment]. Don't tell anyone else about this. Don't help others [to do this]. In instructing others, don't tell them to practice solitude and quietude in this way. This would not necessarily be a good thing for them. Use my own words, that is, 'extend or apply innate knowledge of the good into practice.' Don't tell other people to go practice meditation. Tell them to extend or apply their innate knowledge of the good into practice. That will cause no harm. If they go meditate, possible this will cause harm, it might not be the right thing for them to do." That is to say, this kind of learning of Master Yangming's had to be able to effect a "complete understanding" toward human life and life being. Finally it must... But it must not be forced. You just do it this way, extending or applying their innate knowledge of the good into practice."

不是这样。在彻悟上，阳明先生他有他的彻悟，我不够。

阳明先生的门下有好几个重要的人，都是受到阳明先生的指教了。可由于每一个人的天资不相同，天资有高有低，有偏于这边的，有偏于那边的，所以阳明先生的门下著名的、了不起的有好几个人。有一个姓钱的（疑为钱德洪），他也是阳明先生的门下，后来很出名的，阳明先生的年谱就是他来编订的。他以前没有跟着阳明先生求学，后来跟着阳明先生求学。他就一面呢跟着阳明先生，听阳明先生的教诲，一面嘛他跟许多师兄、前辈请教，很诚心诚意地去求。但是总觉得不行，他自己说啊，没悟道。所谓没悟他就是摸不着头脑，进不去门。后来呢，他就啊，跑到和尚庙里头去静坐。"习静"，关起门来，跟人不接触，在和尚庙里头"习静"。那么，悟于深的静的时候啊，他就恍然，如同从那个黑暗中看见天日一样，这个就是说他彻悟了。他彻悟了就赶快跑来问老师。阳明点头，他说对了，对了，对了，但是告诉他——告诉钱平江（疑为钱德洪），你不要告诉人，你不要帮助旁人，你指点旁人，不要说是这样子去"习静"。虽然你得利于"习静"。但是你这样子指点旁人，不一定好，你还是用我的话——用阳明先生的话了，你还是用这个话，"致良知"，不要告诉人去"习静"。你告诉人家，指点人去"致良知"啊，不出毛病，你告诉人去"习静"啊、去静坐啊，可能出毛病，可能不对。这个就是说啊，阳明先生的这种学问，必须能够有一个——对人生、对生命——有一个彻悟才行，最后一定……，不过不要勉强，你就是这样子好了，"致良知"。

This extension of innate knowledge of the good calls for putting forth effort in society. Even though Qian went into a monastery to isolate himself, practiced the skill of meditation and in this way achieved complete enlightenment, Yangming still said: When you are helping and instructing another, do not tell him to follow this path of yours. It might easily result in problems. You still have him "extend his innate knowledge of the good into practice" and apply his efforts to society. Do not have him isolate himself from society, avoid complex environments, and go into a monastery. That kind of way of hard work cannot help the average person. Do not advise the average person to go this path. What path should he go? That of applying his efforts to society. So, I very much admire Master Yangming. This way of his is completely right. He was completely right in keeping the interests of the average man in mind. This way, although a profound enlightenment would not be easy, a gradually attained enlightenment was possible. The way of putting it for the average man is to apply efforts to society, and to apply innate knowledge of the good into practice in society. There is a phrase in the *Doctrine of the Mean* which goes "to raise the way to its greatest height and brilliancy, so as to pursue the course of the Mean."

Alitto: You used that phrase in your book *Eastern and Western Cultures and Their Philosophies*.

Liang: I want to continue this statement. I will tell a story of Master Wang Yangming. This story fully shows Master Yangming's philosophy, not intellectual knowledge, but his skill. What skill? His attaining of thorough and complete understanding. Master Yangming achieved, as the old saying goes, "familiarity with one's disposition." This is an uncommon achievement. To truly understand one's own real nature is quite uncommon. Didn't I say that I saw that as though through a mist at a great distance? This is a long way from "truly understanding one's own real nature." But Master Yangming did achieve this. Master Yangming's life-being was on a far, far higher level than ours.

There are some other matters [that demonstrate this]. The Ming emperor in his time was a disaster, confused and muddle-headed. He was also surrounded by eunuchs. Master Yangming had already captured the rebel [Zhu] Chenhao in Jiangxi. But the emperor told Wang Yangming to release him because he wanted to capture the rebel himself! This emperor was a real joke, very muddle-headed. All of those advising him were

"致良知"呢是随世用功，尽管这个钱他是到庙里头去避开人，自己去"习静"，这么样得到彻悟的。可阳明先生说，你帮助人、指点旁人的时候，不要用你这个路子告诉他，这个路子容易出毛病，你还是让他"致良知"，让他随世用功，就是不要躲开众人、躲开复杂的环境，跑到庙里去。那种用功的方法，不能够帮助普通人，对普通人你不要让他走这个路。要走什么路子呢？就是随世用功。所以我非常之佩服阳明先生，他这个完全对，为普通人设想，他这个完全对。这个样子也慢慢地能够深入，这个虽然不容易深入，可是也能够慢慢地深入，对为普通人说法，就是随世用功，随世"致良知"，引用《中庸》上的老话，就是"极高明而道中庸"。

艾：是，"极高明而道中庸"，《东西文化及其哲学》里您是用过这个话。

梁：我想接着这个话啊，我讲一个王阳明先生的故事。这个故事里头啊，完全见出来王阳明的学问。这个学问不是知识，是见出来他的功夫。什么功夫呢？他的彻悟啊。用一句老话，有这么一句老话，阳明先生是做到了这个了，"明心见性"。那很不寻常，明心见性很不寻常。我不是说，我是在一种好像天上下雾，在雾中远远看到？那就是离这个还远，离明心见性还远。可是阳明先生他是做到这个了，就是阳明先生他的这个人、他的这个生命已经远远高过我们。

还有一些事情，当时是明朝了，皇帝是很糟糕的皇帝，很糊涂的皇帝，皇帝又被左右的太监所包围。这个阳明先生已经擒了（朱）宸濠，宸濠要反对皇帝，在江西擒了宸濠。皇帝就说把宸濠放了，我自己来擒。这个皇帝是个笑话了，糊涂了。就是因为在皇帝旁边帮助皇帝出主意的都是些个太监，都是些个

eunuchs and slaves. But the emperor believed and trusted the palace eunuchs, he was surrounded by them, and he did laughable things, such as releasing the already captured Chenhao so that he could come capture him himself. This was just nonsense, a joke. He himself led a great imperial expedition, with a lot of eunuchs and troops.

Of course, this expedition was a large and stately affair, and so topped Wang Yangming. Wang also led troops and was a very high official. But when the emperor arrived, he outshone Wang. At the time this event took place in the public square, there were many military officers who had followed the emperor there; they staged an archery contest to see who was the best shot. They thought that Wang Yangming was an effete intellectual, someone with only bookish knowledge, and wouldn't be much of an archer. They regarded him with some contempt. So, the target was set up and the archery contest commenced. Contrary to expectations, Wang's first shot was a dead-center bull's eye! OK, a cheer rang out from the surrounding spectators. Wang took his second shot. Another bull's eye! The crowd acclaimed him. He took a third shot, with the same result. The military men watching the contest all cheered. Wang withered those eunuchs who had held him in contempt. They dared not harm him because he had won the people's hearts. Everyone had eyes and had seen he did have ability, and was not a common scholar-official. This turned the tables. If this hadn't happened, the emperor might have done something else foolish.

Now in this story, why was Master Yangming able to hit three bull's eyes in a row? It was ascribable to this: He was completely enlightened! He had achieved perfect enlightenment about life-existence. He was a sage. He was a sage, completely different from an ordinary mortal; he was not an ordinary human. That is, [he was] an extraordinary person. So his hitting three bull's eyes in a row was not by mere luck; it was a fundamental question that far exceeded mere chance. It was his comprehension of the truth, his attaining perfect self-understanding. He was far, far above ordinary people. He was no longer a common person. He was really something. Master Yangming had attained sagehood, and was no longer an ordinary man, not a so-called mortal man, or a common man. Now if one says that I have some strong points, some area in which I am a cut above other intellectuals, then it is only that I am able to glimpse a little of this, however unclearly. In conclusion, my level of accomplishment is only this. To be immodest, my level is higher than that of an average person, for the average person hasn't even gotten a glimpse. But on the other hand, my level is not high enough, not as high as that of Wang Yangming.

奴隶了。那么这个皇帝还是相信太监，太监包围他，要做那个很可笑的事情，就是要擒了宸濠再放，他自己来擒。他自己要御驾亲征，带着很多太监、很多军队来了。

当然来了嘛，皇帝来了嘛，当然很威严、很大啊。这个盖过了王阳明，王阳明带着军队，王阳明也算是很高的大臣，但是皇帝来了，盖住他了。这个时候有这么一件事情，就是在广场里头啊，随着皇帝来的有许多武将了，武将会射箭啊，那么，要比一比谁射得好。他们以为王阳明是一个书生、文人，恐怕射箭不行吧。他轻视王守仁，那么好，就树靶子在那儿，比较射箭。居然比较射箭的时候，阳明一箭射去，正中那个中心点。好！周围观看的军民呢大声喝彩。再射第二遍，又是正中，啊，又喝彩，欢呼。第三箭还是正中。这三箭一射，周围看的军人都欢呼，把这个来的太监、看不起阳明的都镇住了，不敢动他。因为他得民心，大家有目，看他真有本事，不是普通的文人。这样一下，才把这个局面转回来了，要不然那个皇帝还要乱搞。

我说这个故事啊，阳明为什么能够三箭都射中啊，因为这个啊，他得力于这个地方。他是彻悟，他对生命，他达到了彻悟，他是圣人了，完全不是普通的凡人，那是很了不起的人。所以他把三箭都射中啊，不是机遇，是远高于机遇的一个根本问题。他是悟道，他是明心见性。阳明先生是进入圣人的地位了，不再是个普通人，不再是一个所谓凡人、凡夫。我呢，如果说我有什么长处，有什么比普通的其他读书人好像高一着的地方，如果说有，那就是因为我能够望见到一点，好像是看不太清楚，但是也可以望到一点。结束一句话，我的程度是如此，我的程度，不客气地说，比普通人高，因为普通人连这个也没有，另外一方面呢不够高，没有达到这个地步。

Alitto: Aside from Wang Yangming, who else achieved this "familiarity with one's disposition"?

Liang: Speaking of ancient Chinese learning, in the past, for example during the Qing Dynasty, there were three schools of classical learning. One school was called the school of Han Learning. This school's focus was on texts, on philological evidence. They were interested in verifying the old texts or institutions. This was called textual research.

There was another school called the school of Belles Lettres, e.g., the Tongcheng school, whose focus was also on books, emphasizing reading the old books. But in reality they were most interested in writing style, in writing in the ancient style of the Tang and Song Dynasties' masters Han Tuizhi (Han Yu) and Liu Zongyuan. So this school just wouldn't work either.

I've already mentioned two schools. The third school was that of Song and Ming Learning—Neo-Confucianism. This scholarship proceeded upon this path [that I have been speaking about, pursuit of enlightenment and sagehood]. But in the two or three hundred years of the Qing Dynasty, the school produced no really outstanding men. Before the Qing, during the Yuan Dynasty, there had appeared no really able men in this school either. It was during the Song that the school produced great men, such as Lu Xiangshan[Lu Jiuyuan,with his literary name Xiangshan]. Later people liked to use the term "Lu-Wang" and this too was a school. Wang refers to Wang Yangming. In this school there were two exceptional men whose accomplishments were, relatively speaking, profound. In the Song, there was Yang Jian (Yang Cihu). The other, in the Ming, was Luo Rufang (Luo Jinxi). These were two Confucians of scholarly accomplishment and virtue. I very much admire these two men. The average Confucians, even though they talked Confucianism and revered Confucius, were all outsiders [to true Confucianism].

艾：那谁达到这个地步，除王阳明以外呢，谁达到“明心见性”？

梁：讲这个中国古学问的有……就过去说，比如就清朝说，清朝的时候，讲学问有三派。一派呢就被称为汉学家，这一派的汉学家他的重点、他的学问是书本考订，考订古时候流传下来的文字或者制度，证明过去是怎么一回事，这个叫做考订考据学，考据学这是一派。

还有一派呢叫辞章之学，像桐城派，桐城派也讲学问，特别讲究读古书，但是实际上呢它是一种辞章派，作古文，作韩柳文——韩退之、柳宗元，这是一派，这一派也不行。

第三派，它是讲宋明学。讲宋明学的呢，就是要往这个路上走，它采取的方向是这个方向，不过在清朝二三百年里头，在这方面没有出什么人才。在过去，在清朝以前，元朝在这方面也没有出什么人才。元朝以前，宋朝在这方面出了人才，那就是陆象山（陆九渊，号象山）。后来呢，喜欢说“陆王”，陆王是一个派吧，王就是王阳明。陆王派里头有两个特殊的人，比较算是成功的人。在宋朝，名字叫杨简——杨慈湖；在明朝，叫罗汝芳，号叫近溪。这是两个深造有得的儒者，就我说，我最佩服这两个人。其他的一般人，尽管他讲儒书、孔子，尊奉孔子，实际上是门外汉。

Confucianism and Buddhism: the enlightened person has no problem.

● Difference between Confucianism and Buddhism

Liang: I really want to talk about Confucianism and Buddhism again. Didn't you say that I was the "last Confucian"? I want to say a word more about the similarities and differences between Buddhism and Confucianism. Possibly I have already expressed these opinions before. Confucius and Confucians always speak from the standpoint of humanity, of humans or of humanism. Confucius, no matter what he is talking about, is still in the sphere of the human. But Buddhism transcends humanity. Its central focus is not on the human himself, but rather on an area that transcends the human. So, these two kinds of thought are very different. Yet, there is one area in which they are similar, and that is "egoless self-sacrifice for the salvation of the world." That is, they both seek to forget the self and save the suffering. In Buddhist terms, this object of salvation is "sentient beings." The suffering of sentient beings is the suffering of the Buddhist. In China, let's take Confucians and Mozi as an example. Now, Mozi also sought to do the same. He spent his entire life trying to save people, rushing around for others. So, on the surface, there is no difference between the Mohists, Buddhists and Confucians. The major difference between the Confucian enterprise of salvation and the Buddhist lay in the concept of "self" or "ego." The school that analyzed this problem of self most completely was the Buddhist Consciousness-Only (*Yogācāra*) school.

It talks about the eight consciousnesses. The first six are the senses: seeing, hearing, smelling, tasting, tactile feeling, and also mind. These first six are for coping with the external world; they are all tools, or instruments. They are all directed toward the external. Using these six tools is life, is living beings, e.g., a living person, a living human. This is called "*diqiyuandiba*" (the seventh and eighth consciousnesses control the six others). The seventh mind is called the "manas consciousness"; the eighth is called the "storehouse consciousness." These two consciousnesses apply, use and control the first six. This is called "*diqiyuandiba*." That is, it holds to a self (clinging to the self called "*wozhi*"—*ātma-grāha*—clinging to the idea of a self). There are two kinds of things clinging to the notion of the reality of the ego. One is called "*fenbie wozhi*" (the clinging to this notion of the reality of the ego as a result of intellectual reasoning). The other is called "*jusheng wozhi*" (the inborn instinctive cleaving to the idea

肆 佛家与儒家：高明的人通达无碍

• 佛跟孔子的异同

梁： 我愿意把佛跟孔子我再说一下，因为你不是说我是"last Confucian"吗？我想把佛跟孔子的异同说一下。也许我们已经都说过一下，孔子、儒家他总是站在人的立场说话，他说来说去还是归结到人身上。可是佛家，他是超过人说话，他说来说去，归结点也不归结到人身上，归结到超过人的那个地方，所以好像他们是很不同。不过还有同的一面，就是"无我"——没有我——"而救世"，佛家话就是众生，众生的痛苦就是他的痛苦。就中国说吧，儒墨——墨子也是这样子，都是在他生存的这个时候，他总是一生都在为大家奔走。所以表面上没有很大分别，但是我底下就要说一下孔子跟佛的分别。这个分别就是在"我"的问题上，关于"我"的问题，把它讲得最清楚的，分析得最清楚的，是唯识家。

佛学的唯识家，是讲八识。八识，前六识——眼、耳、鼻、舌、身，这是五个，加上一个"意"，这个就是前六——前六都是应付外面的，都是工具，都是对外的。运用这个前六识的，是生命，是活的，比如说人吧，活的人啦，这个在唯识家讲，叫做"第七缘第八"。第七就是"末那识"，第八是"阿赖耶识"，运用这前六识的工具而为之主的，就是这个"第七缘第八"。怎么叫做"第七缘第八呢"？就是这个时候执着一个"有我"，它叫做"我执"。两种执，"我执"，一种叫"分别我执"、"分别执"；一种叫"俱生执"、"俱生我执"。"俱生我执"就是与生俱来的，

of the self). This refers to the natural, intuitive assumption of the reality of the self, prior to intellectual reasoning. This inborn instinctive cleaving to the idea of the self is extremely deep, very concealed. The clinging to this notion as a result of intellectual reasoning is shallow. The deepest and strongest of the clinging to the reality of the self (*wozhi, ātma-grāha*) is our very life, the root of life. In ordinary activity, in life, the clinging to this notion as a result of intellectual reasoning is also active. But when we are sleeping—the deepest dreamless sleep with the cerebrum being as though completely inactive, very very deep sleep—at that time, the clinging to the notion of the reality of the self as a result of intellectual reasoning does not appear. But the inborn instinctive cleaving to the idea of the self does not weaken in the slightest; in deep sleep it's still this way. Perhaps I've been injured, fallen from a height and it appears as if I were dead. I'm not dead, but just about. At that time the clinging to this notion as a result of intellectual reasoning disappears. But the inborn instinctive cleaving to the idea of the self is still present. So this instinctual grip on the self is very profound, concealed and not obvious, but it has great strength. Now I would like to talk about the differences between Confucianism and Buddhism.

Buddhism wants to refute false tenets, it wants to refute the notion of the reality of the self. I remember once I wrote down on a piece of paper six characters "*qihuo zaoye shouku*." Buddhism looks at all like this. "*Qihuo*"—"the arising of illusions," that is, confusion, bewilderment, insufficient acuity. Where is the illusion? What are you referring to when you say illusion? It refers to this holding on to the notion of the existence of the ego. Buddhism wants to thoroughly destroy illusions. It also says that it wants to "destroy the two illusions." Why "two illusions"? On the one hand there is the "illusions of the reality of the self" (*wozhi*), and on the other, the opposite, "illusions of the reality of things, or phenomena" (*fazhi*). "*Fa*" refers to things. Buddhism wants to destroy these two illusions. Destroying the two illusions is also called "excising the two graspings."

What are those "two graspings (*upādāna*)"? They are "*nengqu*" (ability to grasp) and "*suoqu*" (that which is grasped)—two sides of the same thing. No "ability," no "object." Both are together, meaning that there is no grasping or grasped. What is this? This is Buddha. This is one integrated whole, one integrated whole that contains no binaries. Buddhism holds that differentiation or distinction is a mistake, and wants to restore one

就是不等到分别就有。"俱生我执"很深、很隐——"隐藏"的"隐","分别我执"就浅。最深的也就是最有力量的"我执"啊，是我们生命、生活的根本。通常在活动中、生活中，都有一个"分别我执"在那儿活动。可是假定我们睡眠——最好的、最深沉的睡眠，一点梦都没有，大脑完全好像没有活动，睡得很深很深了——那个时候，"分别我执"就不显露了，可是"俱生我执"那还是一点也没有减弱，睡得沉的时候是这样。或者我受伤了，从高处摔下来受伤了，好像死了，虽然没有死，跟死差不多了，那个样子的时候也是"分别我执"没有了，可是"俱生我执"依然还在。所以"俱生我执"是很深的、很隐藏的、不大显露的，可是非常有力量。底下我就要说儒家跟佛家的分别了。

佛家是要破执，破"我执"，我记得我在一张纸上写过一次，写过六个字——"起惑造业受苦"，佛家看都是这样。起惑——惑是迷惑了，糊涂了，不够明白了。惑在哪儿呢？你说的惑是指什么说呢？就是指这个，指"我执"，惑就是指"我执"说。佛家是要彻底地破执，彻底。他又说破"二执"，为什么用"二执"呢？就是一方面有"我执"，还有一面跟"我执"对面的"法执"——"法"就是一切的事物。"我执"是一面，对面还有"法执"，佛家就是要破这二执。破二执有时候又叫"断二取"。

那么"二取"是什么呢？——"能取"跟"所取"。能取、所取就是一个这边，一个那边，佛家的意思，是断二取，没有"能"，没有"所"，能、所是归在一块的，意思是没有取的。这是什么？这个就是佛，这个就是一体了，一体就没有二了。佛家的意思就是说，分别就是错误，就是要恢复到一体，复原

integrated whole, to re-establish one integrated whole. The cosmos is a blended, indiscrete single body. This is Buddha. Ordinary people think that Buddha is a deity. That is wrong.

We'll continue further with the differences and similarities of Buddhism and Confucianism. Confucianism—Confucius did not destroy the inborn instinctive cleaving to the idea of the self; if that were destroyed, then there would be no activity. Life is situated in the inborn instinctive cleaving to the idea of the self. Only with this illusion of the existence of the self are there all activities coming from the natural instincts of humans. In all of these activities the "inborn illusion of self" prevails.

So since Confucianism does not depart from human life, it is unlike Hinayana Buddhism's desire for the calm and quiet of Nirvana and desire to leave home and be a monk. Confucianism by no means wants that. Confucianism wants activities in the human world. Confucianism wants completely real human beings like us. It does not want to be a deity. It wants the same as we are, wearing clothes, eating food, "drinking, eating and sex." But we are not completely the same. There is one aspect that is completely the same as us—the primal wants, life, rest, sleep. Where is the difference [with what Confucianism wants]? He doesn't want this [clinging to this notion as a result of intellectual reasoning]. Confucianism is with "an all-encompassing, empty and impartial mind" in the process of satisfying primal wants. The eight characters—*kuorandagong, wulaishunying* (with an all-encompassing, empty and impartial mind, taking things as they come)[11] —these eight characters are Confucian. Although the Confucian satisfies the primal instincts and all the activities are just like ours, in life the Confucian has only the inborn instinctive cleaving to the idea of the self, not the notion of the reality of the self as a result of intellectual reasoning.

Why doesn't it have the latter? It's an all-encompassing, empty and impartial mind, and taking things as they come. For example, my loved one dies, and I cry. This is with an all-encompassing, empty and impartial mind, taking things as they come. The weather is good, and I'm delighted and happy. This is taking things as they come. At this time there is no clinging to the notion of the reality of the self as a result of intellectual reasoning, but it never departs from the inborn instinctive cleaving to the idea of the self. Only because there is this latter "me" do I cry or laugh. That there is no obstructing of laughter or tears is also an all-encompassing, empty and impartial mind. This is Confucianism. But Buddhism isn't like this; it transcends this. For example, if my body is hacked with a knife, I will be in pain. Even if it was Confucius, he couldn't but feel pain. But if you plunge a knife into Buddha, it makes no difference, he doesn't suffer. Confucius suffers. The Buddha transcends this. They are not the same.

到一体，宇宙浑然一体，这个就是佛。普通人以为佛是神啊是什么，那不对。

再说儒佛的异同。照我的说法，儒家啊，孔子不破"俱生执"，破了"俱生执"就没有活动了，生命就坐落在"俱生我执"上，有"俱生我执"才有饮食男女的一切活动，这些活动都有"俱生我执"在那里为主了。

那么儒家既然不离开人生，他不像佛家小乘佛法要涅槃寂静，要出世，儒家并不要那个样子，儒家就是要在人世间活动。儒家就是要像我们这样一个完全真的人，他不要做神，他就是跟我们一样，穿衣吃饭，饮食男女，他就是这样。跟我们还不同了——跟我们有完全相同的一面，饮食男女、生活、休息、睡觉，这是同的一面——不同在哪里呢？他不要这个（"分别我执"）。"廓然大公"，他就是穿衣吃饭的时候他还是"廓然大公"。八个字，"廓然大公，物来顺应"，这八个字是儒家。尽管他穿衣吃饭，一切活动与我们一样，可是他活动中只是"俱生我执"在那里活动，没有"分别我执"。

为什么没有"分别我执"？他"廓然大公，物来顺应"。比如我一个亲爱的人死了，我哭，这个还是廓然大公，还是物来顺应。天气很好，我很高兴、愉快，这就是物来顺应。这个时候都没有我，都没有这个"分别我"，可是离不开"俱生我"。因为有这个我，才哭啊、才笑啊，有哭有笑没有妨碍，还是廓然大公，这个是儒家。可是佛家不如此，他超过这个了。比如说，拿一个刀砍了我的身体，我痛，即使孔子他也不会不痛的。但是你如果拿刀去扎佛，没有关系，他没有什么痛苦。孔子有痛苦，佛超过这个，不一样。

● Intellectual inclination toward Buddhism & life along the Confucian path

Alitto: In these [past] sixty-some years of life, you have both followed Confucianism, and had a Buddhist side...

Liang: I only love, like, and admire Buddhism, but that's as far as it goes. I only like, admire, and am inclined toward Buddhism, but I'm an ordinary person.

Alitto: I understand. From *Eastern and Western Cultures and Their Philosophies*, it seems that like a lot of Chinese historical figures, you went from Buddhism to Confucianism. Like a lot of Neo-Confucians, such as Wang Yangming... In any case there are a lot of people like this. You openly declared "I was a Buddhist previously, and now I am going to Confucianism," then...

Liang: I'd add a word here. I led a life as an individual, but intellectually I was inclined toward Buddhism. My intellectual inclination was toward Buddhism, but I still led an individual life. An individual life should be following the Confucian path, but I still wanted to lead a good life but didn't succeed entirely. If I would explain further how it was insufficient, it was in the areas of destroying the notion of the reality of the ego and having an all-encompassing, empty and impartial mind. I had hoped that I would be able to be that way, but it was not enough.

Alitto: You just mentioned that you were insufficient in those areas—that is the standard attitude, especially of Neo-Confucians. That is, whatever I do, it will never be good enough, not thorough enough. In the U.S. recently, there has been a discussion of this question: Did the Song and Ming Neo-Confucians have a philosophy of life similar to that of the Western Puritans? The conclusion of many is that there are many similarities—forever progressing toward goodness, forever perfecting, continuously practicing self-cultivation. This is the same as the Puritans. You just said that this is the standard attitude of Neo-Confucians. What I can't make out, however, is in the end how to divide the Buddhist and Confucian intellectual parts. In the past sixty years, intellectually, you have been more inclined toward Buddhism, meaning that you didn't become a monk, and that your life was Confucian. Some scholars say that Neo-Confucianism from the Song and Ming on has some elements of Buddhism.

• 我在思想上倾向佛家，生活上走儒家的路

艾： 您 60 年来的生活，有佛教的一面跟儒家的一面……

梁： 我仅仅是爱这个佛教、喜欢佛教、佩服佛教，可是仅仅如此而已，仅仅喜欢佛教、佩服佛教、倾向于佛教，可我还是一个平常的人。

艾： 我明白了。您在《东西文化及其哲学》里，也是好像跟中国历史上好多人物一样，由佛转儒，好多人——像理学家……王阳明啊，反正很多了——好多人都是这样。您公开地宣布，我以前是佛教徒，现在呢我就转入儒家了，那么……

梁： 我再补一句。我是在生活上做一个人的生活，我思想上还是倾向佛家。思想上倾向佛家，人还是做一个人的生活。做一个人的生活应当是走儒家的路，可是我是一个想要做好而不够的一个人。如果再说明怎么样不够，那就是我在"破执"上、在"廓然大公，物来顺应"上不够。我希望我能够这样，但是不够。

艾： 您刚才说的自己那方面不够，就是最标准的尤其是理学的儒家的态度了，就是永远自己做得不够好、不够彻底。最近美国有一些人在讨论这个问题：中国的宋明理学家，有没有像西方的清教徒这一类的人生观？很多人的结论就是有很多类似的地方——永远向善，永远要改善、求善，继续不断地修养，这是你们跟清教徒一样的，您刚才说了，也是很标准的理学的儒家的态度。我弄不清楚的是，到底您怎么分佛的意思那层和儒的意思那层。您 60 年来思想比较倾向于佛，意思就是说没有做和尚啊，生活还是儒家的。有学者说，宋明以来的理学有几分佛教的成分在里面。

Liang: I think that others look at it that way; others, it appears, are criticizing them for being too close to Chan Buddhism, and asceticism. I think these views are not correct.

Alitto: Yes, your own view is that these views are not correct. Your works contain this opinion. A lot of foreign scholars of Chinese thought don't mean this in a critical way, but are analyzing the difference between Han Confucianism and Song Confucianism. From the Song on, [they find that] Neo-Confucians have some Buddhist elements.

Liang: In general, people are likely to say that they seem to have been influenced by Buddhism, even to the extent of saying that certain Confucians... For example, there is a famous Confucian of the Song Dynasty Yang Cihu (Yang Jian). Most people say that he was Chan. Actually this was not so. They also say that Wang Yangming himself appears to be close to Chan; or Wang Yangming's student Wang Longxi. Wang Longxi is also quite famous. They say that they appear to have absorbed some of Chan Buddhism, or are followers of Chan Buddhism. This is not completely accurate. Also, some of the Song and Ming scholars were also anti-Buddhist, and held that to be infected even a little was intolerable. There are also those who pull Chan Buddhism and Confucianism together.

Alitto: In your opinion, your situation of being intellectually inclined toward Buddhism and in life striving toward the Confucian ideal is relatively similar to which thinker in Chinese history?

Liang: I hope to do this better, to strive upward. I want to be like Wang Yangming.

Alitto: Are you saying you would follow both Wang Yangming and Buddhism? I mean...

Liang: Actually I understand a bit of Buddhist principles. In my thought and consciousness I understand some Buddhism, but in my real life I hope to follow Wang Yangming's example.

● I am not qualified as a person of learning; I'm a thinker.

Liang: ...I am not qualified as a person of learning. Why? The intellectual foundation of an authentic scholar of China's traditional learning is a mastery of the written language and literature. I haven't paid much attention to the written language which is the foundation of ancient

梁： 我认为是旁人这样看，旁人认为好像是批评他们近禅、禁欲，我认为这种看法，没有对。

艾： 是，您自己的看法是没有对，您著作里有这种意见，很多研究中国思想的外国人也没有什么批评的意思，就是分析汉跟宋儒家的分别，宋以后理学家有几分佛教在里面。

梁： 他们一般都是容易说是好像是受佛教影响，乃至于说某一个儒者，比如说宋朝有一个有名的儒者，叫杨慈湖——杨简，一般人都说他是禅，其实不是。把王阳明看作也是好像说他近禅，或是王阳明的门下有个王龙溪——王龙溪很有名的，都说他们好像是吸收了禅家的，或者是跟禅家、跟佛家好像混同起来，被人这样批评，这些个话都是不完全正确。另外，宋明学者又有一种排佛的，排斥佛教，认为沾染一点禅宗就是要不得的，也有这样的。也有把儒、佛家跟禅宗拉得很近的，也有。

艾： 依您自己看，您这个情形，就是思想倾向佛家，而生活向儒家的理想而努力，这种情形比较接近于中国历史上的哪一位思想家？

梁： 我希望把它做好一点，勉力向上，那我愿意学的还是王阳明。

艾： 您自己觉得王阳明、佛家两个都有？我的意思就是说……

梁： 实际上是我懂一点佛家的道理，在我的思想意识上懂一些个佛家，可是我的实际的生活，我是希望跟着王阳明走。

· 我不够一个学问家，而是一个思想家

梁： ……我不够一个学问家，为什么？因为讲中国的老学问啊，得从中国的文字学入手，才能够有中国老学问的根底。可是中国的文字学我完全没有用功，所以对于作为古书根底的

books. I have not read China's ancient books. When I was small, I didn't read the Chinese classics. Therefore, I really lack a background in traditional Chinese scholarship. On the other side, in modern science, I don't qualify either, because my foreign languages skills are lacking. When I say science, I refer to the natural sciences. When I was in middle school, I studied a bit of science, but it was very superficial. So my foreign learning falls short, too. So speaking from these two areas, I am completely unqualified to be a man of learning.

My area of strength is that I like to think. Therefore, if someone calls me a thinker, I won't decline [the designation]. A thinker and a scholar are different. The scholar knows a lot of things; he has absorbed a lot; in knowing more and seeing more, naturally there is some element of creativity; without creativity, one can't absorb anything. But a thinker is different from a scholar in that, although he also knows some things, his power of creativeness is greater than his power of absorption. Of course if he doesn't master a great amount of knowledge, he can't be a thinker. I do admit that I'm someone who has his own ideas, who acts according to his own ideas and puts them into practice. I am someone of independent thought. I have consistency between my thoughts and my actions. So, I admit that I am a thinker, not a scholar. My thought also has a source of inspiration, and that is Buddhism. So that is what I want to say about myself. I'm not a scholar, but a thinker, and my greatest intellectual inspiration has come from Buddhism.[12]

文字学，我没有用过心。那么，对于中国古书也没有读过，小时候没有读中国的经书，所以讲到学问的话，我的中国学问很差、很缺少。那么再一方面呢，就是近代的科学——外国学问，我的外文又不行，也不能够，所以科学也就不行了。科学主要的还是自然科学，那么在自然科学上，我在中学的时候学过一点，学得很粗浅。所以外国学问也不行。这两面说下来，就是说我完全不够一个学问家。

那么我所见长的一面，就是好用思想，所以如果说我是一个思想家，我倒不推辞、不谦让。思想家跟学问家不同，学问家他知道的东西多，他吸收的东西多，那么在吸收、多知道、多看里边当然也有创造，没有创造不能去吸收。可是在一个思想家来说，他不同于学问家的，就是虽然他也要多知道些东西——不知道古今中外的一些个知识，他也没法成为思想家——但是呢，他的创造多于吸收，跟学问家不同。那么，我承认自己是一个有思想的人，并且是本着自己思想而去实行、实践的人，独立思考，表里如一。我就是这么一个人。那么我的这个思想呢，也受到启发，启发我的是佛教、是佛学。我想说的话，就是这么一段，（我是）思想家，不是学问家，在思想上给我很好的启发的是佛学。

Questions of reality and life

现实问题和人生问题占据着我的头脑

have occupied my mind.

有两个问题占据了我的头脑。

一个呢，现实问题，现实中国的问题。

还有一个问题是人生问题，

对人生的怀疑、烦闷。

一个就让我为社会、为国事奔走，

一个又让离开。

There are two questions that have occupied my mind. One question

is the practical problem of China.

There is another problem of human life: its afflictions and uncertainties,

the misunderstandings of life, and doubts about it.

One makes me involve myself in social and national affairs;

and the other makes me want to leave.

● From joining Revolutionary Alliance to teaching at Peking University

Liang: ...Wang [Jingwei] was released by Yuan Shikai to be a mediator between the Northern and Southern Revolutionaries. Wang organized a Beijing-Tianjin branch of the Revolutionary Alliance (the Tongmenghui). The Revolutionary Alliance was founded by Sun Yat-sen. Its official name was the Chinese Revolutionary Alliance. This new branch was considered its northern branch.

When I was still in middle school, I had already secretly joined a revolutionary organization, which was part of the Beijing-Tianjin branch of the Revolutionary Alliance that I just mentioned, led by Wang Jingwei. At that time I was also a news reporter. The newspaper office was in Tianjin. Later it was moved to Beijing. For a time I led the life of a news reporter. Moreover, I was a field reporter who went out to cover the news on the spot. There was such a period. After the Republican Revolution, I went to Nanjing once. Later I doubled back. After Nanjing, I went to Wuxi, and from Wuxi doubled back. At that time my plan had been to go to Guangxi to sign up for the examination and go abroad to study, but I didn't succeed in going.

...At that time, we were all together in the Revolutionary Alliance because the revolutionary army had arisen, and the Qing court abdicated governmental power. Some of us originally were fooling around with bombs and pistols, but then we began to run a newspaper. We ran *The Republic*. The head of *The Republic* was Zhen Yuanxi. This man also ran a Chinese language newspaper in the U.S. At the time I was a field reporter, not someone who sat in the newspaper office writing essays, but was outside all the time. At that time, *The Republic*'s office was in Tianjin, and my home was in Beijing, so I commuted back and forth between the two cities, covering stories.

Alitto: Did you get to know Huang Yuansheng at this time?

Liang: I got to know him after this.

Alitto: Later? He was assassinated in the U.S. in 1915.[13] So was the first time you met Cai Yuanpei when you were a reporter...

Liang: I met Cai Yuanpei once during this period, but he didn't remember

 从同盟会到北大

• 从参加同盟会到任教北大

梁： ……汪精卫出来了，被袁世凯请出来了，让他做调和人，他就组织了一个……“京津同盟会”——同盟会就是孙先生所创建的中国革命同盟会，这个就算是中国革命同盟会的北方支部。

我是在中学读书的时候，已经就秘密地参加了革命组织，这个革命组织就是属于刚才说的汪精卫领导的京津同盟会。这个时候我还做新闻记者，那时候报馆设在天津，后来搬到北京来了。我有一段新闻记者的生活，并且那个记者是外勤记者，外勤记者就是访查新闻的，做过那么一段。我也曾经在辛亥革命后，去南京一次，可是后来又折回来了。去南京之后我就去了无锡，从无锡又折回来，那次本来意思是想到广西去投考、去出洋留学的，没有去成。

……那个时候，京津同盟会跟我、我们都在一道的，因为清廷退位了，革命军起来了，清廷就让出政权来了，退位了。我们一些原来是搞手枪炸弹的吧，改了，就办报，办《民国报》。《民国报》的社长甄元熙，这个人还在美国，在美国办中文报纸。我就算是一个外勤，不是坐在报社内写文章的，而是在外边。当时《民国报》报社在天津，我的家住北京，我就往来于北京、天津之间，做采访工作。

艾： 那是这个时候您认识黄远生吗？

梁： 黄远生认识在这个之后。

艾： 以后啊？他是 1915 年在美国被刺杀了。那蔡元培先生也是……第一次见面的时候是您在做记者的……

梁： 那时我做记者的时候见过他，可是他不记得我，等于没有什么

me. Afterwards, in 1917, when he became president of Peking University, I really got to know him. I had sent him my essay "On Tracing the Origin and Solving Doubts" for comments. He said that when he was passing through Shanghai, he had read it and found it very good. He said that he was now going to Peking University, and asked me to come on board.[14] I said that I really wasn't qualified to teach Indian thought. At the time, scholars of Europe and Japan did not include Buddhism as one of the six schools of Indian philosophy. Strictly speaking, I really didn't know much about Japanese or European scholarship on Indian philosophy. I only liked Buddhism, that's all. When Cai invited me, something else had come up, and being occupied with it, I couldn't accept Mr. Cai's invitation to teach at Peking University.

What was I busy with at the time? By that time Yuan Shikai had already died and the North and South were reunited. The major force that overthrew Yuan was in the Southwest. In Guangxi, the important figures were Cai E and Lu Rongting. In Guizhou, it was Liu Xianshi. Among the forces overthrowing Yuan inside the government was Liang Qichao (Rengong). In the North, when Yuan was dying he had asked Duan Qirui to come into politics. Duan was, among the Beiyang militarists, a very honest, decent, fine person. Duan resolutely and firmly opposed Yuan Shikai's becoming emperor from the first. So a group of Yuan's supporters wanted to assassinate him. He was at the time Minister of the Army. He resigned and went to live in the Western Hills of Beijing. They still wanted to assassinate him. The upshot was that he was never killed. Yuan's plan for becoming emperor failed. In order to maintain the power of the Beiyang clique, he had to ask Duan to return to Beijing. Because Yuan was intent upon becoming emperor, he had already abolished the State Council and had set up a Political Bureau within the Presidential Palace. At the time he knew that he was dying, that he was done for, and he asked Duan to abolish this organ, restore the State Council and assume the post of Premier. Because Duan was honest and upright, and because he had opposed Yuan's plans to be emperor, the Southwestern forces still recognized Duan. In any case the Southwestern forces didn't have sufficient military forces to attack Beijing, so they came to terms.

An older relative of mine entered the government as a representative of the Southwest. This was Zhang Yaozeng, who drafted me to be his confidential secretary. There were secret telegrams and letters between him and the anti-Yuan forces of the Southwest—Guangxi, Yunnan and Sichuan; I managed

关系。到了后来，到了民国六年（1917 年），他来北京就任北大校长的时候，那个时候才认识。因为那个时候我拿《究元决疑论》向他请教，他就说：我路过上海，看到了，很好；我现在到北大，也请你帮忙。当时我说：我还不会讲印度哲学。因为在欧洲或者日本，谈到印度哲学，都是谈到六派哲学，而六派里头不包含佛学。认真讲，欧洲人讲的、日本人讲的印度哲学，我不太清楚，我不过喜欢佛学就是了。同时，我那个时候正好旁的事情很忙，不能够答应蔡先生到北大。

那个时候什么事情很忙呢？那个时候，袁世凯死了以后，南北统一，推倒袁世凯的势力是在西南——广西，主要是蔡锷、陆荣廷、贵州刘显世。倒袁势力内部有梁启超——梁任公。这个时候北方就是袁世凯死了，袁世凯死的时候，他才把段祺瑞请出来。段这个人在北洋军人里头是一个很正派的、很好的人，自从袁有意要做皇帝，他就反对，坚决反对。另外一些包围、帮助袁世凯做皇帝的人要刺杀他，要刺段祺瑞，段祺瑞自己本来是陆军总长，自己辞职不干，住在北京的西山，他们还要刺杀他，也没有刺死。袁世凯做皇帝做不成，只好维持北洋军人的势力，请段出来，从西山上把段请回北京。并且这个时候，由于袁世凯想做皇帝，他已经把国务院撤销了，不要国务院，他在总统府内设了一个叫做政事堂（的机构）。这个时候他要死了，他晓得是不行了，要请段出来，撤销政事堂，恢复国务院，段是国务总理。这样子因为段的人很正派，也是反对袁世凯做皇帝的，西南对段还是承认的，并且西南也没有兵力可以打到北京来，所以就妥协，妥协就组织一个南北统一的政府。

我的一个亲戚（张耀曾），也是一个长辈，就代表西南入阁、进政府。张耀曾就拉我做机要秘书，他跟西南方面的广西、云南、四川倒袁的势力往来有秘密的电报、函电，我就替

these affairs for him. So when Mr. Cai asked me to come to Peking University to teach, I could not go. I asked a friend of mine to substitute for me. The next year the political situation changed, and Duan left. Zhang also fell from power. Only at this time was I able to go to Peking University.

• Work with Chen Duxiu and Li Dazhao

Alitto: What do you think of Chen Duxiu?

Liang: Chen Duxiu was really a formidable person.

Alitto: You met him only after you went to Peking University, or...

Liang: I ran into him right before I went to Peking University. There was someone who was known by everyone, Li Dazhao. He had some guests over to his house for dinner. He invited Chen and also invited me. That was the first time I met Chen. At that time, Chen had just come from Shanghai to Beijing. He had intended to persuade people to buy shares from him for an "East Asia Library" publishing house he was creating. Each share was 50 silver dollars, and two shares were 100 dollars. He hoped that his old friends would persuade everyone to buy shares in order to finance this publishing house of his. He came to Beijing for this purpose. Right at that time Cai Yuanpei had returned from abroad and assumed the presidency of Peking University. He needed a corps of teachers, obviously. He couldn't teach everything himself. He was an old friend of Chen Duxiu's, so he told Chen, "Alright, since you have come to Beijing, forget about this publishing house project. Don't mess with publishing houses. You come help me out?" So, in this way, the three of us—Chen Duxiu, Li Dazhao and myself—entered Peking University at the same time.

Alitto: My impression is that your relationship with Chen Duxiu wasn't as good as yours with Li Dazhao.

Liang: Right. My relationship with Li started slightly earlier than with Chen. When I ran into Chen, it was at a banquet at Li's. But we three entered Peking University at the same time.

Alitto: With Chen Duxiu, you...

Liang: Chen left a very strong impression on me. Chen was someone who could really make breakthroughs, a man of great power.

Alitto: What do you think of the role he played in history?

他主管这个事情。所以蔡先生要我到北大，我就不能去，我就请了一个朋友替我。转过年来，第二年，政局变了，段也走了，张耀曾也下台，这个时候才帮助他。

- **与陈独秀、李大钊共事**

艾：您觉得陈独秀怎么样啊?

梁：了不起啊，这个人了不起。

艾：您是到北大以后才认识他的，还是……

梁：刚好在进北大之前就碰见他。就是有一个人人都知道的人——是李大钊。李大钊有一次请客人吃饭，请的有陈独秀，请的也有我，第一次见面是这样子。那次呢，陈独秀来是从上海到北京，他的意思是到北京来劝人募股，他搞一个叫做“亚东图书馆”这么一个出版社，要大家入股凑钱。50 块钱一股，100 块钱就是两股，希望找一个熟的朋友劝大家入股，凑成他要办的亚东图书馆，他是这样来的。刚好这个时候蔡元培先生从国外回来，接任北大校长，他得需要一个班子，他一个人不行啊。他跟陈独秀本来是老朋友，他就说：“好啦，你到北京了，不要搞什么图书馆了，不要搞什么出版社了，你就来帮我吧。”这个时候陈独秀、李大钊连我，我们三个人同时进北大。

艾：我的印象是，您跟陈独秀的关系没有和李大钊的关系那么好。

梁：对，跟李的关系比陈稍早一步，跟陈碰见，还是在李的宴会上，可是进北京大学是陈、李、我同时的。

艾：跟陈独秀，您……

梁：我对他很有印象。那个人是一个能够打开局面的人、很有力量的人。

艾：在历史上您觉得他扮演的角色是怎么样呢?

Liang: He started the Communist Party.

Alitto: Right! Very important?

Liang: Very important.

Alitto: He and Li Dazhao, naturally they together founded the Communist Party.

Liang: The friendship between the two was very good, but their personalities were different.

Alitto: So, Li was relatively...

Liang: On the surface Li was a very gentle person. Everyone who had personal contact with him liked him. In fact, though, he was a very radical person in his heart.

Alitto: His personal relations with others were comparatively good.

Liang: Better than Chen Duxiu did in his relationships. Most people's attitude toward Chen Duxiu was to respect him but give him a wide berth. Everyone was afraid because he was often very rude in his speech with others. At meetings of the university, he was the dean of the College of Arts. There was a College of Sciences, which was headed by Mr. Xia Yuanli. These two were of the same rank, one in the Arts and one in the Sciences. During meetings Chen would be very rude toward Mr. Xia and embarrass him. So...

Alitto: Li Dazhao wasn't that kind of person. Which of these two people do you feel yourself...

Liang: Of course my relationship with Li Dazhao was better.

Alitto: Was the most important reason that Li was gentle, or...

Liang: Yes, Li was gentle.

Alitto: In thought, was Li's close to your own? So [your good relationship with him] had to do with thought, or with the way he conducted himself?

Liang: It was very strange. What was strange? Both Chen Duxiu and Li Dazhao were members of the Chinese Communist Party, but Li never said anything to me about joining it. I don't know why. We were good friends but he never tried to get me into the Party.

Alitto: What about Chen Duxiu? I remember he had talked about this

梁：他是共产党的发起人。

艾：是啊，很重要的？

梁：很重要。

艾：他跟李大钊，当然也是一起组织成立共产党。

梁：他们两个人的朋友关系非常好，但两个人的性格不同。

艾：那李呢是比较……

梁：李呢，表面上是非常温和的一个人，表面上很温和，同大家一接触，人人都对他有好感，实际上骨子头里他也是很激烈的。

艾：他个人跟别的人的关系搞得比较好。

梁：比陈独秀搞得好。大家对陈独秀都有点敬而远之，怕他，因为他对人常常当面就不客气。在学校里开会议，他算是文学院长，开头叫文科学长，另外还有一个理科学长，搞物理的夏先生——夏元瑮，两个人地位是相同的，一个是文科，一个是理科，在会议席上他有时候对夏先生就很不客气，让人下不来台，所以……

艾：李大钊不会这样。您觉得这两个人，哪一位和您自己……

梁：我当然还是跟李的关系好。

艾：那主要原因是李温和，还是……

梁：唉，李温和。

艾：那李的思想有没有比较接近您自己的？是不是跟思想有关系，或者说是为人的关系？

梁：很奇怪。很奇怪是什么呢？陈独秀、李大钊都是搞共产党，可是李先生没有说过一句话拉我入党，不知道为什么。朋友关系很好，可是从没有介绍我也参加共产党吧，他没有。

艾：那陈独秀呢？我记得是有，跟您讲过，《中国人民最后觉悟》

with you. In *The Chinese People's Final Awakening* [referring to *The Final Awakening of the Chinese People's Self-Salvation Movement*] you mentioned Chen Duxiu's criticism of your conception of the rural reconstruction, calling it some petite bourgeois fantasy. At that time Chen Duxiu wanted you to join the Party. You didn't...he also didn't...

Liang: No, he also didn't ask me to join the Party.

● Bring Xiong Shili to Peking University

Alitto: Did Mr. Xiong also teach at Peking University?

Liang: He taught there.

Alitto: You met him at that time or after he had arrived at Peking University? Or before then?

Liang: I knew him before that. In fact, it was I who brought him to Peking University. Mr. Xiong and I were together for forty years.

Alitto: So when you were in Shandong, he went too?

Liang: He was with me in Shandong for a period. He didn't follow me from beginning to the end. In 1924, I went to Shandong to start a school. We went together. When I returned to Beijing from Shandong, we again were living together. In that period when I went to Guangdong, he went to West Lake in Hangzhou. Those two years we were separated. Later, when the War of Resistance started, I withdrew to Sichuan, and we were again together.

Alitto: As far as his publications go, can he be considered close to your own thought philosophically...

Liang: Xiong Shili was worthy of being called Confucian. From start to finish, his thought was Confucian. Other people mistakenly call him Buddhist, mistakenly term his theories Buddhist. Actually, this is not so.

In China there was a Buddhist group. It was in Nanjing, and was called the Institute of Buddhist Studies. (Alitto: It was Ouyang Jingwu?) Yes, the institute was run by Ouyang Jingwu. I knew Xiong very well, and I advised him to go to this institute to study.

How we became friends was kind of funny. At that time Mr. Xiong was teaching Chinese language at the Nankai Middle School. He had

（应为《中国民族自救运动之最后觉悟》）这本书，提到陈独秀批评您乡村建设的观念，说是小资产阶级的什么幻想，那个时候陈独秀是要您参加党，您没有……他也没有……

梁： 没有，他也没有让我参加党。

- **介绍熊十力到北大任教**

艾： 熊先生也是在北大教过书？

梁： 教过书。

艾： 您是那个时候认识他的，还是他到了北大以后呢？还是以前认识的？

梁： 早认识了，他到北大还是我介绍的。熊先生同我在一起有40年了。

艾： 那您在山东的时候，他也去了？

梁： 在山东他同我在一起有一段时间，没有始终跟着我，民国十三年（1924年），我到山东去办学，我们同去的。从山东回到北京，又是在一块儿同住。有一段我去广东的时候，他去杭州西湖，有那么两年分开、分手。后来抗战起来，退到四川，又在一起。

艾： 以他的著作来说呢，算不算是接近您自己的思想，哲学方面的……

梁： 他可以称得起是一个儒家，他始终是一个儒家思想。旁人误会他是个佛家，旁人以为他是一个讲佛学的，其实不是。在国内有一个佛学的团体吧、机关吧，就是在南京，叫支那内学院。（艾：是欧阳竟无？）是欧阳竟无。我跟熊先生认识在前，我介绍他去内（学）院。

我们发生朋友关系，说起来好像很可笑。那个时候熊先生他是在南开中学教书，教国文，教中文，他曾经在梁任公办的

written articles for Liang Qichao's journal called *The Justice*. These articles were written from a Confucian position vilifying Buddhism, saying that Buddhism was no good, that it made people lose their moorings spiritually and philosophically... In my article I criticized him. I said that in "this place" (referring to China) "a common fellow" (an ordinary Chinese) was "striving for survival," such and such. I said that his words were nonsense, that he was wrong. The article was published and he read it. In 1920, he wrote me a postcard from Nankai Middle School to Peking University. His postcard said, "You reprimanded me quite deservedly. I'm now on summer vacation and am coming to Beijing. I want to meet you." And so it was in this way we began our relationship. So he arrived in Beijing that summer. His personality had its cheerful side. When he was talking in high spirits, he would laugh heartily, and would gesticulate wildly, waving his hands and stomping his feet very exuberantly. He criticized Buddhism from a Confucian perspective, but I was myself a Buddhist, so I told him that he didn't understand Buddhism, that the Buddhist doctrine was extremely profound. He said he was going to explore Buddihism. I said, "All right, I'll introduce you to Ouyang Jingwu and his Institute of Buddhist Studies." So there he went through my introduction, and for three years, from 1920 through 1922, he studied there.

Now, I was at Peking University teaching; at first I was teaching Indian Philosophy and later added Consciousness-Only Buddhism. Consciousness-Only is an extremely specialized type of learning, technically very difficult. It originated with Xuan Zang of the Tang Dynasty. A follower of his, Kui Ji, also contributed to it. This type of doctrine is actually very scientific, with a lot of "names and phenomenal appearances." That is why it is sometimes called the "appearances school" (*dharma*-character school). It has a lot of technical terms that make extremely fine distinctions. These terms cannot be used arbitrarily, or casually. In using these terms one must be precise. The entire body of doctrine is highly structured and systematic, very scientific-like.

At the beginning, I taught Indian philosophy at Peking University, then I also taught Confucianism, Buddhism and Consciousness-Only Buddhism. When I was teaching Consciousness-Only Buddhism, I quoted a lot of Western scientists in order to explain it. The Consciousness-Only doctrine speaks of eight *parijñana* (kinds of cognition or consciousness). The first five are the senses (seeing, hearing, smelling, tasting, tactile feeling). The sixth is *mano-vijñāna*, the intellect. The

刊物叫《庸言》上写了些稿子，那些稿子站在儒家的立场诋毁佛家，他说佛家不好，佛家让人“流荡失守”。我的这篇文章里头就批评到他，我说“此土”——“此土”就是说中国了，“此土凡夫”，是个凡夫、凡人，“求生存”，怎么怎么样，他这个话是胡说，说的不对。文章发表了，他也看到了。民国九年的时候，1920（年），他在南开中学教书，他写一个明信片给我，寄到北京大学转给我，明信片上说：你骂我骂得很好，我现在放暑假了，我要到北京去，我们要见面。这样子开头相交的。他暑假就来到北京。他这个人有他那个敞亮的一面，他说话说得高兴的时候，他会哈哈大笑，可以手舞足蹈，很畅快的样子。他这个时候站在儒家的立场批评佛家，可是我是个佛家。我说你对佛家不明白，佛家的道理是非常地深的、高深的。他说我要去探求佛家，我说好，我可以介绍你到欧阳那个地方。所以，经我介绍，他就参加了欧阳的支那内学院。民国九年（1920 年）、民国十年（1921 年）、民国十一年（1922 年），有三个年头，他都在那里。

这个时候我在北京大学教书，起初教的是印度哲学，后来增加了讲佛家的唯识哲学。唯识这个东西，在佛家里头是很专门的东西，传统做这种学问的是唐朝的玄奘，玄奘的徒弟叫窥基。这个学问内容讲得很科学，它说名相，被称为相宗。它的名词都不能够随便讲的，都是需要很明确、确实，它全盘的学问很有组织、很像科学，唯识论啊、唯识法相。

我在北京大学起先讲印度哲学，后来也讲儒家，也讲佛家，讲唯识。开始我讲，引用许多西洋科学家的话来讲佛家，讲唯识。唯识是讲八识，头五识是眼耳鼻舌身，第六意识——

six ones enable us to cope with our external environment. The seventh is called *klistamanas* [the discriminating sense] and the eighth, the *ālāyavijñāna* [the "storehouse consciousness" from which come all "seeds" of consciousness]. These last two come from egoism and the ego. Not only do we humans have the ego, but all [other] animals do. All of us satisfy our desires from the external environment. So, with all animals we distinguish between the self and the "other," the internal and the external.

I was writing and lecturing on the Consciousness-Only school, and published two books on it. When I tried to continue writing, however, I felt that I was not really competent to deal with Consciousness-Only, and was not at all sure if I was correct. So I thought, well, the people at the Nanjing Institute of Buddhist Studies are true experts in this field. They can really penetrate and grasp the doctrines of Xuan Zang, Kui Ji and their school, so why don't I ask one of them to come teach this subject at Peking University? I had a discussion with President Cai Yuanpei about it, explaining that I was not really qualified to teach this subject, had no confidence and so on, and that I wanted to get one of the scholars from the Buddhist Institute at Nanjing to do it. President Cai agreed to provide the position, so I went to Nanjing. Of course, Ouyang Jingwu himself could not be moved from the Nanjing Institute, so I thought that I would invite one of his disciples, a man named Lü [Lü Zheng]. Lü was an excellent scholar who knew Tibetan and Sanskrit, a man of great erudition. But Lü was Ouyang's right-hand man and so he would not let Lü leave.

At that time, Mr. Xiong was already starting his third year at the institute. This was the winter of 1922, and it was I who, after all, was responsible for his being there in the first place, and he was an old friend. So, when I couldn't get the man I wanted, I invited Mr. Xiong to come instead. I invited him to teach Consciousness-Only Buddhism at Peking University. Ah! How could I have known that he would do the opposite of what I had hoped! I didn't have any confidence in my own understanding, and was afraid that I was teaching a confused jumble, distorting what Xuan Zang introduced from India. My original aim was to get an expert on Consciousness-Only to come teach instead of me, as I thought that this would be a more suitable arrangement. Who would have thought that after Mr. Xiong arrived, in fact he would do precisely the opposite of what I had hoped? He wanted to create an entirely new pattern of things, to start a whole new entity. He entitled his lectures on Consciousness-Only the "New Consciousness-Only." For fear that I might distort or lose the original message of the ancients, I asked Mr. Xiong to come teach Consciousness-Only for me, and he simply took his own interpretations very subjectively to be the substance of Consciousness-Only! But since he had already arrived at Peking University as a professor, there was no way I could then ask him to leave. So I was stuck.

眼耳鼻舌身意。前六识是意识外面的，应付环境的，根本上有个第七识和第八识。我们人呢，不单是人，一切的动物，一切动物它都有"我"。昨天我说了，一切动物都是向外取，满足自己，所以它都是分成一个外边、一个内边，一个物、一个我。

我慢慢地写文章讲唯识学，出了第一册、第二册，继续写的时候自己也很不自信，这个讲法对不对？我就想南京内学院他们是内行，他们是能够本着玄奘啊、窥基啊、法相宗的学问，我就请他们。我跟蔡校长蔡元培先生说，这门功课我讲不了了，我不敢自信了，恐怕讲得不好、不对，我要去内学院请人来讲。蔡校长同意了，我就去请。一请呢，当然欧阳大师是请不动了，我就想请欧阳大师的大弟子，姓吕的（吕澂）来讲。吕的学问也是好得很，他可以通藏文、通梵文，学问好得很。欧阳大师不放，他的左右手，不放。

这个时候，熊先生在内（学）院已经到了第三个年头了，本来是我介绍去的，我的熟朋友，请不动旁人，我就请熊先生。我说"你来吧"，请他到北京大学讲唯识。哪里晓得跟我的所想的相反。怎样相反呢？我是不敢自信，恐怕我讲的是自己乱讲的，不合当初玄奘从印度学来的那个学问——唯识学。我的意思请个内行人来讲妥当，哪晓得熊先生请来以后大反我所预想，他要开辟新局面，他讲的唯识标明是"新唯识论"。我是唯恐失掉古人的意思，他就是主观地按自己的意思来讲古人的学问。可是这时候已经请他来了，他担任这个课了，尽管不合我的意思，我也没有办法变更了。

● Gu Hongming of an analytical mind but quite tendentious

Alitto: Did you know Gu Hongming?

Liang: I ran into him.

Alitto: In Beijing?

Liang: At Peking University. Didn't I tell you that I withdrew from Hunan? When the troops pulled out, I came out with them, and wrote a small pamphlet—"If We do not Take Action, What about the People?" At that time I went to Peking University. I ran into Mr. Gu in the Teachers' Lounge—there was a lounge for the teachers to use before going to the classroom to teach their classes. He was very tall, and wore the old style dress, the dress worn during the Qing Dynasty—a long robe, a riding jacket. The robe was blue and the riding jacket was maroon. He wore a small cap with a red bump on it. He wore a queue. Didn't the Qing people wear queues? He was very tall. Didn't I write the pamphlet, "If We do not Take Action, What about the People?" I had put several copies of it on the table in the Teachers' Lounge for people to see. He picked one up, nodded his head, and said, "A person of high aspirations and determination." He was much older than I, probably by fifty or sixty years. At the time I was only 24.

Alitto: I knew his granddaughter in Taiwan.[15] She's already gone to the U.S. I met her when I was studying Chinese. Too bad that her family's papers are gone. What did you think of him? I feel that he was strange. He advocated bound feet and wearing queues. He really was completely conservative.

Liang: In China a man had a wife and several concubines.

Alitto: Right, he also advocated...

Liang: If people expressed opposition or disagreement, he would tell a joke. He said that a teapot could have four cups, but you could not have a cup with four teapots. This man was quite eccentric. He did his utmost to raise up China, and belittle foreign countries. He said such a remark: You foreigners, Europeans, previously you were unable to separate yourselves from the church. Religion taught you morality and restrained you. Later when religion no longer was such a powerful force, national armies kept you under control and dominated. China was not like this. China's common people themselves like peace and quiet.

- **辜鸿铭有见识，但思想主张很偏**

艾： 您跟辜鸿铭认识吗？

梁： 碰见过。

艾： 是在北京吗？

梁： 北大。我不是说我从湖南撤退？他撤兵的时候我也随着出来了，写了本小册子《吾曹不出如苍生何》。那个时候我去北大，在教员休息室——就是说在上课堂教课之前，有个教员休息的地方——在教员休息室碰见辜先生。身体很高，穿旧的服装，清朝人的服装，穿长袍，穿马褂，蓝袍子，枣红的马褂，带小帽，小帽上有一个红疙瘩，有辫子，清朝人不是留辫子嘛，身体很高。我不是写了《吾曹不出如苍生何》那个小册子？我就在教员休息室的台上我也放了几本，随便给大家看。他也捡起来看，点点头，说一句话："有心人。"他岁数比我大很多，恐怕要大五六十岁，那时我只有24（岁）。

艾： 对。他的孙女，我认识她，在台湾，她现在已经在美国了，学中文的时候我认识她的。可惜她家的文件啊这类东西已经都没有了。你对他怎么看，感觉他好奇怪啊，他主张小脚、主张什么辫子，他真是保守到家了。

梁： 中国人有一个正太太，还有好几个妾。

艾： 对，他也主张……

梁： 人家表示反对，不同意，他就说一个笑话，他说一个茶壶可以有四个茶杯，你不能一个茶杯有四个茶壶。他这个人呢，是一个很古怪的人。他极力抬高中国、贬低外国。他说这样一句话：你们外国，欧洲人，以前离不开教会，宗教教训你们、管束你们。后来呢，宗教没有那么大势力了，国家的军队镇压、统治。中国不是这样，中国就是他自己喜欢和平、安静的老百姓。

Alitto: Your books,[such as] *Eastern and Western Cultures and Their Philosophies,* also expressed this idea.

Liang: Russell of England very much admired China.

Alitto: Yes. As for the saying of Gu Hongming just mentioned, if the church didn't control Westerners, they were controlled by the state—it was always a force external to person. The case was different in China. After Confucius, it was ethics for ethics' sake, pure ethics—not gods or laws. This is a very big difference between China and the West.

Liang: Aren't China's common people very disorganized? Disorganization and peace are linked. The more peaceful the more disorganized, the more disorganized the more peaceful. Each goes through life in a disorganized and peaceful manner, unless in certain periods—China underwent a cycle of order and a cycle of disorder. In a period of order, perhaps after a hundred years or whatever, there must be disorder. The disorder is followed by order. What is order? It is everyone settling down, in disorganization and peace. This is different from foreign countries.

Alitto: Did you have any other opinions on Gu Hongming?

Liang: This man did have an analytical mind, but he was also one biased old-timer. His thought and positions were quite tendentious and one-sided.

● My intercourse with the four professors of the Institute of Chinese Studies, Tsinghua University

Liang: I already spoke of my relationship with Mr. Liang Rengong. My relationship with Mr. Liang was not that long. He was in the North. Later I went to Guangdong, to Li Jishen's. When I was in Guangdong, I was 36. Liang Rengong was exactly 20 years older than I. While I was in Guangdong, he died in Beijing in 1929. Most of my contact with him was in Beijing. He was in charge of the Institute of Chinese Studies of

Tsinghua University. At the time, the institute had four professors. Liang Rengong was one. Another was Wang Jing'an (Wang Guowei), another was Chen Yinke. The fourth was Zhao Yuanren. Zhao Yuanren is still alive in the United States.... He possessed an extremely rich knowledge. I heard that he had this kind of ability: he usually spoke madarin as we did. But if he went to a new place, for example, Fujian or Guangdong, within a

艾： 您的几本书，（如）《东西文化及其哲学》，也有这种意思。

梁： 英国的罗素他对中国很欣赏。

艾： 是。辜鸿铭刚才提到的那句话，西方人不是给教会控制着就是给国家控制着，总是人外的一种力量，跟中国人不同了。中国孔子以后，为了伦理而伦理，纯粹的一种伦理，不是什么神啊，也不是什么法律，这是中西之间很大的不同的地方。

梁： 中国的老百姓不是很散漫的（吗）？散漫跟和平相连，越和平越散漫，越散漫越和平，散散漫漫、和平地各自过日子。除非到某一个时期，中国都说一治一乱，一个治的时代，或者有 100 年或者多少年就要乱一次，乱了又治。什么叫做治呢？治就是大家都各自安身了，散漫和平。跟外国不同。

艾： 对辜鸿铭有没有别的意见……

梁： 这个人就是一个有见识、但是又是很偏的一个老前辈吧，思想主张很偏。

• 我与清华国学院四大导师

梁： 再说的就是我也提到过的，跟梁任公的关系。跟梁先生的关系，时间不是太长，他在北方，后来我去了广东，在李济深那个地方。我 36 岁，梁任公刚好长我 20 岁，我在广东的时候，他就在北京死了，故去了，民国十八年（1929 年）故去的。跟他往来比较多的时候是在北京，他主持清华大学的国学研究院。当时清华大学国学研究院有四个导师，梁任公先生是一个，还一个有名的叫王静安先生——王国维，再一个姓陈的，叫陈寅恪，第四个呢是赵元任，赵元任现在还在，在美国。……他的知识很丰富。听说他有这样一个本事，一般地他跟我们一样讲北京普通话，但是如果他到一个新鲜的地方，比如到了福建、到了广东，就那么一天、两天，他就能讲那个

day or two, he was able to speak that place's dialect.... From the rhyme and enunciation, he understood the speech after having been there a day or two, so he could speak local speech. People told me it was that way.

At that time I also lived at Tsinghua, staying at someone else's place. I wasn't working at Tsinghua. But Mr. Liang Rengong was managing the Institute of Chinese Studies, and engaged me to give lectures for a short period, about a month. I lectured on a temporary basis. At that time I had relatively more contact with him. I also met and had contact with Mr. Wang Jing'an at that time. I heard about Mr. Wang Guowei's suicide by drowning at the Summer Palace just a few hours after it happened. I even went off to the Summer Palace to see what the situation was. I also knew Chen Yinke and had some contact with him. He also was someone of rich and broad learning. I did not much seek his instruction. As for Mr. Zhao, I didn't speak with him. Among historical personages, I had a period of closeness with Liang Qichao.

地方的方言。……从音韵上、从运用口齿上，住上一两天，他就晓得怎么样子，所以他能讲当地的话。人家告诉我是这样。

我那个时候也住在清华，算是借住，我没有在清华工作。不过梁任公先生主持那个国学研究院，他也请我在国学研究院作过一个短期的讲演，短期讲学，大概就是讲一个月，临时给他讲。那个时候我同他比较有往来。那个时候我同王静安先生——王国维认识、往来。王国维先生在颐和园投水，我就在几个小时后我就听说了，我还跑去到颐和园去看。我跟陈寅恪也认识，有过接触，他也是学问很丰富、很多，我没有怎么样向他请教。至于赵先生，没有谈过话。过去的人物里头算是我跟梁任公先生——梁启超曾经有一段很亲近。

● My running school in Shandong

Liang: There was some one else with whom I was very close. I don't know if you heard of this person—a Shandongese named Wang Hongyi.

Alitto: Yes, that's in the book [*The Last Confucian*]. There are about ten pages about your intellectual relationship with him. I have read his writings. Did you get to know him at that time? At first he was in Shandong running a school. Later, when the May Fourth Movement began, he came to Beijing and sought out Hu Shi. (Liang: Sought out Hu Shi and Mr. Cai [Yuanpei].) You got to know him at this time?

Liang: Yeah. Because he was someone of influence in Shandong. He was from Caozhou in Shandong. There was a middle school in Caozhou called the Sixth Middle School under Provincial Administration, which he had founded. Later he was very close to someone named Jin Yunpeng, who had been Chairman of Shandong Provincial Government and the Premier [of China]. He had great influence in Shandong educational circles, and in 1921, he supported and welcomed me to go to Shandong to lecture during the summer, to give lectures on *Eastern and Western Cultures and Their Philosophies*. Later he, together with Jin Yunpeng, wanted to organize a Shandong Great Company. The company's funds were from mining and railroads—the Boshan Coal Mines and the Qingdao-Jinan Railroad that the Japanese had returned; they wanted to use a part of these funds to found a university. What university? One called Qufu University, in Confucius' hometown. They were busy with this and wanted me to come run the university. I said that it wouldn't work. I said that I was thirty-some years old. At that time I was just thirty. How could managing a university be that easy? How could so young a person [as I, who had] just [entered] the academic world... This wouldn't work.

Alitto: When you left Peking University, you went to Shandong… (Liang: I did.) I don't quite have this straight. I supposed that you and those who founded the university had different opinions, with the result that you didn't go.

Liang: They wanted me to manage Qufu University. I said: I can't regard

贰 我与乡村建设

- **我在山东办学的经历**

梁： 有一个人跟我朋友关系很好，不知道你听说过这个人没有？一个山东人，叫王鸿一。

艾： 是，这个书里也有（《最后的儒家》），关于他跟您的思想有关系的，差不多10页。他的著作我拜读过，我都看过。您是那个时候认识的？他是先在山东办了个学校，后来五四运动开始，他到北京来，跟胡适请教，（梁：向胡适、蔡先生求教。）您是那个时候认识他吧？

梁： 嗯。因为他是在山东地方上很有势力的一个人，他是山东曹州人。曹州有一个中学，叫省立第六中学，第六中学他办起来的，他同那个做过山东省政府主席的、后来做国务总理的叫靳云鹏，跟靳云鹏很熟、很相好。他在山东教育界很有势力，他主张要欢迎我去暑期讲演，讲《东西文化及其哲学》，在民国十年（1921年）。后来他还要同靳云鹏，他们想要组织一个鲁大公司，鲁大公司的款，是日本退回来的博山煤矿、胶济铁路——把铁路矿山的收入取一部分办一个大学。办一个什么大学呢？办一个叫做曲阜大学（的学校），孔子的家乡，办一个曲阜大学。他们搞这个活动，要我来办。我说不行啊，我说我就30多岁，那个时候刚刚30岁，不行。办一个大学哪里那么容易的事情，哪里这么（个）年轻人，刚刚在学术界……这个不行。

艾： 您离开北大的时候，您就是去山东……（梁：去了。）这个我弄不清楚了。我猜的是，结果您还是与创立大学的人意见不同，结果不去。

梁： 他们要我办曲阜大学，我说不能就这么样子把它看成可以随便

such an enterprise as something that could be done casually. If you want to hand over its management to me, we should have done the work for the preparatory stage. There are two kinds of preparatory tasks. One is the preparation for the future instructors. The other is the preparation for the university students. They said, "Alright, you go manage it." [I then] went to run a senior high school. On the one hand, a senior high school, and on the other...an academy, the Revive China Academy.

Alitto: The Revive China Academy is also in Caozhou?

Liang: Caozhou. These two institutions were together in the same place, the same city. The students were not only going to be drawn from Shandong. Although the school was in Caozhou, Shandong, students would be recruited in Beijing. I had previously issued a document called "Brief Review of Our Opinions on Education," which was how we were going to run the school. It mentioned a slogan, "to Be Friends with You [the student]." [This was] not like the situation in which the teachers talked about some stuff in school and the students received some knowledge, which looked like an instructor selling knowledge. We didn't want it like that. We wanted to be friends with the youth and leading the youth together on the road of life. We recruited students in Beijing. Because this document was issued, a lot of people saw it, and because we recruited students in Beijing, not in Shandong, the recruited students, the later ones, carefully counted, included people from thirteen provinces and cities, some as far away as Suiyuan, Shanxi, Shaanxi, Yunnan, Guangdong, Sichuan, Zhejiang, etc.—students from thirteen provinces and cities. Because we recruited them in Beijing, we brought them to Shandong. But, it was a pity that I myself stayed there just for half a year. I brought several friends there to be instructors who worked there a year.

...At the time there were two cliques of warlords, the Zhili clique and the Anhui clique. There were contradictions between them. When there were contradictions, military activities would influence things.[16]

My school couldn't continue. So I withdrew. The group of instructors that I brought there had lectured for a full year and they also withdrew. Because, as I just said, we wanted to be friends with the youth, many students had emotional attachments and very close relationships with us. So, some students withdrew with us. Everyone lived together in Beijing. At that time, Mr. Xiong Shili was together with me. When I

办起来的事情，你们要交给我办，我们应当做一段预备阶段的工作。预备阶段的工作作两种预备，一个是预备将来主持这个大学的教员，一个是这个大学的学生，就这个预备。他们说好，你就去办，去办就是办高级中学，一方面办一个高级中学，一方面办一个……书院，重华书院。

艾：重华书院还在曹州吗?

梁：曹州。这两个机关在一起，在同一个地方，同一个城市。学生呢，不是单吸收山东的学生，虽然学校办在山东曹州这个地方，可是招生在北京招生。因为我事先发布一个文件，叫《办学意见述略》，讲我预备怎么办学校。提出一个口号，就是要跟青年做朋友，不是像学校里头老师讲一些东西，学生就是来接受一些知识，好像是一个贩卖知识的教员，不要这样；要跟青年在人生道路上做朋友，领导着青年大家共同在人生道路上走。发表了这样一个《办学意见述略》，在北京招生。因为这个文件发表出去，很多人看到了，招生又不是在山东，在北京招生，所以招的学生、后来的学生，细心地数起来，包含 13 个省市的人，有绥远的、山西、陕西的、云南的、广东的、四川的、浙江的……13 个省市的学生。因为在北京招到的，都带去到山东。不过可惜呢，就我自己说，我就是在那边停留了半年，我带去几个朋友，就是教职员，在那里搞了一年。

……当时的军阀里头算是直隶派——直系，还有皖系——就是安徽的，所以他们都有矛盾啊，有矛盾了，军事活动就影响了，我那个学校办不下去，所以我就退出来了。我带去的一班人满了一学年之后，也退出来了。因为刚才说过，我们是要跟青年做朋友，所以许多学生跟我们感情、关系很密切，所以有些学生都随着我们都撤退出来。就在北京嘛，大家在一起住。这个时候熊十力先生也跟我一块儿住，我去曹州，他也

went to Caozhou, he went with me, and left there together with me. Also, there was a period, about one or two years, not a brief period. So, I wasn't doing anything, and I had some students [with me]. One was Li Jishen, one was Chen Mingshu. Every month they would send several hundred silver dollars to support us. After they supported us for these two years, they sent a letter saying that we should not closet ourselves in Beijing talking scholarship, because at that time the National Revolution was in Guangzhou [and] the revolutionary waves were strong—they told us not to talk scholarship behind closed doors, to go participate in the revolution together. I also felt that this national revolution was a new lease on life for China. [I felt that] they weren't the old style warlords. The era of the old warlords had passed. They seemed to be a newly arisen force. At that time Mr. Sun [Yat-sen] was influenced by Russia, and allied with Russia and the Communists, with his "Three Great Policies." I also wanted to go take a look around. Before I went myself, I first had three friends go, and then later I would go. When I went I only wanted to observe the situation, and didn't dare involve myself in [the movement]. But because Li Jishen was an old friend...he didn't tell me beforehand and had the Nanjing National Government announce that I was a member of the Guangdong Provincial Government Committee. I wasn't willing [to serve]. This I said before.

● When I was Yan Xishan's advisor

Alitto: According to some materials, there was a "Village Government Group." Before you joined, there were already some...which consisted of Wang Hongyi, Wang Yike, and Liang Zhonghua. Were there others?

Liang: There were others who belonged to this group. In Henan they started the Henan Village Government Academy and in Beijing they started the *Village Government Monthly*. Both the magazine and the academy used the name "Village Government." The inside story is that money was still needed for the publication of the *Village Government Monthly*. Where did this money come from? From Yan Xishan.

Alitto: Oh! So Yan Xishan was connected to this Village Government Group?

Liang: It was all [through] Wang Hongyi. Wang Hongyi was like an honored guest of theirs. Feng Yuxiang was a big warlord. And so was Yan Xishan. Wang was an honored guest of these warlords. They both respected him, and would speak with him. He was their advisor. Later I, too, was engaged by Yan Xishan as an advisor. Wang Hongyi was also the person who introduced me to Yan.

跟着我一块儿去，一同退回来。第二个就是有这么两年，时期并不很短，那么我什么事情不做，还有一些学生（跟着我）。……一个是李济深，一个是陈铭枢，每个月给我们几百块钱维持。维持了这么一两年，他们就来信，说你们不要在北京关着门在那儿谈学问——因为这个时候广州正是国民革命，革命的潮流正在很盛——你们不要关着门谈学问了，你们来，我们一道参加革命。我也感觉到他们广东的这种国民革命好像是中国的一个生机——不是旧军阀，旧军阀那个时代过去了，他们好像是一个新的力量起来了。那个时候正是孙先生受俄国的影响，联俄联共，三大政策。我也想去看一看。去看之前，我先让三个朋友去。然后自己也去。去的时候我只是想看，不敢自己投入到里边去。可是因为李济深是个老朋友，他没有先跟我说，他就让南京国民政府发表我（为）广东省政府委员，我不肯就，过去说过一下。

- **我做阎锡山顾问的时候**

艾： 有些资料说有个“村治派”，您参加以前已经有一些……就是王鸿一、王怡柯、梁仲华，还有一些别人啊？

梁： 还有一些别人。因为河南的，在河南就成立了村治学院，北京呢成立了《村治月刊》社，出版刊物，一本杂志，都是用村治的名字。这个背后呢，《村治月刊》社出版东西是需要钱的，这个钱谁出的呢？阎锡山。

艾： 噢，那阎锡山和村治派怎么有关系？

梁： 都是那个王鸿一。王鸿一好像是一种座上客。冯玉祥是一个大军阀，阎锡山是一个大军阀，他是大军阀的座上客，他们都很尊敬他，他可以向他们说话，是他们的顾问。后来不是我也被请为阎锡山的顾问？也都是王鸿一介绍的。

Before the enlarged meeting, I received a letter of appointment as a high level advisor from Yan Xishan through Wang Hongyi. Each month he would send me 500 silver dollars as a fee for advising him. At that time, I spoke to Yan: Since he gave me such a lavish fee for being an advisor, I wanted to contribute my opinion. I told him that now China's present problem was none other than you several big leaders. China's problem was whether or not there would be civil war again—previously there had been civil war. Civil war benefited no one. It would benefit none of you powerful figures, or the common people, and it would sap the vitality of the nation. Rather than having another civil war, it would be better to sacrifice oneself, to fall from power. This was the suggestion I gave him. He should respect the older generation in the Guomindang—the four senior statesmen—Wu Zhihui, Cai Yuanpei, Zhang Jingjiang and Li Shizeng. He should respect them, establish a privy council, and allow them to perform a supervisory function. Each of the big warlords should disarm, and absolutely should not have another civil war. This was my contributory opinion. Later Wang Jingwei and Chen Gongbo went to Taiyuan. He never listened to my council again; instead he organized an enlarged meeting to oppose Chiang. I immediately resigned my position as advisor. Later then, the Great Plains War started.

Alitto: How was Yan Xishan as a person?

Liang: He had his strengths. He was extraordinary. From the Revolution of 1911 overthrowing the Qing Dynasty, he arose to seize the governmental power in Shanxi, and held on to it for several decades. In no other province can you find a second person that controlled a provincial government continuously for several decades. There was no one else. That he had abilities and strengths is out of question, but he was still selfish. He was always grasping at power. He wanted his subordinates to adopt a kind of religious ceremony, to take a vow to the spirits that they would be loyal to him, and never betray him. People took this oath, which said what punishment Heaven would befall them if they were not loyal to the vow. He went in for this sort of game.

So I say that he was selfish, he had no [greater] ability. It was limited to this. No more. His moral character, personality and ability stopped with this, and didn't go higher. So as soon as Wang Jingwei and Chen Gongbo arrived there, he cast my advice aside, set up an enlarged meeting to oppose Chiang, and so in this way there was the Great Plains War, with Yan and Feng [Yuxiang] on the one side, and Chiang on the

扩大会议之前，通过王鸿一，我接受阎锡山一个高级顾问的聘书，每个月送我 500 块钱，顾问的工资。当时我就对阎谈了，他这样厚礼顾问，我要贡献我的意见。我说现在中国当前的问题，不在别人，就在你们几个巨头。中国问题就是，是不是还要再打内战，过去打了内战，今后是不是还要打内战。打内战是谁也没有好处，你们巨头之间谁也没有好处，老百姓、国家元气更受伤，再也不要打内战，宁可牺牲自己，我下台，不打内战。那么我给他建议，要尊重国民党内部的老前辈，就是吴稚晖、蔡元培、张静江、李石曾四大元老，尊重他们，成立一个枢密院，让他们来发挥一种监督作用。各军阀巨头要裁军，绝对不要内战。我贡献的意见是如此，可是后来汪精卫、陈公博来了，到了太原，他就没有再听我的话，他就搞起了扩大会议，对蒋，那么我就马上辞了这个顾问。以后就中原大战打起来了。

艾：阎锡山他怎么样，为人怎么样啊?

梁：人有他的长处了，很了不起了。他从辛亥革命推翻清廷的时候，起来掌握了山西的政权，一直掌握了几十年，在全国各省找不到第二个人掌握一省政权始终掌握几十年的，再没有别人。他有他的本事、有他的长处是没有疑问的，但是还是有私心。他就是说老想掌握大权，他要部下啊，好像是采取宗教的仪式，对着神灵发誓，发誓我要忠于阎先生，决不背叛；我发了这个誓，以后我要是不能忠于这个誓，天怎么样地降罚给我——他就搞这一套。

所以要不我说他那个自私啊，也就是他没有本事吧，他的品格、人格、本领也就止于如此，没有更高的。所以汪精卫、陈公博一到他那里，我劝他的话他都扔到一边，搞扩大会议，要对蒋，这样就有中原大战。阎、冯（玉祥）是一边，蒋是

other. They lost the Henan War. How did they lose? Zhang Xueliang of the Northeast was bribed by Chiang, and entered at their rear. Naturally they lost. He was selfish and unclever.

● Han Fuju and Rural Reconstruction Institute

Liang: Chiang Kai-shek wanted to get three [bodies of] people out of the way—the Guangxi clique, Feng Yuxiang, and Yan Xishan. At that time [when Han Fuju was governor of Henan Province] Feng was under great pressure from Chiang. Feng didn't want to fight Chiang, so he withdrew his troops westward. He gave up Shandong and Henan. Originally he had occupied both Henan and Shandong. He gave them both up. He withdrew northwestward through Tongguan.

After going through Tongguan, he held a military conference. At this meeting Han spoke against the withdrawal westward, because with so many troops—around 200,000—they would not be able to survive in such poor areas as Shaanxi and Gansu. Moreover, because of the poverty of the region, our [the troops'] presence would also be a burden for the people in the region. At this point, Feng became angry and said, "What do you know? Don't say anything more! Get out of here! Leave the conference room! Go outside the door and kneel as punishment!" Feng always handled his subordinates in this high-handed manner, treating them as if they were his children. So Han had to go outside the door—still in the adjoining room—and kneel. After the conference had been adjourned, when Feng was leaving, he passed by the still kneeling Han, gave him a box on the ear, and told him, "Get up!" Then Feng left.

Now at this point Han was the commander of the general headquarters and also the governor of a province. He had a lot of subordinates of his own. So he just could not take this kind of treatment. So he got up and, with his most trusted officers and their troops, left off the westward march, and instead returned through Tongguan to Henan. As soon as Chiang Kai-shek heard that Han had broken away from Feng, he was overjoyed. He had wanted to separate them. He immediately offered Han the chairmanship of the Shandong Provincial Government. Han was Chairman of the Shandong Government for ten years.

In 1929 I hadn't had any intention to stay in the North, but as it turned out, I did [stay]. It was because the political situation in Guangdong

一边，在河南大战。河南大战失败了，怎么失败的呢？东北的张学良受蒋的贿赂，张学良从后边来了，当然他们就失败了。他是有私心，不高明。

- **韩复榘与乡村建设研究院**

梁： 蒋要解决三个人，第一是解决桂系，第二解决冯，第三解决阎锡山。这个时候，冯呢受蒋的压迫，冯不想跟蒋打，冯就是把自己军队向西撤，放弃山东、河南，本来山东他也占了，河南他也占了，山东、河南他都放弃，从潼关往西北走。

进了潼关之后，开军事会议，在会议席上，韩（复榘）就说话了，发言就是说，我们不应该向西撤，我们军队这么多人，好像 20 万人吧，往西撤，陕西、甘肃这个地方是苦地方，不像山东那样。我们到那里，到这个苦地方，这么多军队啊，于军队也不好，于地方也不好，地方也受苦。冯就发怒，说："你懂什么？你不要说话！"跟他说："你出去！"——从这个会议室出去，到外面一个屋子，到门外面，外面还是一个屋子，"罚跪！"——跪下。冯对他自己的部下，他向来就是有这样一个威严，好像是对自己的孩子一样。韩就只好在门口外头——还是个屋子，跪着了。这个会议开完了，冯散会，冯出去的时候，打韩一个耳光，说："起来吧！"就走了。

韩呢，他已经又是总指挥，又是什么主席，他自己有很多部下嘛，他就受不了。他起来之后，他就把他比较能够最亲信的将领、最亲信的部队，就带出来了。他就不往西去，回河南，从潼关又回来了。这个时候呢，蒋介石知道了这个韩从冯脱离，他非常高兴，他是要分化，他马上发表韩的山东主席，韩就到山东了。韩到山东，做山东主席正好 10 年，韩的势力发展在山东。

我本来在民国十八年（1929 年），没有想到留在北方，

Province changed. Chiang placed Li Jishen under arrest, and so I didn't want to return to Guangdong. Right around that time, a friend of mine established the Henan Village Government Academy. Peng Yuting was the president, with Liang Zhonghua serving as vice president. They welcomed my going to work in the school, and so I became the academic dean. At that time, they had just started the school, and so all the substantive issues—content, curriculum, teaching methods and so on—had not yet been decided upon. I was able to make these determinations, and also to write many of the rules and regulations, and methods. Then Han, following Chiang's orders, was transferred to Shandong. At that time, Liu Zhi was one of the big generals in Chiang's army, and he arrived in Kaifeng, Henan. The vice president of the Henan Village Academy, Liang Zhonghua, closed the academy. He was no longer able to run it. He set out for Jinan and reported to Han. Han answered that it didn't matter (that the academy shut down). He then invited us to bring the school to Shandong. The original body of people involved in the Henan Academy had not yet dispersed, so we all went to Shandong. We consulted together and decided not to use the name Village Government Academy anymore. So the name of the school was the Rural Reconstruction Institute. And so that is how we ended up in Zouping, Shandong.

Alitto: It would seem that Han Fuju felt that local self-government and rural reconstruction were important.

Liang: He trusted and believed in us.

Alitto: How did your own relationship with Han Fuju develop?

Liang: It was for this reason. At first, in Henan, when the academy was still in the planning stages, Peng Yuting came to bring me from Beijing to Henan. We went first to Zhengzhou, and from there to Kaifeng. The provincial government was in Kaifeng at that time. We had just got off the train in Kaifeng and were in the hotel when Han Fuju arrived to visit me. He was extremely modest and unassuming. He said to me, "I have heard you lecture in Nanyuan in Beijing." So this meeting was in Henan.

Didn't I just say that he had already been transferred to Shandong? So, when we went to Shandong, I had known him, and had become well acquainted with him long before. Well-acquainted, so we chose Zouping

可是结果留在北方了，因为广东局面变了，李济深被扣了，我不想回广东了。刚好河南朋友，就办起来河南村治学院，院长就是彭禹廷，副院长是梁仲华，他们就欢迎我参加这个工作，我就担任教务长。这个时候他们刚刚开始，一切的内容，怎么一个办法，都还没定，都是我给他出主意，定了许多的章则、办法。刚才不是说韩奉蒋的命令就调到山东了吗？这个时候是蒋的军队有一个大将，叫刘峙，刘峙驻开封，到了河南。刚才说的，原来村治学院的副院长，姓梁——梁仲华，就结束了河南的事情，河南的村治学院不能办了。他就跑到济南去向韩报告，韩说："不要紧，我请你们都在山东好了。"所以，我们就到了山东。本来村治学院的一批人，很多人都还没有散，那么就转移到山东去了。转移到山东去，大家商量不用那个"村治学院"，不用那个名称，用这个名称，是"乡村建设研究院"。这样子，我们就在山东邹平……

艾： 就是说这个韩复榘，他是好像觉得乡村建设、这个村治啊工作是要紧的，对不对？

梁： 他很信任我们。

艾： 那么您个人跟他的关系……

梁： 也就是这样一个关系。开头在河南的时候，还是要开办村治学院，村治学院在筹备期间的时候，那个院长是彭禹廷，彭嘛就从北京迎接我到河南，到郑州，从郑州再去开封，当时省政府还在开封。我刚刚下了火车，在开封下火车，住在旅馆里的时候，韩就来看我，很谦虚。他告诉我，他说："我听过你的讲，在北京南苑的时候。"这是在河南。

刚才不是说他已经调山东了吗？所以到山东已经算是早已认识了，早已相熟了。相熟嘛就是我们选择了邹平这个县，

County. This county was not far from Jinan, and it wasn't too far from the railroad either. We chose this place as our experimental district. In this district, the institute was divided into three major sections: a research department, a training department, and an experimental department.

Alitto: Yes. There is a lot of material on all of this. What was Han's attitude toward this? What do you think his motive was for supporting you? He was...

Liang: His intentions were the best. He gave us completely free rein. He let us work independently, and completely gave over to us the County of Zouping. The institute was located in the county, and the county was under the control of the institute. We nominated the county magistrate, and then the provincial government would appoint him and announce the fact. Later, we reorganized the county government. All of the measures we adopted were of an experimental nature, just to see what methods and measures would be best. For example, originally there were four bureaus outside the county government. There were an educational bureau, a reconstruction bureau, a finance bureau, and a security bureau. We amalgamated these four bureaus into the county government itself, and these various matters were managed centrally in the county administration. This is an example of the sorts of experiments we carried out.

In the end, Han unintentionally offended Chiang, and so he had Han shot. How did he offend Chiang? When the Xi'an Incident occurred, and Chiang was detained, the CCP sent Zhou Enlai down to Xi'an to consult on what should be done with Chiang. At this time, the various warlords all sent representatives to consult with each other on what action to take. He [Han] sent a cable to Xi'an that proposed that the question of how to punish Chiang should be settled by a conference in which all parties would consult with each other. Now, this proposal was not to Chiang's advantage, but when this cable was sent Chiang had already been released. When Chiang saw the cable, he said, "I have always been good to you. How could you do something like this?" And so he began to hate Han after this. Han had sent his cable too late; Chiang had already been released. So, later Chiang had Han shot.

Alitto: I had understood that Chiang had Han shot because when the Japanese invaded Shandong, Han did not resist with full force.

这个县刚好离胶济铁路不远，离济南也不算很远，离铁路线不太远，离济南也不算很远，我们就选择这个地方做一个实验区。在这个实验区，研究院就主要是三个部分：一个部分是研究部，一个部分叫训练部，一个部分叫实验区。

艾： 是，这些倒是有很多资料啊。就是说韩复榘自己的态度怎么样呢？您看他维持着你们的动机在哪里呀？他是……

梁： 他的意思是很好的。他很放手给我们，让我们工作，他就把这个邹平县交给我们。这个研究院设在这个县里头，而县呢属于研究院。县长由我们提名，省政府来任命、发表。后来我们就对县政府改组，一些事情都采取一个试验的性质，看看怎么样好，怎么样办法好。比如说，原来县政府之外是四个局，什么教育局、建设局，什么公安局、财政局，我们就把这些局都不要，统统归并到县政府里头，在县政府里头合署办公，合在一起办公，如此之类。

韩在无意中得罪了蒋，所以蒋把他枪毙了。怎么样得罪蒋呢？就是西安事变，不是蒋被扣吗？蒋被扣的时候，陕北的中共方面，周恩来到了西安了，蒋被扣起来，好像要商量对蒋怎么样。这个时候，各省的军阀互相派代表商量——得到蒋被扣的消息了——商量怎么样子……韩答复一个电报到西安，他就提议说，怎么样处分蒋，我们大家开会商量。这样一个主张并不利于蒋——共同商量对蒋如何嘛。可是这个电报出去之后，蒋已经出来了，蒋看见这个电报："我一向对你很好嘛，你怎么还要这样子？" 所以他心里头恨这个韩。韩这个电报去晚了，韩去电报，蒋已经出来了，所以后来是韩被蒋枪毙的。

艾： 不过我也听说、了解，韩被蒋枪毙是因为日本人侵略到山东，韩没有抗日。

Liang: Han was a selfish person. He was not able to resist the Japanese completely because he wanted to preserve his own forces, and so he withdrew from Shandong. He was going to move to the west of the railroad.

● My views on rural reconstruction

Alitto: When you were working in Henan as well as in Shandong, Sun Zerang was there as well?

Liang: Right. I was working at the Rural Reconstruction Institute in Shandong. The president was Liang Zhonghua. The vice president was Sun Zerang. I was head of the Research Division, but later Liang Zhonghua resigned, and I took over as institute president. Sun Zerang was vice president. Later because we opened a second experimental district in Heze, there was a branch institute there, and Sun Zerang went there to take charge of things. But later he died; he died in Sichuan.

Alitto: What kind of man was he? What was his background?

Liang: He had entered an agricultural technical school, but he was a courageous and able man. He was Wang Hongyi's student, Shandongese, from Caozhou. He first served as the [Rural Reconstruction] Institute's vice president, and later went to his home area. He went to Heze in Caozhou to set up a branch institute. He was first the county magistrate, and later after an administrative district was established, he became Administrative District Commissioner, administering over ten counties. After the War of Resistance started, he withdrew from Shandong with some armed forces, armed militia, about two thousand men. First they went to Wuhan, then from Wuhan to Hunan, and from Hunan into Sichuan. When in Hunan and Sichuan, the government wanted him to be an Administrative District Commissioner. A commissioner could administer over ten counties. There was an administrative district in Hunan, so he was a commissioner first in Hunan, and later in Sichuan. This man had talent and nerve.

Alitto: Were his views on rural reconstruction different from yours?

Liang: Very different. The kind of rural reconstruction I wanted was for the long term, with far-reaching significance. The devices of the village schools and township schools were designed with quite profound

梁： 韩有一种自私的心，他没有能够在山东这个地方尽力地抗日。他自己保存实力，保存他自己的实力，撤出山东，他预备到铁路西边去。

• 我的乡村建设主张

艾： 您在河南、也在山东工作的时候，有一位孙则让。

梁： 对。我在山东不是搞乡村建设研究院？乡村建设研究院院长是梁仲华，副院长是孙则让，我是研究部主任，不过后来梁仲华辞职了，我就接任院长。孙则让先是副院长，后来因为在菏泽开辟了第二个实验区，有乡村建设一个分院，孙则让就到那儿主持那个事情。但是他后来死了，死在四川。

艾： 他是什么样的人呢？什么来历？

梁： 他进过一个农业专门学校，但是很有胆子，很有才干。他是王鸿一的学生，山东人，曹州人。他先做我们的副院长，后来就到他本地，他是菏泽那儿的人，曹州人，到那个地方设分院，先做县长，后来又成立专区，他做专员，管十多个县。抗日战争起来，他带着许多的武装势力、武装壮丁，差不多有 2000 人，从山东撤退，先到武汉，从武汉到湖南、到四川。到湖南、四川的时候，当时的政府要他做专员——专员是可以管十多个县的，有一个专区——先在湖南做专员，后来在四川做专员。这个人很有才，很有胆子。

艾： 他对乡村建设的看法和您的有没有特别？

梁： 很有不同。我想要搞的乡村建设，我把它的意义是从一个很深远的方面来看。我所要办的村学、乡学，那里边的一些办法、

purpose in mind.[17] But he was not this way. He focused on the [short-term] necessities of the time. What was the immediate need of the time? Because of the Japanese aggression against China, he concentrated hard on training militia and preparing to resist Japan.[18] He focused on this.

Alitto: The book also has this aspect. Heze and Zouping were two different styles of rural reconstruction. Heze style was Sun's. It was like that.

Liang: It was like that.

Alitto: How would you compare your Rural Reconstrlcction Movement with the present movement? In greater detail.

Liang: As far as I am concerned, what I wanted to do with rural reconstruction was to bring some organization and mobilization to the scattered, disorganized countryside and its traditional "familialism," by which each person cared only for his own family, and completely ignored any wider community. So, as far as the Rural Reconstruction Movement's aim of organizing the peasantry into groups, I think that this has indeed been accomplished. Previously, China lacked two things: first, organizations in suprafamilial organizational forms and second, modern science and technology. As far as the latter was concerned, the question was how to introduce science and technology into Chinese agriculture effectively and how to industrialize agriculture. So, now this task can be accomplished, too. So, the two original goals I had for the Rural Reconstruction Movement—group organization and science and technology have been or will be accomplished.[19]

• My second son is Tao Xingzhi's student.

Alitto: You knew Mr. Tao Xingzhi for a long time. You met him in 1928 or 1929? After you toured the Xiaozhuang Normal School, you wrote many articles that referenced this place, such as "My Northern Journey...."

Liang: "A Record of What I Saw [on My Northern Journey]." My second son can be considered his student.

Alitto: Where?

Liang: In Sichuan. When he was eight or nine years old, he was Mr. Tao's student. Mr. Tao was very good indeed, really terrific. He was a very good person. He had studied in the U.S. Previously these were called

设计有相当用意很深的地方。可是他不是这样，他就是着眼于当时的需要，当时的需要是什么呢？就是日本人要侵略中国，所以他着意训练壮丁，准备抗日，他着眼这个。

艾： 书里也有，菏泽式和邹平（式）是两种式样的乡村建设，荷泽式就是孙的。是有这件事。

梁： 是那样的事。

艾： 那您觉得，比如乡村建设运动，您自己也是发起了这个运动，有没有跟现在的情况类似的地方？具体一些。

梁： 就我自己说，我想要做到的——我曾经说过一下了——就是让散漫的农民——各自顾身家、顾我一身一家的农民——能够组织起来，能够组成团体，现在组织起来了。团体组织是一面，是中国所缺乏的，要赶紧往这方面走。还有一方面就是，中国的科学技术上是太缺乏了、太落后了，那么怎么样子把科学技术能够引进到中国来，引进到农业上，引进到农业工业化，这个事情现在也能做了。一个团体组织，一个科学技术，这个两面，从前我搞乡村运动的、我想要做的事情，现在都往这个方向走了。

• 我的二儿子是陶行知的弟子

艾： 陶行知先生您也认识了很久了，1928、1929 年就认识他了吧？参观了晓庄乡村师范，您写了很多关于那个地方的文章，《北游……》……

梁：《所见记略》(《北游所见记略》)。我的第二个儿子算是他的学生。

艾： 是在什么地方？

梁： 在四川。还在他八九岁的时候，他是陶先生的学生。陶先生这个人好得很啊，了不起，人太好了。他本来是留美的，中国

students who had studied abroad, and they wore Western clothes and leather shoes. He also had worn them, but discarded them and wore instead peasant clothes and straw shoes. He founded the Xiaozhuang Normal School. He led a class of students to some empty space outside of Nanjing, where they built the buildings themselves. Really something. This man was great, really good. I never saw anyone like him among those who had studied abroad.

Alitto: Aside from that tour of Xiaozhuang Normal School, what other contact did you have with him...

Liang: When the Japanese came, we withdrew to Sichuan. What work was he doing? Mr. Tao had taken in a group of homeless refugee orphans of both sexes from Wuhan and from along the railway. After he took them in, he brought them to Sichuan, where he trained and educated them. At that time I also sent my second son to him,[20] so he can be considered Mr. Tao's student. That man was wonderful![21]

Alitto: From the viewpoint of the present, how would you appraise his historical role? How would you describe it?

Liang: He should be considered an educator. I want to say something about his death. How did he die? The Nationalist Party government in Nanjing thought that he was a Communist Party member and treated him as such.

Alitto: When was that?

Liang: The peace talks were held in Nanjing between the two parties before he died. The Nationalist secret agents on Chiang's side put him on the blacklist of people who must be killed. The secret agents were to assassinate him. After this list came to light, he himself was a bit frightened. He died in Shanghai. He didn't die of illness. It seems that he collapsed while on the toilet. We were all in Nanjing [at the negotiations]. Zhou Enlai took a special trip to Shanghai to see him off after he had died. When he was in Wuhan, he had taken in a great many homeless refugee children. At that time he set up an orphans' school [Yucai School] on the upper reaches of the Jialing River in Chongqing, slightly upriver from Beibei. The name of the place was Caojiezi. I sent my second son there to be his student.

Alitto: He shared a lot of similarities with you. He also liked Wang Yangming and his philosophy. He also admired Dewey. He also laid stress on rural education...

从前的叫做留洋学生，都是穿西装、穿革履。他也穿西装也穿革履，都脱了，穿中国农民的衣裳、穿草鞋，创办晓庄师范。在南京城外空地，他领着一班学生，自己盖房子，了不起。那个人太好了，太好了，在留洋学生中没有看见那样的人。

艾：您除了那次参观晓庄师范以外，跟他有什么……

梁：日本人来了，我们都退到四川去了。退到四川去了，他做一个什么工作呢？陶先生他把逃难的——在武汉、在铁道旁边有些个没家可归的孩子，男孩子、女孩子，他都收了。收了之后带到四川去，他培养他们、教他们。我那个时候把我第二个儿子也送去给他，所以他算是陶先生的学生。那人太好了！

艾：您从现在的眼光来看他、评价他历史上的角色，您会怎么说？

梁：应当算是一个教育家。我要说一下他死，他怎么死的呢？就是国民党南京政府，认为他是共产党，把他看作共产党。

艾：这是什么时候？

梁：就是他死之前，就是在南京搞和谈的时候，两党和谈的时候。在国民党蒋方特务黑名单一定要杀的人里头，把他的名字列在内，特务去刺杀他。这个名单透露出来之后，他自己很有点害怕。死在上海，不是病死，好像是在大便的时候，坐在上面就虚脱了。我们都在南京，周恩来还特别到上海去送，看他一下，他故去了。他在武汉收了许多逃难的、无家可归的孩子，那个时候，他办了一个儿童学校（名为“育才学校”），在四川重庆嘉陵江的上游，北碚往上一点儿，地名叫草街子，我就把我第二个儿子送去给他做学生。

艾：他跟您有很多相同的地方。他也是喜欢王阳明、王阳明的哲学，他也很欣赏杜威，他也是比较注重乡村的教学……

Involvement in national affairs

● Feng Yuxiang's men both loved and feared him.

Liang: Wang Hongyi introduced me to Feng Yuxiang, in 1924.

Alitto: In 1924, Feng Yuxiang was in Beijing.

Liang: Feng's title was Inspector of the Army. There were about 50,000 men in his troops. He himself held the rank of Divisional Commander. A division was made up of two brigades. There were three more independent brigades, so five brigades altogether. There weren't 50,000 men. Probably around 35,000 men. They were stationed at Nanyuan in Beijing. It was at that time through Wang Hongyi's introduction that I first met Feng Yuxiang.

Alitto: Because Wang Hongyi was in Beijing at that time?

Liang: Yes, in Beijing. He invited me on behalf of Feng to visit Feng at his quarters in Nanyuan, and to give lectures to his troops. That was in the first lunar month of 1924. So I met Feng at Nanyuan. I gave five lectures.

Alitto: To what troops were all the lectures given?

Liang: To his troops.

Alitto: Did you lecture to all of his troops at once?

Liang: No. They were divided into separate groups. He had five brigades, right? I gave one lecture to each of his brigades, only to the officers and noncoms. So, one day I lectured to brigade A and the next to brigade B. The content of each lecture was similar though not necessarily. The content could be different. Feng also attended these lectures. Everyone called Feng the "Christian General." He was a believer in Christianity. The YMCA was part of the Christian church. So he operated a YMCA in his army. The person who ran this YMCA of his was named Yu Xinqing. Didn't Feng later get married? The person he married was Li Dequan. Ms. Li was a member of the church. She was a teacher in a church-run school in Tongzhou.

Alitto: What kind of things did you and Feng Yuxiang talk about when you met?

叁 奔走国事

• 冯玉祥让士兵又爱又怕

梁： 我跟冯玉祥的认识，还是王鸿一介绍的，就是民国十三年（1924 年）。

艾： 民国十三年，冯玉祥在北京。

梁： 冯玉祥官的名叫做陆军检阅使。他的部队大概有 5 万人，他自己也是兼一个师长，一个师有两个旅，另外还有 3 个独立旅，一共 5 个旅。一共 5 个旅……没有 5 万人，大概有 35,000 人的样子，地点驻在北京的南苑。我跟冯玉祥的开头见面，就是王鸿一介绍的。

艾： 因为王鸿一在北京吗?

梁： 在北京，王鸿一介绍，就是王鸿一代表冯玉祥，说冯玉祥请我去到南苑——他驻军的地方，给他军队讲演，这样子我开头去的。这个时间是民国十三年，旧历正月，这个时候我到南苑跟冯玉祥才见面。讲了 5 次。

艾： 都是给什么军队啊?

梁： 就是他的军队。

艾： 是所有的军队，还是给一部分?

梁： 分开，分开。他不是有 5 个旅吗? 给一个旅的官兵讲一次——没有兵，兵的人太多了，他叫官佐。每一个旅有它的官佐，今天给这个旅的官佐讲，明天给那个官佐讲。讲 5 次，内容可以相同，也可以不相同，听讲的人是换的，每一次讲的时候冯陪着听讲。冯嘛是人家称他为“基督将军”，他是信教，基督教里头有青年会，他也在他的军队里头办青年会，替他办青年会的叫余心清。后来不是冯玉祥结婚了? 结婚的那个叫做李德全，那个就是一个教会里头的人，是在通州教会学校里的一个女教员，叫李德全。

艾： 那您跟冯玉祥见面的时候，谈到什么样的事情啊?

Liang: I didn't talk much with him personally, even though Wang Hongyi introduced Feng to me. In Feng's army there was a special custom. Didn't he run a YMCA organization in the army? He had a custom of inviting people to give lectures. For example, the famous military scholar Jiang Fangzhen. Feng invited Jiang Fangzhen to come give lectures. Feng also issued a small book to his officers. There were sayings in this small book—maxims and quotations from people, usually of two or three sentences, five sentences at most. Not long. He would write that somebody had said such and such. For example, "Zeng Guofan has said such and such" or "Zhuge Liang has said such and such." He even had Jiang Fangzhen quoted in this small booklet. So, this booklet was issued to his officers and noncoms. Feng did an excellent job in supervising and educating his troops. So his men both loved and feared him very much. Even with the number of troops that he had he would often, when in the ranks, address people by name. Of course, he couldn't remember every single soldier's name, but he did remember quite a few. So his men both loved and feared him.

Alitto: Feng Yuxiang also had a great interest in rural work, didn't he?

Liang: Right, right.

Alitto: Wasn't he friends with Tao Xingzhi?

Liang: He toured Tao's project at Xiaozhuang.

Alitto: Whether or not it was Feng Yuxiang and Han Fuju who were the sponsors for the Henan Village Government Academy, or...

Liang: It was founded during the time when Feng controlled Henan, but not on Feng's initiative. It was started by Henanese—such as Wang Yike, Liang Zhonghua, Peng Yuting, and so on. These Henanese presented this proposal [to found such a school] to Feng Yuxiang and Feng accepted it. But Feng did not give them any money for the school.

Alitto: You just said that making an evaluation of him was difficult. Is there any other meaning, about him or his political...

Liang: He was a military man. Politically he didn't have any clever opinions or positions. He wasn't that smart. He and Chiang Kai-shek... Chiang liked to be on good terms with people. To get on good terms, the old Chinese way was to become sworn brothers. He was older than Chiang, so Chiang called him elder brother. Chiang was into this routine. He had no way of handling Chiang. He wasn't that smart, but he was a better man than Chiang.

梁：跟他个人没怎么多谈，就算是王鸿一先生介绍。冯的军队有一个习惯，不是他办青年会吗？他有习惯请人讲演。比如那个中国有名的军事学家蒋方震，他就先请蒋方震讲。冯玉祥给他的军官发个小本子，小本子上有一些好像是语录，就是人家讲的话，两句、三句，或者稍微多一点也就是五句，不多。他就写个某某人曰，比如"曾国藩曰"，从前诸葛亮，（就写）"诸葛亮曰"，他也将蒋方震蒋先生列为"蒋方震曰"。他有这么一本小本子，他给他的官佐看。冯玉祥对所谓带兵、管兵、教育兵他很有办法，他的兵非常地爱戴他，也非常地怕他。他那么多兵啊，他有时候在许多兵里头："你，出来，你不是谁谁吗？"——他能叫出来那个兵的名字。当然他也是不能全记得了，所以他的兵都又怕他又爱他。

艾：好像他对乡村工作也很感兴趣，对不对？

梁：对，对。

艾：他跟陶行知算是朋友吧？

梁：他到陶先生的那个晓庄师范去参观。

艾：王怡柯的村治学院呢，不是冯玉祥、韩复榘好像做村治学院的靠山哪，或者……

梁：他是那样，他是在冯玉祥统治河南的时候，成立的这个村治学院，但是村治学院的成立，不是冯玉祥主动的。是河南本省人，比如王怡柯是河南人，彭禹廷是河南人，梁仲华也是河南人，本省人建议给冯，冯采纳，才同意，又不需要冯出钱，这么样成立的。

艾：关于他为人，甚至他政治上的……

梁：他就是一个军人。在政治方面他没有什么高明的见解主张，头脑还是不够。所以他跟蒋介石——蒋喜欢跟人所谓要好，要好嘛，中国的老办法结为兄弟——那么他比蒋岁数大，蒋就叫他大哥，蒋就是这一套。他对蒋毫无办法，他的头脑不够，他人比蒋人好。

● My student Xu Minghong and the Fujian People's Government

Alitto: You had a student named Xu Minghong? (Liang: Yes.) Can you talk in comparative detail about him, or your evaluation of him? Mr. Wang Shaosheng of Hong Kong had written a draft of his biography, but the draft has not been published yet. Only after he let me read it did I know any details about him [Xu], but you know much more than Mr. Wang.

Liang: I possibly know more than he. I still have letters from Xu Minghong. I have a student, perhaps my closest one, Huang Genyong. Huang was from Guangdong. Xu was also from Guangdong. It was Huang who introduced Xu and me. [There were three people—] one was Xu Minghong, one was Huang Genyong and another was Wang Pingshu. The three went south to Guangdong through my introduction, and later they participated in the National Revolutionary Army. During the National Revolutionary Army's Northern Expedition, the three went with the Army to Wuhan. In Wuhan the three had differences. Xu Minghong joined the Communist Party, and was in Wuhan. Wang Pingshu liked the Communist Party's thought, philosophy and theories, especially historical materialism. But Huang didn't join the Communist Party, and didn't exactly like its theories. So the three were different. To put it simply, later in Fujian, Li Jishen and Chen Mingshu started a People's Government.[22] At this time, Xu Minghong had a relatively important position in the People's Government. Huang Genyong also went there. Xu Minghong represented the Fujian People's Government in their dealings with the Communist Party in Jiangxi.

Alitto: I mentioned this in the book [*The Last Confucian*]. Later he was killed.

Liang: He was assassinated. In Shantou, Xu's hometown, he was killed by Chen Jitang. After the Fujian affair failed, Xu fled back home from Fujian, and died a martyr's death there.

Alitto: What contribution do you think he has made to the Chinese revolution?

Liang: He died for the revolution, died a martyr's death. But I had expressed my disapproval of the Fujian affair. How did I express disapproval? I had held back Huang Genyong from going [to Fujian]. I

- **我的学生徐名鸿与福建人民政府**

艾： 您有过一个学生，徐名鸿？（梁：对。）可不可以比较详细地讲他的事啊，或者您对他的评价？香港的王韶生先生就是写的他的传，可是稿子没有出版，他给我看了，我才知道他比较详细的情形，不过您知道的比王先生多得多了。

梁： 可能多一些。我现在手里还有徐名鸿写来的信，他亲笔的信。我有一个跟随我最亲密的学生叫黄艮庸，黄艮庸是广东人，徐名鸿也是广东人，徐名鸿与我的关系还是黄介绍的。徐这个人，也是经我介绍吧，一个徐名鸿、一个黄艮庸、一个王平叔，三个人去南方广东，后来他们参加国民革命军。国民革命军北伐的时候，这三个人都随北伐军到了武汉，到武汉的时候三个人就不相同，怎么不相同呢？徐名鸿就参加了共产党，到武汉去了。王平叔对共产党的思想、哲学、理论还欣赏，特别是关于唯物史观。可是黄呢，没有参加共产党，也说不上是欣赏共产党的理论，三个人就不相同了。简单地说嘛，后来李济深、陈铭枢在福建搞起了人民政府，这个时候徐名鸿在人民政府里算是个比较重要的人。黄艮庸也去了。徐名鸿还代表福建的人民政府去跟江西的共产党接洽。

艾： 这个我也在书里提到了（《最后的儒家》）。以后也是被杀的。

梁： 被刺。他是被广东方面的陈济棠杀的，在汕头，就是徐的家乡。福建的事情失败了，他从福建逃回家乡，那个时候牺牲的。

艾： 您觉得他有什么贡献，对中国革命？

梁： 他为革命而死，为革命而牺牲了。不过我对福建的事情我曾经表示不赞成，怎么表示不赞成？曾经拦阻黄艮庸，

had said to him, "Don't go. Originally Li Jishen and Chiang Kai-shek were both veteran Nationalist Party members. They both followed Mr. Sun Yat-sen. You can oppose Chiang, but do not yourself oppose him from a position outside the Nationalist Party. You should tell him, 'You have betrayed the Nationalist Party that Sun Yat-sen originally created. I am a Nationalist Party member. You have betrayed the Nationalist Party.' Now if you leave the Nationalist Party, and position yourself outside the Party, you then cede legitimacy to Chiang Kai-shek. This would be a mistake." Later, right through to the death of Li Jishen, he [Huang] was still the director of the Beijing Revolutionary Nationalist Party, and avowed himself to be a Nationalist Party member. Why did he go outside of the Nationalist Party?

I had heard that originally Xu Minghong was supposed to represent [the People's Government of Fujian] in contacting the Jiangxi Communist Party, but the Communist Party rejected him. If Chairman Mao had taken a position at the time, he would have approved of the alliance. At the time, Chen Shaoyu and Qin Bangxian were in charge [of the Communist Party]. They had seized Chairman Mao's power. They couldn't hold out in Shanghai, so they ran off to Jinggangshan. They said that the Fujian group were petty bourgeois, and were not sufficiently revolutionary, so they did not help Fujian. In fact, the correct strategy for the Communist Party was to ally itself with Fujian and tackle Chiang together. Well, in allowing Chiang to wipe out the Fujian People's Government, the Communist strategy was wrong.

● Li Zongren's War Zone Party Policy Committee

Alitto: How did you get to know Li Zongren? Where was it?

Liang: Both Li and Bai Chongxi were natives of Guilin. I can also be considered a native of Guilin. When they ruled Guangxi Province, they used a policy called the "Three Selves Policy." That is, self-government, self-defense, and self-sufficiency. They followed these three guidelines.

Alitto: Was it their original policy, or through your...

Liang: It was their idea.

Alitto: These ideas are quite similar to those of Peng Yuting's group in Zhenping.

Liang: They were similar, but they didn't interact, or influence each other.

我说你不要去。本来李济深跟蒋介石都是老国民党，都是追随孙中山先生的。你可以反对蒋，但是你不要自己站在国民党外头反对他，你应当是说：你违背了孙先生当初创造的国民党，我是国民党，你是背叛了国民党。现在你离开国民党，自己站在国民党外边，反而把正统让给蒋介石，这个是错误的。往后呢，一直到李济深死，他还是作为北京的民革委员会的主任，还是承认自己是国民党，为什么要跑到国民党外面来?

那次的失败，我听说，他们本来要徐名鸿去跟江西的共产党联系，可是被共产党拒绝。当时如果是毛主席作主张的时候，他是会赞成联合的。当时是陈绍禹、秦邦宪他们作主，他们夺了毛主席的权，他们在上海站不住了，跑到井冈山去。他们就说福建这一派是小资产阶级，不够革命，所以没有帮助福建。其实如果共产党跟福建联系，共同对付蒋，策略上才是对的；那么让蒋消灭了福建，共产党策略上不对。

- **我与李宗仁的“战地党政委员会”**

艾： 李宗仁，您是怎么认识他的？原来是在什么地方？

梁： 李宗仁同白崇禧，这两个人都是广西的桂林人，我也算是桂林人。所以在他们统治广西的时候，他们提倡所谓“三自政策”，“三自”好像是：自治，地方自治；自卫，自己保卫；自给，“给”就是经济上自给自足。搞这个“三自政策”。

艾： 是原来的政策，还是您……

梁： 不，当然是他们的。

艾： 就是跟镇平那一带的……彭禹廷也有个“三自政策”。

梁： 相似吧，相类似，不过不是互相影响的。他们在广西这个

In Guangxi, they were not happy with Chiang Kai-shek's rule, so they were semi-independent. They also took on board some intellectuals and thinkers and worked together. When they brought out this "Three Selves Policy," they invited me to return to Guangxi [Liang's formal native place] to lecture. I think that was about 1935. That was the first time I returned to Guangxi. Li and Bai were both Guilin men. Bai was a Moslem. That was the first time I went back to Guilin. I was closer to Li than to Bai. When the war started, Li was the Fifth War Area Commander, stationed in Xuzhou. Later he invited me to visit him in Xuzhou.

Alitto: Yes, I have that in my book. He wanted to consult with you on how to mobilize the masses for the war effort.

Liang: Right. I stayed in Xuzhou for more than a month. I lived on a farm in the northern part of Xuzhou. But I went to Li's headquarters every day to have lunch with him, and to talk with him afterwards. I did this every day for about a month.

Alitto: Did you talk about plans, or...

Liang: We didn't talk about anything in particular. At the time there was an organization called the War Zone Party Policy Committee. I was considered a member of that committee. Every war zone had such a committee. The committee members were appointed by the central government. I was a member of the Party Policy Committee for the Fifth War Zone, and was stationed in Xuzhou, and so stayed there over a month. Afterwards, we withdrew to Wuhan. In Xuzhou, there was one convenient thing—my students, my cadre from Shandong could come see me, and I could then give them instructions on what to do. I wrote about this in that little book I gave you.

Alitto: Yes, there was something about that in it. So your relationship with Li Zongren was very close at that time.

Liang: Yes, quite close.

Alitto: Li Zongren... When the CCP had already got to the Yangtze River,

Chiang Kai-shek resigned, and Li Zongren became president. According to some material that I have seen, he wanted to invite you to be...

Liang: He wanted me to become active, to campaign for peace.

Alitto: And you refused?

Liang: Yes.

地方，他们不高兴蒋介石的统治，他是一个半独立性，他也收一些个文人或者有思想的人，一同搞，那么就有“三自”的提出来。这个时候呢，他就希望我回广西，去看、去讲演，那么我回去讲演来着，这个时候好像是 1935（年）吧，民国二十四（年），好像是那样。那是我第一次回广西。李、白都是桂林人，白呢是回族，回教的。我第一次回去。后来嘛，就是跟李相熟得多一点，抗日战争起来，李就算是第五战区司令长官，驻徐州，最后他请我去徐州。

艾：这个我书里有的，他跟您商量怎么动员群众啊……

梁：对。在徐州我停留了有一个月，我住啊，是住在徐州北郊一个农场里头，可是午饭呢，到李宗仁那个总司令部去吃饭，在他那儿坐，随便谈。天天如此，有一个月的样子。

艾：那您讲计划呢，还是讲什么？

梁：没有讲什么。当时算是有个机关吧，叫做“战地党政委员会”，我算是战地党政委员会的委员。战地党政委员会呢，是每一个战区都有一个战地党政委员会，委员呢是中央任命的。我是作为第五战区战地党政委员会的委员，住在徐州，住了有一个月，后来就从那儿回武汉。在那儿对我有一个方便，就是山东的我的学生、我的干部，可以到徐州来见我，我可以指示他们怎么样办。那个小册子上后边有。

艾：是，关于这一点是有的。就是您和李宗仁从那个时候关系比较密切啊。

梁：很熟啊，很熟。

艾：李宗仁这个……，共产党已经打到长江的时候，蒋介石辞职了，而李宗仁做总统的时候，依我看到一些资料啊，他想要请您做……

梁：要我出来，要我出来奔走和平。

艾：您拒绝了他的请求？

梁：嗯。

● My contact with Chiang Kai-shek

Alitto: You also had a lot of contact with him [Chiang Kai-shek], especially during the War of Resistance, and after it. You hadn't met him prior to the war, had you?

Liang: No, because I never participated in government... I always worked in society.

Alitto: I know that in the 1930s, before the war, you didn't seem to have a good impression of Chiang Kai-shek. I seem to recall that in your book *The Last Awakening of the Chinese People's Selfsalvation Movement,* you compare Chiang with Yuan Shikai, saying that they were about the same, simply very successful warlords. I also remember that during the peace negotiations after the war you didn't seem to like him very much, and blamed the continuation of the civil war on him. Did you make any other comments about him?

Liang: If we are going to talk about Chiang Kai-shek and me, we must start from an earlier period. I was in Shandong doing rural reconstruction at the time that Chiang was in Wuhan in what he called his Bandit Extermination General Headquarters. The "bandits" referred to the Communist Party. As he was stationing troops in Wuhan, he reorganized the Wuhan Provincial Government. He wasn't very satisfied with the original administration, [so he] had Zhu Jingnong appointed as the Superintendent of Education for Hubei. Zhu had studied in the U.S., and had specialized in education. But Zhu was the president of Cheeloo (Qilu) University in Jinan, Shandong. A church ran this university. He had to resign his position as president and then take up the position as Superintendent of Education. So, he went from Wuhan back to Jinan. Chiang asked him if he knew Liang Shuming. Zhu answered that he did know me. Chiang said, "When you go back to Jinan, ask him to come to Wuhan to meet me." Zhu returned to Jinan and resigned his university presidency. He saw me in Jinan, and relayed Chiang's invitation to me. I told him, "OK, I have the message." But I didn't go. I couldn't bring myself to go just because he had sent someone with this one sentence. This was the first contact that I had with Chiang.

I had contact with him next in Nanjing, when the Second Interior Affairs Conference was held to discuss the internal affairs of the whole nation. The Ministry of Interior Affairs convened this conference. The

- **我与蒋介石的来往**

艾：政治家蒋介石，您和他也有很多来往，尤其是在抗战的时候、抗战以后啊。抗战以前，就没有见过面吧？

梁：因为我始终是不参加政治，我始终在社会方面做事情。

艾：我知道在 30 年代，抗战以前，您对蒋介石也没有什么好的印象了。我记得您那个《中国民族自救运动之最后觉悟》书里面说，蒋介石是跟袁世凯差不多了，是军阀，就是比较成功的军阀了。也知道抗战以后，和谈、谈判的那个时候，也印象很不好，觉得就是因为他内战。另外呢，有没有什么别的……

梁：谈到我跟蒋，我要从头说起了。还比较早的时候，我在山东做我的乡村建设工作。刚好啊，蒋本人住在武汉，他叫做“剿匪总司令部”——“匪”嘛就是共产党。因为他自己驻军在武汉，他就把武汉省政府改组，原来的省政府他认为不大满意，他就改组。改组嘛，他就用一个姓朱的，叫做朱经农，也是留美的，学教育的。他就改组湖北省政府，湖北省政府里头有教育厅了，他就用这个朱经农做湖北教育厅厅长。可是朱呢，原来是在山东济南做齐鲁大学的校长，齐鲁大学是个教会办的学校，所以他需要辞齐鲁大学校长，来接任湖北教育厅长，所以他就从武汉回济南。回济南的时候，蒋就对朱经农说：“你认不认识那个梁某某人呢？”朱说：“认识呀。”他说：“你替我说一句话，希望梁到武汉来跟我见面。”那么这个朱经农他回去，到济南交卸齐鲁大学校长，在济南看到我，他就把蒋的话传达给我。我说：“好，我知道了。”但是我不去，我不能够因为他派人传这么一句话，我就自己去呀，我不去。这是头一次。

后来，刚好在南京开第二届内政会议，讨论全国的内政，这个是归南京的内政部召集的。这个时候内政会议的部长是

Minister was a Guangxi native, Huang Shaohong. He was eager to adopt innovative and new programs and policies. He wanted to use measures superior to and also inclusive of rural reconstruction, which he called county government reconstruction. This would include the county level and the countryside below the county. At this conference he presented his plans. So he invited me and my colleagues working in Shandong, as well as Yan Yangchu, to attend as specialists this conference in Nanjing to help his program of county government reconstruction. So, because of this matter I traveled to Nanjing.

At that time, the mayor of Nanjing city was an old friend of mine. This man [Shi Ying], was a veteran, an old friend of Sun Yat-sen's. He was old, quite a bit older than I. When only 19 years old, he won the *Juren* degree, and after that studied chemistry in England. Mr. Cai Yuanpei engaged him as a professor of chemistry at Peking University. He had helped Sun Yat-sen while abroad, an old friend of Sun's. At the time he was mayor of Nanjing city, and also a friend of mine, since we had both been teaching at Peking University. Mr. Shi came to see me at the Central Hotel [where I was staying]. He said, "Chiang Kai-shek had wanted to meet you and you didn't come. Now that you are already here in Nanjing, you must see him." I answered that I would see him. Mr. Shi was mayor, so later he called Chiang's secretary to arrange a time, the evening of a certain day. Mr. Shi came in his car to pick me up for the appointment at Chiang's official residence. This was the first time I met Chiang Kai-shek.

Even from the very outset, at this first meeting, I didn't like him. Why? He was insincere and false. He had heard, he said, that I was very famous and had wanted to meet me. He wanted me to come see him, but I had been unwilling. This time Mr. Shi had made the arrangements and brought me to see him, and so on. How was he insincere and false? He held a pen in his hand—a fountain pen, and also a little notebook. When we were talking—naturally we were just talking at random—I do not remember how I happened to bring it up, that at the time the Jiangbei area—northern part of Jiangsu and part of Anhui—had suffered a great flood, and the damage was quite heavy. A friend of mine was doing relief work in the area. I just don't remember how it came up but I did mention this man's name and his work in disaster relief. As soon as he heard this,

广西人，叫黄绍竑。那么他很想办一件新的，采取新的方针、新的政策，他就要搞在乡村建设之上的、而又包含乡村建设的，他叫做县政建设——一个县，县以下是乡村了，所以是县政建设，县政建设是包含乡村建设的。所以他开这个内政会议要提出这个方案来，就把我们搞乡村建设的人——也包含了我，包含了我们山东的朋友，还包含了晏阳初——都找到南京来，作为是一种专家，参加他那个内政会议，来把县政建设的计划搞好。这个时候我到了南京了，为这个事情到了南京了。

到了南京呢，这个时候的南京市的市长是我一个老朋友。这个人（*指石瑛*）是老资格，他跟孙中山是朋友，岁数很大，比我们都大，他是一个在清朝已经中了清朝的举人的，念那个老书啊，中了举人的。中了举人呢，年纪还很轻，他只有19岁，他又到英国去留学，到英国去留学，学化学；学化学回来之后，蔡元培蔡先生请他在北京大学做教授，做理科化学教授。他在国外很帮助孙中山，跟孙中山是一辈的老朋友。这个时候做南京市的市长，跟我也是朋友，我们在北京大学在一起。他到中央饭店、旅馆来看我，他说：你既然到了南京了，以前蒋介石想跟你见面你不去，那你到了南京了，你不可以不跟他见面了。我说好，那么这个样子他作为市长跟蒋的秘书、副官通电话，约好了时间，某一天的晚上，事先是坐着汽车接我一同到"委员长官邸"，去跟蒋见面。这个时候是我第一次跟蒋见面。

可一见面我印象就不好。怎么样不好呢？就是他虚假。他不是以前因为我的有名，要和我见面，要我去我又不去？这次嘛，石先生陪着我来看他了，约好了见面了，他怎么样子虚假呢？他就手里拿一个笔，也是自来水笔，手里拿个本子，谈话的时候——当然随便谈了，我不知道我怎么样子提起来，那个时候啊江北——江苏北部，包括安徽——有水灾，灾情很重，我一个朋友就在那儿做救灾工作，不知道怎样提到这个事情。提到这个事情，我就提到负责救灾工作的那个人的名字了，

Chiang said, "Very good. What is the name of your friend?" He handed his pen and his notebook to me and said, "Write his name down." Of course I wrote my friend's name. It looked very insincere to me, a show of, as we say, "being modest and respectful before a scholar" [lowering oneself before the scholars]. It had the appearance of modesty and respect, of paying great attention to what I said. Sitting there and acting as though he didn't hear the name clearly—so you "write his name down." Actually, his secretary was sitting there in any case, he also wrote down the name. He didn't have to have it written down for him. So, in general, this first meeting with Chiang left me with a very bad impression, and gave me the feeling that he was insincere and false.

After this, of course, I met him many times. At the time of this first meeting, the Japanese hadn't invaded China yet. Later, the War of Resistance began. In the North it was the Marco Polo Bridge Incident of July 7 and in the South the August 13 Incident, which forced Chiang to resist Japan. He had no choice. It was with the Xi'an Incident that he decided to abandon the civil war and resist the Japanese. The national government felt the need for the support of society as a whole. The government itself could not resist Japan all alone. So it established a Political Consultative Conference within the Supreme National Defense Conference and invited persons from non-official circles who could represent society, people of some prestige, to be members of this body. I was also appointed to this body.

The first time I met Premier Zhou Enlai was at these meetings of this body. At this time, there was in principle a cooperative union between the CCP and the Nationalist Party for resistance against Japan. Actually, it was the CCP that was advocating for resistance against Japan with no more civil war at the beginning. But the Chinese Communists did not by any means participate in the national government, so how did the two parties join hands to resist Japan? It was in this consultative conference and the Supreme National Defense Conference. At this time the name list of the conference had Mao's name on it, but Mao never attended. Zhou attended. So, the first time I met Mr. Zhou was there at those meetings.

Who else participated in the meetings? Huang Yanpei, who was famous in the Shanghai region. Shen Junru, who had just been released from detention, was also there. Shen was a member of the National Salvation Society, which advocated for an end to civil war and resistance

他就说："哦？很好，你这个朋友叫什么名字啊？"他把那个本子、笔递给我："你写下来。"我当然给他写下来了。他这个人就看出来有一种虚假，虚假就是"谦恭下士"，很谦恭的样子：你的话我很注意，你说那个人名，你写给我看。自己拿着本子、自己拿着笔，好像听不清楚，你再写一下。其实他另外有个秘书啊，坐得稍微远一点，也记了，不一定他再记。大体上说这次是头一次见面，头一次见面就是我感觉他虚假。

以后就见面机会很多，因为这个时候日本人还没有来中国、侵略中国，后来不是抗日了？抗日一起来，北方就是"卢沟桥七七事变"，南方是"八一三"，这个时候蒋被逼迫着不得不抗战了。不是有个"西安事变"？他决定放弃内战，抗日。那么"八一三"打起来了，国民政府感觉到需要广大社会支持政府，不能单单是政府抗日啊，需要广大社会的支持啊，所以就在"国防最高会议"之内成立一个"参议会"，请社会方面的人，能够代表社会的、在社会上有资望的，来做参议会的参议员，那么我就被聘当参议。

这个时候可以说一句话，就是我跟周恩来第一次见面就在这个地方，因为这个时候算是国共合作、一同抗日。本来是中共要求抗日嘛，不要打内战，共同抗日，可是中共方面并没有参加国民政府，怎么样子两党能够携手抗战？就是在这个参议会，在国防最高会议里头参与抗日的事情。这个时候名单上发表的有毛泽东，而毛没有来，周来，所以我跟周公第一次见面是在这个地方见的面。

那么参议会里头找来的还有些个什么人呢？有黄炎培，在上海一带很有名的；有刚刚放出来的沈钧儒，沈钧儒是救国会了，救国会就是主张赶紧抗日、不要打内战的，本来他都是把沈钧儒

to Japan. He had been arrested and kept in prison in Suzhou, for Chiang had felt that "you were all going with the Communists." But at this time, the two parties had started to cooperate, so the "Seven Gentlemen," Shen included, were released, and they participated in the Political Consultative Conference. Hu Shi also participated, and so did Zhang Boling of Nankai University, the great military scholar Jiang Fangzhen and the famous Peking University scholar Fu Sinian, and so on. They also found people familiar with diplomacy, for linking up internationally with allies against Japanese. So, because of this, they asked Yan Huiqing and Shi Zhaoji to participate too. They also asked several Nationalist Party veterans who had long been alienated from the Nanjing government, such as Ma Junwu, a Guangxi native. All were asked to participate in the Political Consultative Conference under the Supreme National Defense Conference.

At this time, my contact with Chiang increased somewhat from this conference on. Chiang was busy with directing military operations, however, and so Wang Jingwei was chairman of the conference. We held all of our meetings at night, because the Japanese planes were bombing. Wang presided over meetings, as Chiang was very busy with military affairs. At the end of a meeting, Chiang dispatched a secretary of his to see me, and said that Chairman Chiang [as Chair of the Military Affairs Committee] invited me to go to his official residence the next morning at a certain time to talk, e.g., 8 o'clock. I agreed to see him, of course. The secretary approached me right as I was coming out of the meeting hall together with Jiang Fangzhen, so Jiang Fangzhen knew that I would be seeing Chiang the next morning. So he said to me, "When you see Chiang tomorrow, tell him that I want to go to Shandong to inspect matters related to defense." I agreed. So, when I was meeting with Chiang, I told him this on behalf of Mr. Jiang Fangzhen. Chiang agreed, and asked me to go together with Jiang Baili [Jiang Fangzhen's sobriquet] to Shandong.

● My impression of Hu Zongnan and Chen Cheng

Liang: It was pretty good that I would go to Shandong with Jiang Baili. [Later] Jiang Baili told me that there was someone who wanted to meet me, and asked me if I was willing to see him. I asked him who it was. He answered that it was one of Chiang's generals, Hu Zongnan. I answered

扣在苏州监狱里边，他认为你们是跟共产党跑的，可是这个时候两党合作都要抗日了，所以把沈钧儒（等）“七君子”都放出来，放出来也参加这个参议会；还有社会有名的人——胡适、天津南开大学的张伯苓，还有一个有名的军事学家叫蒋方震，还有北大学生里头很出名的傅斯年，如此之类。他还找一些通习外交的人，这个时候抗日根据国际（形势）要采取联系，所以他就把颜惠庆、还有一个施肇基都请来。国民党的老辈，久已跟南京政府很疏远了，可是国民党的老辈，像是那个马君武，广西人，都请来，这个就叫做“国防最高会议参议会”。

这个时候是我跟蒋接触稍微多一点的时候，从这儿来的。我现在就是在这个会议上，蒋嘛因为他要指挥军事了，军事上忙得很，所以这个会是汪做主席。我们开会都是在夜间开会，为什么呢？因为日本的飞机都来轰炸了。因为汪主持这个会，蒋自己忙军事，很忙，就在我们开会的时候，蒋派一个人，派一个他的秘书吧，来在我们散会的时候看我，说蒋委员长请梁先生明天早晨几点钟，比如8点钟，到官邸见面。那么我当然答应了。这个时候我刚好从会里跟蒋方震一起出来，蒋方震当然就知道我明天要见蒋了，蒋方震就对我说，明天你去跟蒋见面的时候，你替我说，我愿意去山东，去山东看一看山东的防务、国防。我说好，所以等到我跟蒋见面的时候，我就替蒋方震说了这个话。他说很好，就请你——就请我啊，你陪着蒋百里先生（蒋方震字百里）去山东视察。

• 我对胡宗南和陈诚的印象

梁： 那么很好了，我就要陪着蒋百里先生去山东了，蒋百里先生就问我，说有一个人呢，想同你见面，你可以不可以见他啊？我说是谁啊？他说是蒋介石的一个大将，叫胡宗南。我说是什么人

that I was willing to meet with anyone, no matter whom, especially at this critical moment for the War of Resistance. The greater the degree of solidarity, the greater the chance of success in resisting Japan. He said, "Alright, tomorrow we will pass through Xuzhou (Hu Zongnan was stationed in Xuzhou). We'll go together to have a talk with Hu." The next day, we went by railroad through Xuzhou. Hu Zongnan, his chief of staff, and his secretary general were all waiting at the station for us. We went to Hu's headquarters and talked the whole night. The next day the same train, at the same time, passed through Xuzhou and we boarded and went on to Shandong. Later in Xi'an, I had some further contact with Hu. He was a politically ambitious man. He didn't want to be just a military man so he wanted to make friends with us.

I also had contact with the subordinate that Chiang Kai-shek trusted most, Chen Cheng. This was at the time of the retreat back to defend Wuhan. Chen Cheng was living at Wuhan University. Wuhan University was located in Luojiashan. Chen lived there. He asked me to his house for dinner and to talk. He was one of the most powerful of Chiang Kai-shek's subordinates. A car was sent to pick us up. So we got in and went to his house at Luojiashan within Wuhan University campus—the university had been closed. He was not in. But after a few minutes of sitting there waiting, he came in. He talked, but talked about his own topic continually—criticizing, maligning and berating the Minister of the Interior, Huang Shaohong. He said that Huang was a big dummy. He kept talking continually and didn't let me get a word in edgewise. He just kept on, in a very disorganized manner, very angrily. Later one of his staff came in to report that it was time for dinner. So he invited us to go in to dinner. Now, during the time he was eating, of course, he couldn't talk much, but he was by no means quiet. After he finished eating, he continued his non-stop diatribe, giving me no chance at all to say anything.

I took the opportunity when he was speaking relatively slowly to say something because I wanted to say something about the condition of my people. We had brought out some men and rifles from Shandong, over 800 men and more than 800 rifles. We also had tens of thousands of silver dollars in cash. As the administrative commissioner and the county magistrate, we brought out the cash and the armed militia. So I told him that we wanted to go back to Shandong. The militia wanted to fight its way back home. Finally, after much effort, I brought up the matter

都可以见，特别这个时候要共同抗日嘛，那么大家越能够联合、越能够团结越好嘛。他说那么样子，我明天从南京坐火车路过徐州——胡宗南正驻在徐州，我们在徐州下车，同他见面谈一谈。后来果然我们一同坐火车路过徐州的时候，胡宗南带着他的参谋长，带着旁的什么秘书长，很多人，在车站等候，接我们。我跟蒋百里就一同到他的司令部，住一夜，谈话。然后第二天，火车在同一个钟点再过来的时候，我们上车去山东。后来我跟胡宗南还有一些接触，后来在陕西西安有些接触。胡宗南他是一个在政治上有野心的人，他并不是想单做一个军人，所以他愿意同我们交朋友。

跟蒋的部下、蒋的很信任的人，比如陈诚，陈诚也同我有往来，那是退守武汉的时候了。退守武汉的时候，陈诚他住在武汉大学里头，武汉大学那个地名叫珞珈山，他自己住在珞珈山武汉大学里边，他请我到他家里头吃饭、谈话，他算是蒋下面很有力量的一个人。车来接我们，我当然就坐车去了。到他住的地方珞珈山武汉大学里边——学校是停了，他没回来，可是坐了有刚刚几分钟他就回来了。回来了他就谈话了，他老是谈话，老是说他的话，老是骂人、批评人，特别批评那个内政部长黄绍竑，他说那是个草包，这个样子。几乎没有空让我说话，我插不上话去，因为他老说、老说，话说得很乱，气很盛。后来伺候的人来报告，说是要开晚饭了，请进去吃饭，吃饭的时候嘛，不能多说话了，他也还不闲着，吃完饭后还是说话，我想跟他说的话，几乎没有空说。

当然我还是勉强趁着一个机会，他话稍微慢一点了，我马上说一句话跟他，因为我是要介绍我这方面的人的情况，我们从山东带出来一批人，并且都是带着枪的，武装的，八百多人，有八百多条枪，还带着十几万块钱——因为我们在山东做专员、做县长有现款、有壮丁，都带出来了。后来嘛跟他说，说我们要回去，我们从山东出来的人要打回老家去，为了跟他

by cutting off his tirade. So, after this experience with him I felt that he wasn't a man of great ability; he was too shallow and superficial. This is an example of the contact I had with people on Chiang's side. Later on, in Taiwan, Chen Cheng was "vice president" and so on.

● Chiang Kai-shek's greatest contribution

Liang: When General George Marshall came to China to help make peace between the two parties, I had a lot of contact with him. He came to see me at my house once. That was when I was living at Lanjiazhuang in Nanjing. That was where the headquarters of the Democratic League was located. I couldn't speak English, so a friend of mine, Ye Duyi, interpreted for me. I felt that General Marshall was a truly good person. He was a devoutly religious man. Chiang Kai-shek was really bothered by him. Didn't Chiang go hide himself off at Lushan? At the time, the weather was not really all that hot. Of course, Lushan was a cool place, but he didn't go off there to escape the heat. He wanted to hide from Marshall. This put General Marshall in a bad position. He repeatedly went to Lushan. He went up to Lushan nine times.

Alitto: Speaking of Chiang Kai-shek hiding out, in your opinion, after the War of Resistance was concluded, it seemed he... In terms of this kind of behavior he exhibited in those days, it would seem that it was very stupid. He brought trouble upon himself and so in the end exited the stage pitifully. In your opinion, why did Chiang act so stupidly? Did he just underestimate the strength of the Communists or was he just stupid?

Liang: Well, he was not stupid, all right. However, if it was stupidity, it was just because he was so selfish.

Alitto: Selfish? The basic problem was that he was selfish?

Liang: He didn't trust people. His word never...

Alitto: Meant anything?

Liang: Right! He acted this way thinking himself to be very clever. But what he did was to make himself utterly isolated.

Alitto: So, in your view, if after the War of Resistance had concluded, he had been earnestly reasonable with the Communist Party and with the Third Parties, then possibly he would have been able to organize

说这个事情。仅仅是末了当他话稍微停下来的时候，我才能把我的话跟他说。这样看起来，这个人不是十分有能力的人，太浅，太粗浅。这也是蒋方的人我接触的一个例子。后来不是到台湾他还是做“副总统”吗？

- **蒋介石最大的贡献**

梁： 马歇尔元帅不是来中国吗？极力要促成中国国内的和平。我跟马帅有多次见面，他还到我住的地方来过一次，我住南京兰家庄的时候，民盟的总部，来过一次。我不会讲英语了，都由一个朋友——姓叶的叶笃义，替我做翻译。我对于马帅，我觉得他这个人是很好。他是一个信仰宗教信得很真的人。他很为蒋介石所苦——蒋介石他躲到庐山上去，天气并不一定很热，庐山固然凉快，可是他不是为凉快去庐山，他是躲人，他要躲马帅。那么这个样子马帅就辛苦了，他一趟上庐山，再一趟上庐山，他九上庐山。

艾： 说到蒋介石躲人啊，依您看呢，他是抗战结束以后啊，他好像……现在看他当年这个行为，好像很笨啊，是自己找自己的麻烦而终于下场也很惨。依您看呢，是因为他估计共产党的力量估计得太低的关系呢，还是因为他人就是很笨呢？

梁： 笨是不笨，如果说笨呢，他就是太自私。

艾： 自私？基本的问题是他自私？

梁： 他不信任人，从来说话……

艾： 都不算话。

梁： 对啊。他自己以为这样最得计，其实是弄得众叛亲离。

艾： 那您看他是，就是说抗战结束以后，假如他比较认真地和共产党、和第三方面的人比较讲理，那说不定会组成一个联合

a coalition government. Was it just because he wanted to maintain his dictatorial powers that he refused to be reasonable? (Liang: Right.) Because he thought that he had more troops, had good weapons, (Liang: He had U.S. backing.) he had an air force, the CCP didn't have an air force—no matter what, the Nationalist was much stronger than the CCP. (Liang: Many conditions were stronger.) So because of this, he then refused. (Liang: He looked down upon the CCP.) He looked down on the CCP. For example in 1938, the CCP was obviously quite strong, especially in North China and the Northeast. Why didn't he see that the situation was not good, and so make concessions or at least be relatively earnest in the peace talks?

Liang: His attitude towards the peace talks was to take any small advantage. So, one time Premier Zhou came to him with a proposal that was a concession on the CCP's part, and thought that this would satisfy him. But Chiang came back and said that there was still a problem, and this problem called for a further concession from the CCP. So he kept pressing them continually. The CCP knew quite well that it did not have as much power as Chiang did, and knew that it didn't have international recognition as the government of China as Chiang did, or have American help. So, the situation was like, as the saying in ancient Chinese goes, "troops full of righteous indignation will certainly prevail; troops full of pride will certainly be defeated." It was the CCP's troops that had been continually pressed and filled with righteous indignation.

Alitto: During the peace negotiations you must have had some opportunities to speak sincerely to Chiang, and try to persuade him to be more serious and conscientious with the peace talks.

Liang: I had great difficulty in getting to see him. Not only did I have difficulty, even the Nationalist Party leaders had difficulty in seeing him. It was a big headache for General Marshall. He hated Chiang. Didn't he serve as Secretary of State after returning to the U.S.? At that time, he wanted no part of helping Chiang Kai-shek.

Alitto: A lot of Americans who had lived in China for a long time felt that way. For example, there was John Stuart Service. He was in Chongqing. He also read my book manuscript and urged me to publish it without revision. He wrote a few words in it, saying that this book wasn't bad, and so on. Another example was John Patton Davies. I don't remember his Chinese name. Still another was my teacher John Fairbank. They all said

政府。那么会不会就是因为他要保存他这个独裁的权力啊，而结果可以说是拒绝讲理？因为他想：我这个军队多啊，武装也好啊，（梁：有美国做后盾。）空军是有的，他们没有空军，无论怎么样，我们比他们强得多。（梁：很多的条件都强啊。）就是因为这个，他就拒绝，（梁：轻视共产党。）轻视共产党，比如到了民国二十七年（1938 年），共产党尤其在华北、在东北很明显地是力量不小。他为什么不看情况不妙而让步，或者起码比较认真地和谈呢？

梁： 他在和谈上他采取的方针、策略，就是他多占一分便宜就多占一分便宜。有一次，周恩来代表共产党让步了，让步了以为可以满足他了，他说还有一个问题，在这个问题上又让步了，还有一点，如此，就是这样。他就是老是逼人，共产党也自己知道自己没有他那样大的力量了，没有像他还有国际的……，国际承认他是中国，美国的帮助啊，所以中国这个老话，老话讲军事上啊，“哀兵必胜，骄兵必败”，你骄傲，刚好就是共产党是哀兵，受逼迫的。

艾： 那这个谈判过程中，您也许有机会很诚恳地劝蒋介石，要他认真一点吧？

梁： 我们很难见到他呀。不但我们很难见到他，就是国民党的政府负责的人，见他都不容易。马帅很头疼，很恨他，回到美国之后不是担任国务卿吗？那个时候，他完全不想帮助蒋介石。

艾： 有很多住中国住得久的人，例如谢伟思，他是在重庆，他也看了我这个，就是因为他看了这个稿子，他劝我就不要再改啊，立刻出版，在这里写了几个字，就说这本书不错什么的。谢伟思是一位，还有戴维斯，中文名字我不记得，姓戴维斯，连费正清啊，他们都说蒋介石是错的，而且政府是腐败的，没有

that Chiang was wrong, and that the Chiang regime was corrupt. A lot of Americans feared a Communist success, especially feared the Soviet Union; they thought that the CCP was nothing but a tool of the Soviet Union.

Do you think that Chiang Kai-shek made any contribution at all to China and the Chinese Revolution? We have regarded his performance, especially after the War of Resistance, as terrible. As for his overall career, is there any contribution to China?

Liang: His greatest contribution was to make the CCP successful. If he had been a bit more trustworthy, if his character were somewhat better, the CCP would have been unable to beat him. His greatest contribution was to have created the CCP success.

● Zhou Enlai is a paragon.

Alitto: You were also familiar with Zhou Enlai.

Liang: I knew him very well.

Alitto: What dealings or contact did you have with him?

Liang: It was in politics. First it was in Chongqing. Because North and East China had fallen; we all lived in Chongqing. At that time, I had dealings with him, very close dealings. Later Japan was defeated, and all of us went to Nanjing. The Chinese Communist Party office was at Meiyuanxincun. Our Democratic League office was at Lanjiazhuang. At this time we were coordinating peace talks between the two [major] parties....

Alitto: Do you have other evaluations or views of Premier Zhou?

Liang: When the two major parties were conducting peace talks, General Marshall from the U.S. very much wanted to make the two major parties have peace talks. I was the general secretary of the Democratic League. I was also engaged in this work, and wanted to pursue domestic peace and establish a new China. At the time Mr. Zhou was first in Chongqing and later in Nanjing, so we were very close, and I had the most dealings with him. Finally there was a transitional government organized, with 40 members: 20 Nationalist Party members, and the remaining 20 positions divided up among the parties outside the Nationalist Party. That book I just mentioned discusses this question. What did it discuss? That the Nationalist Party allowed the Communist Party and the Democratic League 13 positions. Whether it should be 13 or 14 was still debated.

用处。美国很怕共产党，尤其怕的是苏联，以为中国共产党就是苏联的这个走狗啊，或者它的猫手、猫爪。

您觉得蒋介石对中国、对中国革命有没有什么贡献呢？我们已经谈到了他，尤其在抗战以后啊，实在不行，不过就是说他的整个的事业了，会不会对中国有什么贡献？

梁：他最大的贡献哪，最大的贡献是给机会让共产党……他造成了共产党的成功。如果他这个人还有一点信用，人格还好一点，共产党打不过他啊。所以他最大的贡献，就是造成共产党的成功。

• 周恩来是一个完人

艾：周恩来您也……

梁：很熟了。

艾：您和他有过什么来往、接触？

梁：就是在政治上嘛。先是在重庆了，因为中国华北、华东都沦陷了，我们大家都在重庆，那个时候来往了，来往得很密。后来日本失败了，大家都去到南京了，中共的办事处在梅园新村，我们民盟在兰家庄，这个时候两党和谈我们彼此是配合的……

艾：您对周恩来总理有什么别的评价、看法？

梁：在两大党和谈的时候，美国来的是马歇尔元帅，他是很想促成两党的和谈的。我是作为民盟的秘书长，我也是做这个工作，想求得国内的和平、建设新中国，所以那个时候周公先在重庆、后在南京，我们是最密切的，往来最多的。最后要组织一个过渡的政府，国民政府委员 40 名，国民党占 20 名，剩下的 20 名国民党以外的大家分，我刚才提到的那个书里（梁漱溟借给艾恺的某本书）讲到这个问题，讲到什么呢？讲到国民党许给共产党跟民盟 13 名，是 13 名嘛还是 14 名嘛，还在那里争论……

The Chinese Democratic League was not one group, it was an alliance, and so he made this gesture. The Nationalist Party's *Central Daily News* and some Shanghai newspapers ridiculed the Democratic League as the tail of the Communist Party, as going along with the Communist Party. I made a statement to the press that the Communist Party was following the Democratic League's lead, and not the vice versa. What did I mean by that? I meant that the Communist Party was a revolutionary party. It was an armed party that wanted to seize all of China. We had urged them to renounce armed force and cooperate with the Nationalist Party in creating a new China. We had urged it to renounce armed force. It had agreed to do so, and so it agreed with me to follow the path of the Democratic League, and it was by no means a case of me following the Communist Party. This was discussed in that little book. But one thing was quite clear: at the time the Democratic League was cooperating with the Communist Party. The Nationalist Party totally regarded us as doing so.

Alitto: Leaving aside Premier Zhou's political aspects, what kind of man was he?

Liang: I was very close to Premier Zhou. I am confident that I understood him. In ancient Chinese, the best person was called a "paragon," and I totally regarded Mr. Zhou as a paragon. There was nothing you could find fault with, no matter whether in his public or private morals. For example, he and Deng Yingchao had no children. Madame Deng seemed to have said that he could take another woman, but he didn't want to do so. In this area of marital relations, which was a private matter, he was very clean. In his work, he helped Chairman Mao in dealing with both internal matters of China and with the international area. One could say that before and especially after the founding of the state, if Premier Zhou was not handling things internal and foreign, well, Mao alone could not have handled it and would have failed; he relied on Zhou for both.

Zhou worked like blazes. Everyone knows that he sometimes did not eat; he had no time to eat, so he was given something in the car and had a few bites, and immediately took off. He would work into the night. He received many foreigners, straight into the night, and slept very little, and didn't care much about food. One could say that he gave himself completely to his nation.

中国民盟不是个单一的团体，是个联合的，所以它作出这个样的一个表示。这样一个表示呢，国民党的《中央日报》，还有上海的报纸就嘲笑民盟，说民盟是共产党的尾巴，跟着共产党跑的。我就有一个声明，对新闻记者的谈话，我说是共产党随着民盟走的，而不是我们随着共产党走。怎么样子说这个话呢？因为共产党……是革命党，它是有武装的，它要夺取整个的中国的，我们是劝它放弃武力，跟国民党在建设新中国上可以合作。是我们劝它放弃武力的，它同意了，所以是它同意了我的话，走民盟的这个路子，并不是我跟着共产党走，那个本子上都讲了这个话。但是一个很清楚的事情就是，当时民盟跟共产党是合作的，国民党完全是这样来看待我们的。

艾：周总理政治方面以外，是个什么样的人啊？

梁：我同周总理算是很熟悉了，我自信我很了解他。中国古话说最好的人叫做“完人”，完全，我看周公是一个完人，无论是在公德方面、私德方面，都没有可以挑剔的。比如他同邓颖超没有孩子，邓好像说是你可以结合另外一个女人，他就不要。在这种男女夫妇的关系上——这算是一个私人的事情，他很干净。在工作方面他帮助毛主席，无论是国内应付各方面、国际上应付各方面，全是他啊，没有周那不行的。新中国，可以说从建国前夕，特别是建国后，没有周总理应付内、应付外，那毛一个人办不了，成不了事情，都是靠周啊。周是拼命的，最辛苦了。大家都知道，他常常是没有法子吃饭，没有空吃饭，跑到汽车上人家给他送来饭，吃几口，马上就开走了。夜里头都办公啊。许多外国人，他会客，一直到深夜啊，睡眠很少，吃东西也很不讲究，勉勉强强，可以说是把自己一切全贡献给国家了。

If China hadn't had Zhou these several decades, it would not have succeeded. Zhou best understood Mao's wishes. My critique of him is that he was by nature a second fiddle. He asked Mao for instructions practically constantly and for everything. Mao would hint at something and he would immediately understand. Mao didn't have to say much. But he [Zhou] himself had very few specific opinions. He went along with Mao completely. One could say that he was Mao's best assistant. He was number two, never the first in command. An old Chinese saying is "a sage ruler and a worthy prime minister." He was the virtuous prime minister. When Zhou died, people from all sides, even the common people... There was no one who didn't miss him, admire him and grieve for him. Even when Mao died, it wasn't like this. Of the three [Mao, Zhou and Zhu], Zhou died first. Many people honored his memory in front of Tian'anmen.

● My intercourse with Mao Zedong: different ideas of China's future

Liang: You know, I went to Yan'an in 1938, six months after the Marco Polo Bridge Incident and the outbreak of the war. Our dialogue began then. We both had a great desire to talk together, and both of us were very interested in each other's ideas. Why did I go to Yan'an almost immediately after the war broke out? That was because after the Japanese came, the entire country collapsed. For example, right after the Marco Polo Bridge Incident, in the South in Shanghai, on August 13, a battle started. But we didn't have any capacities of resistance. Shanghai fell, and we pulled back to Nanjing. Nanjing fell and we pulled back to Wuhan. In the North, Beijing and Tianjin fell. All of Shandong fell. People were running in all directions to get away from the Japanese. It was a complete collapse, as though no one was in charge. It was obvious that Chiang's government had no way, no capacity to do anything about the situation. I was extremely disappointed in the performance of the Nanjing government.

Alitto: Oh, because in those several months, the Japanese occupied a lot of places, and the Nanjing government had no way of stopping it, you went to Yan'an then....

Liang: When we reached Wuhan, where the national government had retreated to, I got Chiang's approval to go take a look at Yan'an. Before I visited Yan'an, I was extremely downcast and pessimistic. What to do perplexed me. Everyone was fleeing. The Nanjing government was totally

中国过去的几十年没有周是不行的，国际上、国内都是靠周。周呢，最能懂得毛的意思，我对他的评价：他是天生的第二把手。他是几乎随时、任何一件事情他都请示毛，毛一点，他就明白了，不要多说。可是他自己很少自己的明确的主张，他完全跟着毛走，可说是毛的最好最好的助手了。他是第二把手，不是第一。中国古话有……"圣君贤相"，他是个贤相。他故去了，各方面的人啊，乃至老百姓，没有人不想他的，没有人不佩服他的、追念他的。毛故去都没有这个情况。他们三个人周是最先故去的，在天安门前头多少人纪念他啊。

• 与毛泽东相交：对中国前途的认识

梁： 卢沟桥事变 6 个月我就去了延安，很早。从那个时候起，从那开头吧，好像彼此都很愿意谈话，彼此交谈都很有兴趣。我记得我第一次到延安，卢沟桥事件刚刚 6 个月，我为什么那么早去延安呢？就是因为日本人来了之后，全国有一种崩溃之象，北方就是卢沟桥七七事变，南方上海是"八一三"打起来。就是都不行了，上海退南京，南京退武汉，北京、天津都沦陷了，山东也沦陷了。全国人都是在逃难，你逃难，我逃难，大家各自逃难，崩溃，好像无主了。蒋的政府眼看没有什么能力，没有什么办法。我对他很失望，对南京政府很失望。

艾： 噢，就因为这几个月，日本人占领那么多地方，南京政府没有办法，您就到延安去……

梁： 退到武汉的时候，我取得蒋的同意，我说我要到延安去看看。到延安去看的时候，我心里是很悲观的，不知道怎么好，大家都在逃难，南京政府毫无能力，怎么好啊？怎么办呢？我就想

incompetent. What to do? So, I thought I'd go see if the Communist Party had any way of dealing with the situation. So, with this mind, I went to see Mao, and found that Mao was not the least bit pessimistic. He told me, "China must undergo this great disaster. But the Japanese should not be joyful too soon. I expect they will be defeated." At the time I went to see him, he was in the midst of writing "On Protracted War," so he told me in effect the contents of his essay. He said that the Japanese had overrated their own strength. They were dreaming vainly of swallowing up China. A vain dream, a joke. China was a big country, too big, and Japan was just too small. Moreover, it wasn't just a Sino-Japanese question. The world powers would not stand idly by and watch Japan annex China. "An unjust cause draws meager support. A just cause draws myriad support." Later the world powers all stood againt Japan.

...We of course had to discuss Old China, our view of it and our theories about it, and it was in this area that our opinions differed. The most important disagreement was on the question of class. He maintained that China had always had class struggle, and I said that in Old China, from the Qin-Han period on—we were unclear of the society before then, so I wouldn't address it especially in the last 600 years since the Ming-Qing period, although there naturally were differences between rich and poor, there was circulation and communication between high and low (there was economic, social and political mobility). These distinctions were not like classes in the West, which were fixed and fully formed. In China, society and social groups were loose, unorganized and fluid. Because of this mobility, society was fluid and unorganized, and so the struggles were not all that intense or sharp. It was not a situation of two opposing classes—aristocrats versus serfs, as in the Western Middle Ages, or capitalists versus workers in capitalist society. China didn't have any such thing. Chinese like harmony and compromise. Yes, there was struggle, but it was not habitual, nor did it have any great dynamic force.

Mao could not completely deny this. We debated for a long time.

Finally he said, "Mr. Liang, you are overly emphasizing the peculiar, distinctive nature of Chinese society, but Chinese society is still a human society, and so still has its qualities which it shares with all human societies." I answered, "I completely agree with you. I completely agree with you that Chinese society has qualities in common with other human societies, but I insist that its peculiar or distinctive features are more important. For example, let's say we are speaking of a person. You say, I

看看共产党是不是有办法，我就这样去。一去，看到他完全不悲观，我是悲观地去的，他告诉我：没有问题，中国非有这样一天不可，非有这样一个大灾难不可，不过日本人他不要高兴太早。……这个时候，他正在写《论持久战》，把《论持久战》的话讲给我听，他说日本人是不自量，他想吞并中国，那是妄想、笑话。中国是大国，太大了，它太小了。也不是中日两国，世界列强不能看着日本人来侵吞中国。"失道寡助，得道多助"，后来列强都反对它。

……他对老中国的看法跟我的看法不一致。主要的一个问题是什么问题呢？就是阶级问题。他是阶级斗争，我就说中国的老社会，秦汉以后的社会，特别是从明代、清代600年以来的社会——早的社会我们不太清楚、不大敢说——明清以来的这个社会，在我看，贫富贵贱当然有，可是贫富贵贱可以上下流转相通，它不是像外国那样的一个阶级——很固定，很成型，没有固定成型，而是上下流转相通。中国社会散漫，流转相通呢，它就散漫。散漫就斗争不激烈，不像两大阶级，一个贵族，一个农民或农奴——中世纪的，或者后来的资本主义社会——资本家跟工人两大阶级，中国缺乏那个东西。中国人喜欢调和，斗争还是有，不过不大习惯斗争，斗争的两面，强大的也没有。

我说这个话，他也不能完全否认。辩论很久了，他最后就说了：梁先生，你过分强调中国社会的特殊性，但是中国社会还是一个人类的社会，还有它的一般性嘛。我说对，你说的话，我完全同意。不过，正因为我完全同意你说中国有它的一般性，也有它的特殊性这样子，可是我要强调特殊性要紧。

'know' that person. Only if you can say what the special characteristic of that person is, what is distinctive about him, can you then say you 'know' him. If you speak about the person only from the aspect of his characteristics that he has in common with others—that he is a male, middle-aged, and so on, it won't do. You must speak of his special features as an individual, and only then can you really know him." So, I told Chairman Mao, "Your approach is not as good as mine. I grasp the special, distinctive features of Chinese society and so really know her better than you." Well, because of this kind of disagreement, we reached an impasse, and our discussions were concluded.[23]

● I am different from the others engaged in political activities.

Alitto: Could you give your views on the relationship between the Democratic League, the smaller political parties, and the process of national construction?

Liang: I think that I am, and was, somewhat different from the others [non-Communist Party and non-Nationalist Party intellectuals who engaged in political activities]. Almost all the others vainly hoped for the establishment of British-style rule by political parties. That is, in the national assembly, there would be two large parties; when one was in power, the other would supervise the governance. If the party in power made any mistakes, or did something that was objectionable to the party out of power, the latter would then take power. So the two parties would take turns being in power. This is the situation in England, and to an extent, in the U.S.A. So the others all dreamed of establishing this kind of government. I said that this kind of government did not meet the needs of China, because economically, industrially in particular, China was so different from the Western countries. China was not an industrialized, developed country, so this kind of government would not work. China's most urgent task was to develop economically as quickly as possible. In order to accomplish this, China needed a truly national, central political authority to adopt a fixed, definite guiding principle, a fixed course of action. This fixing of a definite course of action would be through a national governmental power or regime, and should maintain stability for several decades. Only in this way would China be able to develop economically and catch up with the foreign countries. So, I felt and feel that this alternating of political parties in power simply would not work because the national course of action would change whenever the other political party out of power came into power. So, today one policy, tomorrow another. That just won't work.

比如说，一个人，你说你认识这个人，你要说这个人的特色是怎么样一个人，那么算是认识了这个人。不能从"一般的"去说，说这个人是个人，或者这个人是个男人，这个人是个中年人，这都不行，你得说出这个人的特点，你才算是认识了这个人。因此，我说你这个不如我，我是抓住中国社会的特色的一面。谈话就结束了，说不下去了，一般性跟特殊性的比较是这样。

• 我和其他政治活动家的不同

艾：请您就民主同盟或者以前别的小的政党和国家建设之间的关系，或者重要性，作个评论。

梁：我跟其他跟我以外的、搞政治活动的人有一点不同，就是他们几乎都是梦想英国式的政党政治：在议会里头主要是两个大党，这个党上台，那个党在底下，监督着这个政府；或者上台的那个，有什么做错的，或者不得人心的，下台，它就上去了，两党轮流执政，这就是英国的情况。我以外的人他们都是梦想这个东西。英国，美国也是两党。我就是说，这个不合中国的需要，因为中国在物质文明上、在经济建设上，主要说是在工业上，同国外比较，差得太远了，太落后了。这样一个太落后的中国，那非赶紧、赶快、急起直追，把这个缺欠把它补上去不成。要补上这个事情，必须是有一个全国性的政权，采取一定的方针路线，依靠这个全国性的政权，确定一个方针路线，几十年的稳定的局面贯彻去搞、去建设，才能够把那个补回来。不能够你上来，我下去，你上来，我下去，这样子就不行啊！这样今天是这样方针计划，明天又那样子，那不行。

I maintained this view consistently. The others all disagreed with me, as they all had in mind an Anglo-American style of a two-party political system. Later, the situation in China, astonishingly enough, ended up precisely the way that I thought it would.[24] The Nationalist Party was driven out, and the Chinese mainland was united. The CCP took power and did accomplish some things in these years. It's too bad that during those decades of control, there were several periods of political and social turmoil. But now, it looks as though these periods of turmoil are over and will not recur, so that from now on China can stride forward rapidly. So, as I said, I am very optimistic about the future. This is my view, and this is my hope.

...For example, during the War of Resistance against Japan, I went rushing around between the two major parties to avoid civil war. Well, I did it. My plan was successful. I founded the Democratic League. Other people thought that I wanted to found a party, but that was not my intention. My own feeling was that China didn't need any new political party, like America or England. So, although I founded the Democratic League, my purpose was for this organization to represent society in general, in between the two major parties, and to make the two parties compromise with each other and to further the war against Japan and the building of the nation. Finally, when I felt that the organization was no longer needed, I withdrew. So, the Democratic League and the China Democratic National Construction Association still exist, and I don't belong to them.

所以我一个人总是梦想这个样子，可是旁人，就是说我以外的其他的党派，他们都不是这个意思，他们都是想学英、美，学两大党。可是后来嘛，局面居然落到我所想的，把国民党赶出去了，大陆上统一了，统一了，共产党掌握政权，一直掌握几十年，刚好做了不少事。可惜这里头还有些动乱，可惜在这个过去的30年里，还有些个动乱，可惜。可是看现在这个样子，动乱过去了，今后可以迈大步前进，所以我很乐观。这是我的一个看法，我的希望。

……比如我本来抗战起来之后，就奔走于两大党之间，事情都做了，也还都算是顺利。发起民主同盟，旁人以为我是想搞一个党派，我的意思不是，我的意思是中国不需要什么党派，不像英国、美国那样。所以我虽然发起同盟，主要是在两大党之间代表广大社会来牵扯着它们，不要它们两个打架、斗争，而推动或者抗战、或者建国。随后我觉得不需要了，我就退出了。现在民盟、民建都还有，我没有参加。

• It would be better to preserve my middleman status.

Liang: Many years later, Mao was in Beijing creating the new nation. I arrived in Beijing in early 1950.[25] The first time we saw each other again—in March—we started up right where we left off, arguing the same question. Why did we meet in March? Because in February, he and Premier Zhou were in Moscow, and he returned in March. When we did meet in March, the first thing he said to me was, "Now you will take a position in the government, right?" I wasn't able to make up my mind, and only after I thought deeply for a while did I answer, "Is it so bad to keep me on the outside of the government?" Now, I had my hidden purpose in this reply, but he became angry at it. In offering me a government post, he wanted to get a bit friendlier with me, but I didn't want to get any closer to him. At that time, I really didn't want to attach myself too closely because I misunderstood the whole situation. How did I misunderstand it? It was that I didn't know that the overall situation in China was going to stabilize. I wouldn't permit myself to be that optimistic. In the past, China had been fighting civil wars continuously. How many decades we have had endless civil wars!

...Although the Nationalists were defeated, couldn't they return and fight again? Now, I had always been in the middle between the two major parties, and was like a very fair-minded representative of society as a whole. So, I was able to talk to both sides. That is, I could talk to the Chiang Kai-shek side and could also talk to the Communists, so it seemed that it would be better to preserve my middleman status. It was because of these kinds of situations I answered the way I did when he wanted me to take a government position. It made him quite unhappy. He wanted to get closer to me and I didn't want to get close to him! On the one hand, he was a little bit unhappy; on the other hand, he just wanted me not to keep such a distance from him. So, after that he often sent his car to bring me over for a talk. When he had time from his duties, he sent for me. We never had a real topic, but just chatted at random, and sometimes we dined together.

Just whatever we felt like talking about, we talked about. But there were two things that often came up. The first, I wanted to understand more about the methods of the Chinese Communist Party. Just what

 1949年以后的岁月

• 我想保留一个中间人的地位

梁： 后来，他（毛泽东）在北京建国。1950 年我到北京，一开头还是讲这个话。在北京见面是 1950 年的 3 月份，为什么是 3 月份呢？因为 1950 年的 1、2 月他同周总理在莫斯科，3 月他才回来，他回来我才同他见面。1950 年的时候，先头他问我一句，他说："你现在可以参加政府吧？"我有点沉吟，思索了一下才回答。我说："把我留在政府外边，不好吗？"这话在我有我的用意，可是在他听起来他不高兴，他想拉我拉近一点，可我不想靠近。我当时不想靠近，还是把事情看得错误，怎么错误呢？我不知道中国的大局就能够统一、稳定下来，我不知道，我不敢这样乐观，因为过去中国内战老打不完，多少年老打不完。

……国民党虽然失败了，它会不会回来呀？我一向是在两大党之间，好像是一个很公正的、代表社会的一个人，各方面都可以说话，跟蒋方我也能说话，共产党方我也能说话，我想还是保留一个中间人的地位好一点。所以我这样一个念头，他让我参加政府，我就说留在外边不好吗？这样的话，他听了不很高兴，我不肯跟他靠近嘛。不跟他靠近，但是他倒是有一点——一方面是不很高兴吧，一方面还是有点拉着我，希望不要隔得太远。以后他常常接我到中南海他住的地方去谈话，有空他就……没什么问题，就随便地谈谈，坐下来吃饭。

……几乎可以说是想说什么就说什么吧。不过有两个情形可以说一下，一个就是我很想了解共产党的一些做法，他们

did they do in their work, what sort of way did they do it? After they got control of the political power of the entire nation, how would they act, what methods would they employ? The other thing is, in the light of this desire, I wanted to go around the country and view their operations from the grass-roots level, so I could ascertain exactly how we [our rural reconstruction ideas] differed, and see if I could offer advice, or could talk to him on these matters. It was right then that Mao himself suggested such an inspection trip. He said that since I had worked before in rural reconstruction, both in Henan and Shandong, and had known about the situation in the rural areas, I could go to some rural areas to see what kind of changes there had been since Liberation. So, I said, "Okay." It so happened that his own wishes coincided with my own.

● Zhang Dongsun, a professor of philosophy

Alitto: What about Zhang Dongsun? Do you have any... During the War of Resistance, you worked with him in the Democratic League. Did you know him previously, or...

Liang: I knew him much earlier. He liked to talk philosophy. The man was famous in the academic world. He and Zhang Junmai—the two Zhangs—were close both philosophically and politically. Zhang Junmai was kind and simple-hearted. But Zhang Dongsun was artful, even to the extent of being slippery. In the end, he came very close to bringing on a disaster, just short of bringing on something terrible [upon himself]. Why did we say so? Chairman Mao of the CCP fixed Beijing as the national capital, and at the start the government was called the Central People's Government. The Central People's Government had a sixty-person committee. He and Long Yun from Yunnan were the last two members of the committee. Because Mao's troops were entering Beijing, he [Zhang] was in Beijing, rushing about arranging matters to [have the troops] peacefully enter Beijing. At the time the Nationalist Party force in Beijing was Fu Zuoyi's, which was holding Beijing. The CCP wanted to enter Beijing, and there were negociations between the two armies to avoid damaging Beijing. Several people were mediating in between. Zhang was also one of those. So after the CCP army entered Beijing, the CCP respected him, and he and Long Yun were the last two of the sixty members [to be appointed].

掌握了全国政权以后，要怎么样做，怎么样干，我想了解。另外一方面呢，根据这个，我是需要出去看。我想从这个事实上，摸清楚彼此的不同，看我能够进言、能够对他说什么话。刚好这个时候他也提出来，他说从前你是做乡村工作，你在河南也做过，在山东也做过，你看到一些地方的乡村情况，你现在可以出去看看，我们解放之后有什么变化。我说好，我就接受他的，这个意思也是我的意思。

- **哲学教授张东荪**

艾： 那么张东荪先生，您对他有……，抗战的时候您跟他一起（在）民主同盟，以前您是认识呢，还是……

梁： 很早就认识。他喜欢谈哲学，这个人本来在学术界也很有名誉的，他同张君劢两个人，二张啊，他们在一起，在哲学上、在政治上，他们两个始终在一起。张君劢这个人很忠厚老实，可是张东荪呢，很巧，乃至油滑，最后几乎闯祸，几乎不得了。为什么几乎不得了？就是在共产党毛主席定都北京了，开初的政府叫中央人民政府，中央人民政府有 60 个委员，他同那个龙云——云南的那个龙云，（是）60 名委员里最后两名委员。因为毛主席军队入京，他在北京的时候，为了和平入北京奔走——那时北京的国民党的势力是傅作义，傅作义的军队守北京，共产党要进北京——在两军之间奔走和平，不要破坏北京。好几个人在奔走，他也是奔走的一个人。所以进了北京之后嘛，共产党对他也很尊重，中央人民政府 60 个委员，他和云南的龙云在 60 个人里头是居末的两个。

But he had a weakness, a fault which I just mentioned—slipperiness; he was not kind and simple-hearted. At that time he was at Yenching University, where there were a lot of Americans. He was a professor at Yenching University. He thought that the U.S. was extremely powerful, and didn't dare make a judgment on whether the CCP could unite the entire country, stabilize it and move on steadily down the road. Right then, there was a certain person who could be considered bad, a swindler. This con-man was thirty-something years of age. During the Japanese rule of Beijing, he had been in jail with Zhang Dongsun. The Japanese had arrested him, and so the cheat became friendly with Zhang in prison. Later after the CCP entered Beijing, this cheat had contact with him, and sometimes would go to Yenching University to see him. Zhang Dongsun thought that the U.S. was extremely rich, strong, and powerful. Whether the CCP could rule China with stability was not certain, it seemed [at the time]. The cheat bragged to Zhang Dongsun that he had connections with the U.S. State Council, and Zhang believed him. So Zhang Dongsun gave some documents that he had acquired through participating in the People's Government for him to read. This man sent them off to the U.S. Later Beijing Mayor Peng Zhen caught this man; he asked him if he had any fellow conspirators. He mentioned Zhang Dongsun.

It was at this time that I was having regular contact with Chairman Mao. He often sent a car to bring me to the Zhongnanhai to talk. Chairman Mao spoke to me of the Zhang Dongsun incident. He said, "Peng Zhen said that he was to arrest him. I said to Peng Zhen that this scholar was not capable of rebellion, and so it wasn't worth taking him seriously, but he cannot meet with us again. At present we should only warn him, punish him and have him write a self-criticism." I heard that Chairman Mao didn't pass on his first self-criticism; it wouldn't do, was insufficient; and he had him write another. The second self-criticism still didn't pass. The third one—I seem to remember that I also read that one—Chairman Mao approved.

When Zhang's "problem" was discovered, he was terrified. Zhang's wife knew me, and before I went to meet Chairman Mao, his wife came to ask for my help as a favor, hoping to find out how serious this incident was. I said OK, and also spoke to Mao about it. Mao's answer was

不过他这个人呢，就是有缺点吧，有毛病吧，刚才我说了油滑，不是那么很忠诚老实。他那时在燕京大学，燕京大学有很多美国人，他是燕京大学的教授，他是很觉得美国是一个非常有力量（的国家），看共产党是不是能够统一全国，稳定、安定下去，不敢判断。刚好有一个，也算是坏人吧，一个骗子，这个骗子大概是三十多岁，在日本人统治北京的时候，刚好跟张东荪在一个监狱里头，日本人把他扣起来了，骗子在监狱里跟他熟了。以后共产党军队进入北京了，这个骗子还跟他有往来，还是有时候去燕京大学去看他。张东荪呢，觉得美国是最富强的、有力量的，共产党的统治中国是不是能稳定下去呢？好像不一定吧。而那个骗子对东荪说，他同美国国务院都有联系，他自己夸张说。张东荪就信了这个骗子的话，信了这个骗子的话啊，他就把一些个参加人民政府会议的文件，他都给这个人看，这个人都给运走了，给送到美国。这个人后来在北京，被北京市长彭真抓住了，抓住了就问他你还有什么同谋的人，他就把张东荪说出来了。

这个时候刚好还是我跟毛主席有往来的时候，他常常派车子接我到中南海去谈。毛主席就对我讲起来张东荪的事情。他说：彭真说要把他抓起来，我对彭真说，这种文人秀才造不起反来，不值得重视，但是呢，他也再不能够跟我们坐在一起开会了。现在应该警告他，要惩罚他，要他自己检讨，自己写文章检讨。我听说，第一次写了检讨，毛主席看了不通过，不行，不够，再一次。再写还是没有通过。到第三次检讨，一次、二次我没有看，第三次好像我还看过了一下，第三次嘛，毛主席批准了。

当他的问题发觉的时候，他是很恐慌的。他的夫人，张东荪的夫人认识我，在我跟毛主席见面之前呢，他夫人还来托我，说是你看到毛主席的时候替我探探口气，究竟这个问题严重到什么程度。我也就说了，我也去跟毛说了，毛答复的话

like this: Peng Zhen reported to me such and so forth; Peng Zhen had arrested a swindler, and so on. I told Peng Zhen: Don't arrest him; there is no need to arrest Zhang Dongsun; an effete intellectual doesn't have the capacity to rebel; don't mind him; but we cannot forgive him a second time. Chairman Mao told me this personally. I also told this to Zhang Dongsun's wife. I also saw Zhang Dongsun, who was panic-stricken. His crime was "having illicit relations with a foreign country." At that time, there was hostility between China and the U.S. He was mentally disturbed and panic-stricken. He almost couldn't sleep. It seems that I read his third self-criticism essay. Chairman Mao also read it, and approved it. His self-criticism was profound. It could pass and he was not punished. He was given, moreover, a stipend of one hundred yuan a month, but he was kept under house arrest of a sort. He could not have any contact with anyone outside, so that afterwards I could no longer see him.[26]

Alitto: Do you have any impressions of his philosophical writings?

Liang: A thoughtful man of ideas. I think I myself have quoted him.

Alitto: Do you think he could be considered modern China's...

Liang: A thoughtful person, but as a man, he was not kind and simple-hearted; he was a finagler who was looking for personal advantage. This man was not as good as Zhang Junmai. The two Zhangs were extremely close, but Zhang Junmai was loyal, considerate and honest, not like Zhang Dongsun who was a slippery character.

● I was too arrogant, too bigheaded in September of 1953.

Alitto: I think that your life hasn't been completely smooth sailing. There have certainly been heart-breaking events. Do you want to talk about them? It might serve to encourage and stimulate later scholars who find themselves in difficult straits. You have encountered a lot of setbacks, right?

Liang: I think that it seems I haven't actually had any heart-breaking events. I only feel that there are things that I haven't done well, things that I've failed or made mistakes about. For example, speaking of mistakes, that event in September of 1953 was my own mistake. I was too arrogant, too bigheaded, and so refused to go along with His Honor Mao. After that event I thought that I shouldn't have acted that way. I should have respected him more, and should not have fallen out with him.

就是，就是说那个话：彭真来向我报告，说是如此如此，彭真抓住那个骗子了，如此如此，我告诉彭真，不用抓他，张东荪不需要抓，文人秀才造不起反来，不用管他，但是我们也不能饶恕他——这是毛主席亲口对我说的话。我又把这个话回答张东荪的夫人。我也看到张东荪，张东荪惊恐得很，他的罪名是“里通外国”，那时中美之间是互相仇视的。他恐慌得很，差不多精神发病了，简直不能睡眠了，精神错乱了。到了第三次他自己批评检讨的文章好像我还看到了，毛主席也看到了，通过，他自己批评检讨得还算深刻，还可以通过，不治他的罪，并且还要给他的生活费，每月 100 元。不过，等于软禁这样子，他不能同外人往来，所以以后我也没看到他。

艾： 您对他的哲学著作有没有印象呢?

梁： 他还算是有思想、有见解。好像我还有引用他的地方，好像有。

艾： 您觉得他还算是个中国现代的……

梁： 有思想的人。人呢，就是不够忠诚老实，有些取巧，想个人占便宜的这种思想。这个他不如张君劢。

• 1953年9月，自己心太盛、气太高

艾： 我认为您的一生并不是全是一帆风顺的，其中一定有一些令人伤心的事，您愿不愿意谈一谈呢? 可以对处身于困难的后学，产生一些鼓舞、激励的作用。您遭遇到不少挫折，对不对?

梁： 我觉得，我倒好像没有什么伤心的事情。我只是倒觉得自己有没有做好的事情、失败的事情，或者错误。比如说，说到错误吧，那个就是 1953 年 9 月，那个就是自己的一个错误，就是自己气太盛、气太高，所以就跟毛公就抵住了。那个事情后来我自己想，不应当那样的，应当我多尊重他一些，不应当跟他闹翻。

Alitto: So at that time did you feel sad?

Liang: I didn't feel sad. I just felt that I had made a mistake, that I had been in the wrong, but that can't be considered feeling sad. If I have been sad in my life, it was at the death of my first wife. I was a bit grieved. Because I felt that she really was so good, and so her dying was a saddening event. Right when I was 40-some years old. Previously the Chinese ancients had a saying, "It is a great misfortune to lose a spouse in middle age." That is, if it were a bit earlier, not in middle age, for example at thirty... Is it considered a great misfortune to lose a spouse at thirty? Naturally it is considered still a great misfortune, but it is easier to forget when younger. After a while, the sadness passes, and is forgotten. The great misfortune of losing a spouse in middle age is also different from in old age when both spouses are going to die soon and it seems it's not that bad. Right in middle age, right when the feelings of the two spouses are deepest, their emotions are intense. This time is different from youth and old age. So, if I've had a saddening event, it was [the death of] my first wife, who was also the mother of my two sons.

● Perseverance in the turbulant days

Alitto: Aside from this incident, were there others, or say, some other incidents of persecution or of damage to you during the Cultural Revolution?

Liang: I remember on August 24, 1966, Red Guard militants came to our house. They said that they had come to rebel, and there was some damage, and they injured my wife.

Alitto: Did they know who you were?

Liang: You could say that they knew, and yet they didn't know that much about me. They were junior high school students, and their school was just north of my house. It was just about half a kilometer or slightly more away. It was quite convenient for them to go from the school to the house. They were junior high students, and so had very little knowledge. You could say they didn't know anything about me. At the time, I wanted to write to Chairman Mao asking for help. I wasn't sure whether the letter might reach him, or whether it could elicit sympathy from him even if he got the letter. I did write letters, one to Mao and one to Zhou [Enlai], but there was no word from either.

艾： 那您那个时候是不是感到伤心呢？

梁： 没有伤心，我就感觉到自己错了，我不好，不算是伤心。如果有伤心的话，那就是我前头的太太，我的内人，她的死，我有一点伤心，因为我觉得她实在是很好，所以她死呢，是一个很伤心的事情。刚好是一个四十多岁的时候，从前中国古人有这么一句话："中年丧偶大不幸。"就是说假定早一点，不是中年，比如说在三十岁、三十多岁的时候丧偶，算不算大不幸呢？当然也算大不幸，不过比较年轻的时候容易忘，过些日子就把伤心过去了、忘了；中年丧偶大不幸呢，跟老年不同，老年大家彼此都快死了，好像也不大怎么样；中年刚好，刚好彼此两个人关系很深、感情很深，这个时候跟青年不同，跟老年也不同。所以，假定说我有伤心的事情，就是我前头的内人，也就是我现在的两个儿子的母亲。

• 动乱岁月里的坚守

艾： 有没有别的，或者说是"文革"时候的一些迫害，或者一些对您不利的事情？

梁： 我记得 1966 年 8 月 24（日），红卫兵小将来了，他们说他们来造反，就有了一些个破坏，还打伤我的内人。

艾： 那他们知不知道您是谁啊？

梁： 也可以说知道，也可以说不是很知道。说知道，是因为学生是初中学生，而这个初中呢，就在我住家的北边，大概也就是一里路或者是一里多路，从他们学校到我这儿来很方便。再一个，他们是初中的学生，知识很少，可以说是对我不甚知道。当时我自己想写信向毛主席求救，信恐怕也许达不到，也许达到了而他没有什么反响，不清楚。我信是写了的，一个信写给毛，一个信写给周，可是结果都没有消息。

Alitto: Another question. When they burst in, what did they say? How were they going to rebel?

Liang: A group of kids—young teenage boys and girls burst through the door. At the time I lived in the northern main room of the house. I said, "You coming to inspect, right?" They said, "No, we have come to rebel." I didn't want to say anything. I just let them do what they wanted. So, they destroyed a lot of things. They dragged a glass case outside and smashed it. They confiscated trunks. They carted away some things. Openly done robbery. They took apart our bedding, as well as our mosquito netting. They were of low morals. They burnt things to a great pile of ashes. It took more than a day to carry the ashes away.

Alitto: Did they beat your wife when they first came, or did they beat her later?

Liang: In the middle of the several days.

Alitto: Did they explain the reason when they were beating her?

Liang: They didn't give any reasons. They also had her kneel in punishment, right when the sun was the hottest; they had her kneel in the sun.

Alitto: Didn't they say why they beat your wife but not you?

Liang: They didn't explain this either.

Alitto: Did they criticize your past actions or your past publications?

Liang: No, neither.

Alitto: They just made trouble, just like that.

Liang: Yeah.

Alitto: Aside from your books and furniture, did they destroy anything like paintings or calligraphy?

Liang: Some of mine; there were some of my father's things, my grandfather's things, and my great-grandfather's things. Because [these things] provoked them [the Red Guards]. For example, China has always prized painting and calligraphy, the kind of painting and calligraphy that you can hang up. Moreover, they occupied my place for twenty days, perhaps twenty-one days.

艾： 还有一个，他们冲进来的时候，他们是怎么说的呢？什么样的造反法呢？

梁： 一群年纪轻的、十几岁的男孩子、女孩子，破门而入，我当时住在北上房，他们就进来了。我说：你们来是不是检查吧？他们说不，我们来造反。我就没有话要讲了，听他们要怎么样就怎么样吧，所以就破坏了很多东西，玻璃柜拖到外面都砸烂了，箱子扣出来，有些东西用车子拉走了。……抢东西，公开的。把你睡的床铺、蚊帐都给你拆开，……道德低下。烧，烧的灰一大堆，要把灰拿出去，一天都弄不完。

艾： 那个时候他们刚来的时候就打了您的夫人，还是以后打的？

梁： 就在中间。

艾： 打她的时候说什么原因吗？

梁： 不说什么原因。还有罚跪，就是太阳很热的时候，在太阳底下跪。

艾： 他们有没有说为什么打您的夫人而不打您？

梁： 这个没有说。

艾： 他们有没有批评您过去的行动或者过去的著作呢？

梁： 都没有。

艾： 他们就是闹？

梁： 嗯。

艾： 那您的损失包括书籍、家具，没有别的什么字画之类的？

梁： 我自己的、我父亲的、祖父的、曾祖的，有一些东西。因为都招他了。比如中国历来就讲究书画，可以挂起来的那种书画，那种东西。他们并且盘踞我的地方达 20 天之久，21 天好像。

Alitto: When they left, did they explain the reasons?

Liang: No.

Alitto: Not then either? Then they didn't talk to you during the entire process?

Liang: They were busy. Very busy. They made the northern hall where I lived their base area.

Alitto: A base area?

Liang: That was because at that time we had a telephone installed. They used that telephone; they could have communication with their own school through the phone. They also went to the neighboring families to rebel, manhandling them, and driving those people back to their hometowns. Anyway, whoever wasn't of Beijing was sent away. My niece and her husband were Cantonese, and they were sent back to Guangdong. The trains were packed with people who were being sent back under escort to their hometowns. This was one matter. Another matter was to have young students go run around everywhere—young students didn't need tickets to ride the train. For example, there was a Mr. Chen Weizhi whom I just mentioned. At the time he was a junior high student and took advantage of this opportunity to go at will to Xinjiang—a very far place—and in the south he went to Yunnan, Guangxi and Guangdong.

Alitto: Right. I just remembered. In 1974 and 1975, when I was studying at University [of California, Berkeley], there were two brothers surnamed Pan. Before Liberation, their parents were in the United States. [My friend] and his brother stayed in Beijing. He was a junior high school student at that time, and traveled around everywhere.

Liang: Yes, they were running around everywhere, as they pleased.

Alitto: Did any of your friends come to see you at that time?

Liang: No one visited anyone else, because they were afraid of getting into trouble, so if possible no one left home. People didn't even go to buy food and drink. (Alitto: How could that work?) If possible they ate whatever was left in their own kitchens. People didn't go out to shop for more than ten days, much less to visit friends and relatives.

Alitto: Did any of your relatives and Red Guards have...?

Liang: You have already seen, I have an elder son, and a second son. They

艾：他们走的时候，有没有说出原因来？

梁：没有。

艾：也没有？那他们岂不是整个过程中都没有跟你们讲话？

梁：他们很忙，很忙。他们拿我住的北房做一个根据地了。

艾：做根据地？

梁：因为那个时候我家里装了电话，他们用那个电话，他跟自己的学校可以用电话联系。他到附近人家，也是去造反、欺负人，把那些人赶回乡。不是北京的都送走，我的侄女、女婿都是广东人，就把他们送广东。火车装满了人，都是全押送回乡，这是一种情况。还有一种情况，就是让青年学生到处去……，青年学生上火车不用买票，各处跑。比如说我刚才提到的那个陈维志，当时是个初中学生，他就借那个机会，就跑到新疆，很远，南边还到了云南，到了广西、广东，随便跑，完全随便跑。

艾：对，我想起来了，在 1974、1975 年，我在读大学的时候，有一对兄弟，姓潘的，解放前他的父母就在美国了。他和他的哥哥留在北京，他也是初中的学生，他什么地方都跑过了。

梁：是，都到处跑，随便跑。

艾：那个时候有没有老朋友来看您？

梁：彼此不来往，谁跟谁都不来往，怕惹事，尽可能地不出门，像是出门买菜、买饮食啊，都不出去。（艾：那怎么办？）尽可能地在自己厨房里头还剩下什么东西都吃，十几天地都不出门，不出去，更不往来，朋友、亲戚不往来。

艾：那您自己有没有亲戚和红卫兵小将的……

梁：你已经看见过的，我一个大儿子，一个二儿子，他们也都没

didn't live with me. They came to see me, but they could do nothing at all. Moreover, the Red Guards said, "Don't you come around here!" Usually they left. Friends and relatives did not visit each other. They couldn't even fend for themselves. That was a very rare, strange situation.

Alitto: When this situation developed, what were you thinking?

Liang: When I became the object of these assaults, I was a bit unhappy at first. After a while, I took it easy and began to write again. At that time, I had no reference books, as my books had all been destroyed, but I relied on things in my mind to write. That manuscript of mine is still here—I wrote "A Comparative Study of Buddhism and Confucianism," discussing their commonalities and differences.

Alitto: So you were able to remain cool as a cucumber.

Liang: Actually, it was nothing at all.

● The commander of forces can be carried off; the will of a common man cannot be taken.

Liang: Under the leadership of Chairman Mao, everyone must study. In my small study group of about ten-odd or twenty-some people, as in all these small groups, you can talk freely, you can express criticisms randomly. Whatever is on your mind, you can express it to everyone. They have a slogan "an Exchange of Views." That is, you express your views, and we'll express our views. You can criticize me and I will criticize you. So then, you have debates, you "cross swords." Now the other members of the group criticized me, for example, during the "Criticize Lin Biao and Criticize Confucius" Campaign in 1973, everyone in the group was criticizing Confucius. I said, "Probably for the Communist Party leadership it is necessary politically to criticize Confucius. I'm not too clear on this. But Chairman Mao has said that different opinions can be retained. Okay, I have reservations about criticizing Confucius." At first, I expressed that I would retain my opinions on Confucius. However,

I also wouldn't say anything negative in the anti-Confucius campaign. I would simply remain silent. But the members of my study group often intentionally taunted or tempted me into expressing some opinion, so as to criticize me. So I expressed my opinion and ended up being attacked on all sides. Once, in the midst of being attacked by everyone in the

住在一起。他们来看我，完全没有办法，并且红卫兵说你们不要来，平常也就走了。亲戚、朋友都不相往来了，各自都是自顾不暇。那是很少有的、很奇怪的那么一种。

艾：那当时这样的情况发生的时候，您心里在想什么呢?

梁：我开头就是受到这种冲击心里有点不愉快，可是很少的几天我就过去了，就没有什么不愉快了。过去了我就开始写东西、写文章。这时候没有参考书，书都毁了，但是我就凭我脑子里有的东西写，我现在那个稿子还有，写的是《儒佛异同论》，儒家、佛家异同论。

艾：那您真是沉得住气啊。

梁：其实是很没有什么。

• 三军可夺帅也，匹夫不可夺志

梁：比如在毛主席的领导，让大家都要学习，学习就有学习小组，大概十几个人啦、二三十个人啦，大家可以随便谈啦，彼此听听，有什么心里话，要大家说出来。他们的一个口号叫做“思想见面”，你把你的思想拿出来，我把我的思想拿出来，彼此见面。那么，各自拿出来了，也就彼此有些批评，见面了，我也可以批评你，你也可以批评我。这个时候也是有争论的、有交锋的，那么我也就是曾受过旁人的批评。毛主席他有一次批林批孔，那是1973年，在小组会上大家都批孔，我就说：在领导党、党的方面要批孔，也许在政治上有它的必要，需要批孔，我不大清楚；不过呢，毛主席也说过，有不同意见可以保留，那么好，我保留。我第一次表示我保留，保留不同意见，但是我也绝不说反面的话——不要批孔，我也不说这个话，我就是要沉默，我不说就是。可是尽管如此，一同学习的人，他常常还有意地引逗你，引逗你让你说话，你说出来，就好批评你。……最怕的是引起围攻，很多人围攻，有过这样的事情。

group, I said, "Okay, I'll quietly listen to everyone's criticisms and won't say anything more." I think that happened in 1974 or 1975.[27]

After Liberation, Chairman Mao wanted everyone to study and reform themselves in small study groups. Weren't there some democratic political parties, like the Democratic League and the Revolutionary Committee of the KMT? There were also the China Association for Promoting Democracy, the Jiusan Society, the All-China Federation of Industry and Commerce, the China Democratic National Construction Association, and also some members without party affiliations, who were combined together and called the "group directly under the People's Political Consultative Conference." It was in this study group that I said those words. Although I started the Democratic League, later I left it and was without any party affiliations. So, the story I just told was with the small study group without party affiliation. Now the five groups I just mentioned got together in some joint sessions to criticize me.

Alitto: So were these joint sessions in 1973, 1974 or...

Liang: These sessions were held through 1974 and 1975. Of course the group of all democratic personages was much larger, five small groups involving over one hundred members. So, there was a speaker's platform, and I remember over ten people spoke, one after another, criticizing me. I remained silent, refusing to express an opinion, even when they tried forcing me to. To remain silence was not good either,...anyway I did not say a word till the meetings were over. After the enlarged meetings at which I was criticized, my own small group of non-party affiliated personages asked me, "What did you think of the criticisms leveled at you at the enlarged sessions?" I answered with a quotation from *The Analects* of Confucius, "The commander of the forces of a large state may be carried off, but the will of even a common man cannot be taken from him."[28] After I said this, I didn't say another word.

Alitto: So this kind of attitude is good for your health.

Liang: Yes. I am always steady and stable, with inner equilibrium. So, at the time when I said this, I used eight Chinese characters: ***dulisikao, biaoliruyi***—independent thought; unity of inner feelings and outer action. I am not someone who goes along with the crowd. Whatever I think, I say. My interior self and exterior self are identical. I don't hide anything. Generally, everyone is good to me.

围攻，那么我就说："好，我静听大家的批评吧，我不说话了。"在过去，在 1974 年、1975 年，都有批孔。

自从解放后，毛主席提倡大家要学习。不是有一些个民主党派？像是民盟、民革——民革就是从前的国民党，还有一个民进——"进步"的"进"，还有九三学社，还有工商联、民主建国会——民建，还有不在这些里的无党无派，也把它合起来，叫做"政协直属组"，直属于政协。刚才我说的话就是在直属组，我虽然是发起成立民盟的人，可是后来我离开了，所以我后来都一直算是无党无派，刚才说的就是我在无党无派小组会上的那个事情。他们要围攻我，所以呢，五个组，就是说九三学社是一组，民革是一组，民盟一组……一共五个组，开一个联组会，在联组会上批判我。

艾： 联组会它是 1973、1974 年的时候，还是……

梁： 1974 那个时候，在 1974 年、1975 年都有。联组会就人多，五个组成百了。有人就上台去发表言论批判我，先后大概有十多个人批判我，我就静听，不发言。不发言也不好，……不发言这个会也就过去了。批判我的会过去了，可是我自己本组那个小组会上，他们还有人问我说："在联组上大家批判你，你听得怎么样呀？"我就回答，我说古书上——其实就是《论语》上——《论语》上有一句话："三军可夺帅也，匹夫不可夺志（也）。"我就是引了这个话，答复了大家，我不说别的话了。

艾： 原来讲的是跟您身体特别好的关系，就是……

梁： 就是从那引起来说的话。自己很稳定。我当时也说了这么一句话，表明我自己是怎么一回事，八个字，中文是八个字，头四个字是"独立思考"，"表里如一"——表面跟里头一样的。"独立思考"就是不是人云亦云，人家说什么跟着说，不是那么样。"表里如一"，我心里有什么就说什么，表面跟里头是一样的，不隐瞒。一般地说，大家都还对我还好。

Two greatest things in my life

Alitto: By reading about that time of your life in books and essays you wrote, I got the impression that it was only after the Republican Revolution that you wanted to leave home and become a monk.

Liang: I have often said that there are two questions that have occupied my mind. One question is the practical problem of China. China was in a kind of national crisis, and the social problems were very serious. This practical problem stimulated me and occupied my mind. There is another problem. I just mentioned a practical problem. There is another problem that transcends practicality, which is the problem of human life. What should be done with its afflictions and uncertainties, the misunderstandings of life, and doubts about it? Isn't this what I just mentioned about wanting to leave home and become a monk? These two problems are not the same. One makes me involve myself in social and national affairs for society and the country; and the other makes me want to leave society.

Alitto: Early in your life, you worked at a great number of different projects. After you participated in the revolution, you were a journalist, and after that, a Buddhist lay devotee, and you taught at a university. Which of these occupations, as far as your later life is concerned, had the greatest influence?

Liang: Although I had been a journalist, and an instructor, in fact the more important occupation of all was my work in social movements and politics. Didn't I have a relationship with Mao Zedong and Chiang Kai-shek, and the two parties? When George Marshall was in China, I had a lot of contact with him. He very much wanted to have the two parties find a compromise and peace.[29] I also worked on this, so worked quite a bit in political movements and social activities; working in rural reconstruction is a social movement. Political and social activities probably occupied a great part of my life. As for teaching, I had done this at Peking University. Later I also had a lot of students. Well, I was a journalist when I was young, and later I went to Hong Kong to run *Guangmingbao*, and so again was a journalist. The thing I very seldom did was to be an official. I had a very good friend, Li Jishen. When I was 36 years old, I went to Guangdong Province to see him. I went to live in the countryside about 30 kilometers outside of Guangzhou.[30] He didn't

伍 我一生最重要的大事

艾： 看您所写的几本书，或者是文章，关于您那个时候的生活，给我留下的印象是辛亥革命以后您才真正地想出家。

梁： 我常说自己，有两个问题占据了我的头脑。两个问题，一个呢，现实问题，现实中国的问题，因为中国赶上一种国家的危难，社会的问题很严重。这个现实的问题刺激我，这个问题占据我的脑筋。可还有另外一个问题，刚才说的是个现实问题，还有一个问题是一个超过现实的、也是人生问题，对人生的怀疑、烦闷——对人生不明白，怀疑它，有烦闷，该当怎么样啊？这不是刚才说想出家吗？这是两个问题，两个问题不一样，一个就让我为社会、为国事奔走，一个又让离开。

艾： 您早年曾经从事过好几个不同的工作，您参加了革命以后做记者，以后做居士——佛教的居士啊，在大学教过书。您觉得哪一种工作对您后来的生涯影响最大？

梁： 我的生活，固然做过记者了，教过书了，做过教员了，可是实际上比较重要的是做社会运动、参与政治。我不是跟毛主席、跟蒋介石两大党我都有关系吗？马歇尔在中国的时候，我跟他接触很多。他是极力想给两党找出一个妥协和平来。我也是搞这个东西，所以我实在搞了不少政治活动、社会活动，搞乡村建设是社会活动，社会活动、政治活动恐怕是占我一生很大部分。教书嘛，我曾经有过这个事情，北大教过书，后来也带着很多学生。那么，做新闻记者，开头年纪轻的时候做过，后来我到香港办《光明报》，又做新闻记者。那么比较少的，很少很少的，就是做官。我一个很好的朋友，就是李济深，我 36 岁的时候，我到广东去看他。我去离广州 60 里的一个乡下去

get my agreement, but he issued the news to the National Government in Nanjing that I was a member of the Guangdong Provincial Government Committee. I did not take up the office and indicated that I wouldn't do so. So, you could say that I have never been an official. In my entire life, I've never been an official, but I have done social and political activities.[31]

Alitto: That is, aside from having been the county magistrate of Zouping.

Liang: Right, you saw that! We were administrating Zouping County, which was under the Rural Reconstruction Institute, and for a period of about two months, we couldn't find someone for the post of county magistrate, so I myself held this office part-time.

Alitto: Right, so it could be said that you have been an official.

Liang: Yes.

Alitto: Looking back on your life, what do you think was the most important thing in it?

Liang: The biggest was working in society and in social movements. Rural reconstruction was a social movement; this kind of social movement had considerable influence. For three years straight we held an annual nationwide rural work symposium. Rural work was an important task at which I labored in the past. Another was the task of uniting the parties to resist Japan. Because I had gone once to the guerilla area, and had seen there the troops of the two parties fighting with one another, I became fearful that this would lead to civil war, so I first organized the "Comrades' Association for United and National Construction," and later the "Democratic League." Others mistakenly thought that I wanted to organize my own political group. Actually this was wrong. I did not hold that, aside from the two major parties, China needed a third group. I never meant that. The Democratic League was not a third political group, so what was it? It was to promote the two major parties to unite in resisting Japan, and cooperate in constructing the nation. As long as there was unity in resisting Japan, it would be fine; as long as the nation would be cooperatively constructed, it would be fine. I did not want to create some kind of political group, so now the Democratic League still exists, but I am not a member. In the first phase [of my life] I devoted myself to social movements; in the second phase, to national affairs.[32]

闲住的时候，他没有得我同意，就要南京国民政府发表我为广东省政府委员，我没有就，发表了我不干。所以我可以说没有做官，一生之中啊，没有做过官，可是做过政治运动、社会运动。

艾： 除了在邹平的时候，有一阵子您当过县长的。

梁： 对，这个你还看到了。因为邹平县归我们管，属于乡村建设研究院，有那么一个时期，大概两个月，那个县长刚好找不到人，那我就自己去兼这个县长，兼任两个月。

艾： 是，所以可以说是您做过官。

梁： 可以。

艾： 回想、回顾您过去的生活，您以为您生活中最重要的大事是什么？

梁： 大事一个就是为社会奔走，做社会运动。乡村建设是一种社会运动，这种社会运动起了相当的影响。我们曾经连续三年，每一年都开一次全国性的乡村工作讨论会。乡村工作是我过去主要的奔走的一样。再一个就是为国内的党派的团结抗日。因为我去了游击区一次，在游击区看见两党的军队自己打，我就很怕引起内战，引起内战就妨碍了抗日，抗日期间不可以有内战啊，所以我就先搞“统一建国同志会”，后来搞“民主同盟”。旁人就误以为我是想搞一个自己的党派，其实不对。我不认为中国需要两大党之外，还要一个第三个党派，我没有这个意思。民主同盟不是第三个党派，是什么呢？是想推动两大党团结抗敌、合作建国。能够团结抗敌就好了，能够合作建国就好了。自己不想成一个什么党派，所以现在还有民主同盟了，可是我不参加。第一段是搞社会运动，第二段是奔走国事。

Alitto: In your private life, what was the important event? You just mentioned the two important things for society, for the nation, for the people. What was important in your personal life?

Liang: My writing of books, especially the largest and the most important one, called *The Human Mind/Heart and Human Life* (*Renxin yu Rensheng*). I asked a friend of mine who has good English, "How should the name of my most recent book *Renxin yu Rensheng* be translated into English?" He said that this term *renxin* is not one word in English, but rather there were two words that had some relationship to it. One was "Mind," and the other "Heart." That would be "Mind and Heart and Life."

Alitto: Yes. I also think it's not suitable, although directly translated into English is like this. The word *xin* has two meanings, but it is still a bit not... (Liang: Strained?) It isn't pleasing to the ear. How about this: if you want, I would be happy to translate the book into English, no problem.

Liang: I think that this is the most important thing in my life; having written this book is the most important thing.

艾： 您私人生活的重要的大事？您说的是为社会、为国家、为人民服务的两个大事，那您私人生活没有重要的大事吗？

梁： 那就是我的写书了。我写的书，特别是最大的一本书、最重要的一本书叫做《人心与人生》。我曾经请教英文好的朋友，我说我这本重要的书《人心与人生》，要翻成英文说，这个名字怎么翻呢？他说“人心”这个字，英文不是一个字，有两个字跟这个有关系，一个是 mind，还一个是 heart，所以要是给你翻译一个英文名字，那就是“Mind and Heart and Life”。

艾： 是。我也觉得不怎么妥当，虽然是直接翻成英文是这个样子，不错，“心”有两种意思，不过还是有点不……（梁：勉强？）不顺耳。这样吧，假如您愿意，我也很高兴把您的那本书翻成英文，没问题的，我想。

梁： 我想我一生，这个是最重要的事情，写成这本书是我的最重要的事情。

My views of other people,

我对他人、世界和自身的看法

the world and myself

我可能比其他的普通人不同的一点的，
就是我好像望见了，远远地看到了，
看到了什么呢？看到了王阳明，
看到了孔子。
我的程度只是这么一个程度。

I'm possibly an ordinary person who is a bit different from
other ordinary people.
That is, it's as though I have seen something from afar.
What do I get to see?
I catch a glimpse from afar of Wang Yangming, and Confucius.
Viewing them at a great distance—
my level [of understanding] is only to such a degree.

Historical figures

- **Yan Yangchu has no head for philosophy concerning rural reconstruction.**

Alitto: As for Yan Yangchu... (Liang: I had a lot of contact with him.) Do you have any comments on him?

Liang: He was a very nice person. I heard he's in the Philippines now.

Alitto: What was the greatest difference between Yan's and your views of rural reconstruction and its practice?

Liang: Yan lacked a theoretical grasp. He had no head for philosophy. He was originally working in a mass literacy movement. This literacy movement was related to his religion. Religious people very often engage in some philanthropic work and help poverty-stricken people.[33] During the First World War, French manpower was in short supply because of the war, so they needed laborers. They hired a lot of Chinese peasants as laborers for their factories. Of course, it was a good deal for the peasants, as they could earn more than they could back in China. But they were illiterate, far from home and so could not write letters to the families. So in this way Yan Yangchu started to teach the Chinese laborers to read, so that they could communicate with their families back in China.

Afterwards, the situation changed. The French didn't need foreign labor any more, and the Chinese workers returned to China. So did Yan. But he still wanted to continue to do literacy work. At first he worked in Beijing. Someone told him, "If you want your literacy movement to help poor people, the most important sector of poor people are the peasants. The bulk of the people in China are peasants. Most peasants are illiterate. Rather than do as you are doing you should go to the countryside." Only in this way did he go to Ding County. His original term was "Poor People's Education." Later he called it the "Four Great Educations." He said that

Chinese peasants had four urgent faults—poverty, ignorance, physical weakness and selfishness, and his Four Great Educations were targeted at these four shortcomings. His work was like that.

Alitto: What is your evaluation of his work and his thought?

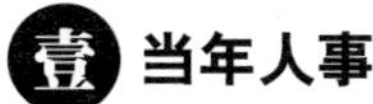

壹 当年人事

• 晏阳初对乡村问题缺乏哲学的头脑

艾： 晏阳初，我不知道您对他有没有……（梁：很熟悉。）您对他有什么评论、评价？

梁： 他人很好，听说现在在菲律宾。

艾： 您看，把您自己对乡村问题的看法和晏阳初对乡村的看法比一比，最大的区别在哪里啊？

梁： 晏阳初在头脑、思想方面，缺乏哲学的头脑。他原来是一个"识字运动"家，他这个"识字运动"跟他的宗教有关系。宗教家总是要做慈善工作，帮助穷苦人，所以他最初是在第一次欧战，第一次欧战法国人就去打仗了，就到中国来招募华工去工厂做工，那么中国农民当然很高兴去做工，可以有好收入，比在农村生活好。可中国农民不识字，远隔了——跟家庭，家庭里也常常要通信给他，他也想通信给自己家里，可是不会写字。这样子晏阳初就是帮助工人写字、认识字，好可以看信，好可以写信。开头就是对法国华工做识字运动，这样子开头的。

事情后来变了，法国不大需要做工作，他就回中国。回中国他还是想做识字运动，起初到了北京，可是有人告诉他：你要做识字运动，帮助穷苦人，那么主要的还是农民，人数最多的是农民，不识字的也是农民，你与其到北京不如下乡。他这样子才去了定县。在定县他就把他的——他原来号称"平民教育"——他就把"平民教育"说作"四大教育"，他说中国农民有四个毛病——"贫愚弱私"，针对"贫愚弱私"搞"四大教育"。他是这个样子。

艾： 您自己来评价他的工作或者他的思想，您觉得怎么样？

Liang: I think he had no head for philosophy. His theory about "poverty, ignorance, physical weakness and selfishness" was not a very brilliant or clever idea. For example, this "poverty"—at the time, the problem of China was not poverty. Why not poverty? Wasn't China very poor? I thought that the problem was not just "poverty" but "increasing poverty." When a child was born, it was not a problem of having nothing. If there was a chance for development and creativeness, he would be able to do well. So, the problem was not just poverty but a tendency toward greater and greater poverty. In Chinese society of that time the problem was one of sinking ever downward, sliding down a slope. So the important task was to reverse this tendency and get Chinese society going upward again. But Yan did not understand this. It was insights like this that he lacked.

Alitto: So he could be considered as having too superficial a view of the situation?

Liang: Exactly, superficial.

● Hu Shi has very shallow views of things.

Alitto: He [Yan] and Hu Shi had quite a few views in common.

Liang: Yes, that's right. Hu Shi also had very shallow views of things.

Alitto: I mention Hu Shi quite a lot in my book for comparison and criticise him on this point. Do you think that the similarities between the views of these two men had anything to do with their education in the U.S.?

Liang: Not necessarily. I just thought of something. During our last interview wasn't I unable to remember someone's name, someone who also had been educated in the United States? I now remember that his name was Jin Yuelin. He had studied political science in the U.S., but what he loved was logic. They ran into each other at a Peking Union board meeting. Hu had just published an article. Hu asked Mr. Jin,

"I have an article. Did you see it?" Jin replied, "I saw it. Very good, very good." Hu was very happy. Jin continued, "Too bad that you left out one sentence." "What was that?" [Hu asked.] "When it comes to philosophy, I'm a layman," [was Jin's response.] Because Hu Shi had been unenlightened to say, "What is philosophy? Philosophy is just bad science," meaning immature, indifferent science.

梁： 我觉得他缺乏哲学头脑，"贫愚弱私"这个看法不高明。比如说"贫愚弱私"的"贫"，当时的中国的问题，不是"贫"的问题。那么是什么问题？怎么会不是贫的问题，农民很贫了？我认为真实的问题是"贫而越来越贫"的问题。人一生下来——一个小孩子生下来，什么也没有啊，没有不要紧，创造、发展就行了。所以不是"贫"的问题，而是"贫而越来越贫"的问题，就是说中国的社会在那个时候是向下沉沦的问题，向下沉沦，走下坡路，一定要把中国广大社会从走下坡路扭转为走上坡路才行。可是晏先生他缺乏这种看法。

艾： 那他算不算是看得太浅？

梁： 就是，看得浅。

- **胡适的头脑是粗浅的**

艾： 他和胡适关于乡村问题、关于中国的问题，有很多类似的地方。

梁： 对，胡适也是浅。

艾： 书里面常常提到胡适，比较批评他的就是这一点。是不是就是这样，晏阳初、胡适原来都是留美的，会不会跟他们留美有关系？

梁： 那不一定。我刚才想起来，上一次我说的，我忘记了人名了，后来我想起来了，叫做金岳霖。他是留美的，本来是去学政治的，但是他喜欢逻辑。在协和医院开会，胡适刚好发表一篇文章，他们两个碰上了，胡就问金先生说："我有一篇文章，你看见了吗？"金说："看见了，很好很好。"胡很高兴。他（金）说："可惜啊，少说一句话。""什么话啊？""我是哲学的外行。"就是这个故事。因为胡那个话是很不高明的了。他说："什么叫哲学？哲学就是坏的科学。"就是一种不成熟的科学，不高明的科学。

Alitto: I also wanted to ask something. You also think that John Dewey's thought is of some value, and Hu Shi's thought was not his own creation, he just followed Dewey. Now, you and Hu Shi's opinions differed. Both of you, it would seem, have toward Dewey...

Liang: He can be considered Dewey's student. Dewey came to China...

Alitto: That is to say, although you two differ in many areas in thought, you still have toward Dewey...

Liang: Of course, Dewey has great value. He seemed to call it "popularly based education." His mind was by no means shallow; it was quite dynamic and thorough. His books were rather profound. Even simple people can read his books. Brilliant, profound people can perceive Dewey's excellent and valuable qualities. Hu Shi was unable to understand Dewey. Everyone's mind is different, and Hu Shi's mind was shallow.

● Kang Youwei's works of the early period have their value.

Liang: ...But I disliked Kang Youwei, very much. Wasn't he working on some kind of Confucian Church? But that problem was relatively small. The most important problem was that he was hypocritical and deceitful in many matters. For example, he used to predate his writings. That is, he would put a much earlier date on them before he actually wrote them. Why? This was dishonest.

Alitto: Right. I had thought that possibly you opposed some parts of his *The Great Commonwealth*?

Liang: Didn't he write *The Great Commonwealth*? I still have it on my shelf. I think that his Great Commonwealth ideal is by no means profound or advanced and not worth all the lavish praise. Well, it's fine to think of the very distant future, what society will be like, and fine to write it down, but it should be recognized that the worth of such an enterprise is certainly not great. Science should be emphasized, and not simply spout fantasies and pipe dreams. Of course, fantasies can be articulated, but they have no great value. The only kind of thinking that has real value is seeking the truth from the facts, and come down out of the clouds.

Alitto: You mentioned in your book *Eastern and Western Cultures and Their Philosophies* that you opposed this ideal thought.

艾： 我也想问，您也觉得杜威的思想是很有价值的，胡适的思想好像没有自己创造的，都是跟着杜威，您和胡适意见不同，您两位都是对杜威好像有……

梁： 他算是杜威的学生，杜威到中国……

艾： 就是说你们两位，虽然思想上有很多不同的地方，但是您还是对杜威这个……

梁： 当然，杜威有他的价值，他好像是叫做“民本教育”。他的思想并不浅薄，很活，他的头脑活动得很，活动，能够深入。他的书就是相当深的，粗浅的人也能看，看了也好。高明的人、深刻的人能够看出来杜威的长处、优点，可是胡适没有能够。一个人与一个人的头脑不相同，胡适的头脑是粗浅的。

- **康有为的价值是在他比较早的时候**

梁： ……我很不喜欢康。他不是要搞什么孔教会？不过这个问题还小，最大的问题是他这个人虚假，很多事他作假。比如他写文章，有倒填年月的事情，后来写的东西，他把它作为多少年以前写的东西。这何必来呢？不老实。

艾： 对，对。我以为可能您对他的《大同书》会有反对的地方吧，有不同意的地方吧？

梁： 他不是有本《大同书》吗？我书架上还有。我觉得这种“大同”的理想，并不高深，不值得去那么样子吹捧。设想远的未来的社会怎么样子怎么样的，可以设想，可以去作一些个想象，也可以把它写出来、说出来，不过应当认为价值不大。应当重视科学，不要作些什么幻想。幻想也可以说嘛，不过不会有很大价值，实事求是的这种研究才是有价值的。

艾： 大同这种理想啊，在《东西文化及其哲学》您也还反对，觉得大同是……

Liang: I didn't really oppose it. In some of the classical books, especially the "Liyun" chapter of the *Classic of Rites*, there are some statements like "Thus men did not love their parents only, nor treat as children only their own sons" and "a public and common spirit governed all under the sky." That is the form human society will develop into sometime in the future. I meant that people should not always place all of their hopes on the future and, in the process, minimize and ignore the present. This kind of psychology makes people unable to go all out concentrating on the present.

Alitto: You previously said that you very much dislike Kang Youwei. Can you give your reasons in some detail?

Liang: Kang Youwei always cheated people. When he first started out, he was really extraordinary. He promoted and led the reform movement. That, too, was really something. At the time this must be considered great wisdom and foresight. Of course we respected and revered him for it. But later in his life he always cheated people. He lied continually, but at the same time he was as proud as a peacock, with an overweening opinion of himself. This sort of thing is just intolerable. We should say something here: "Everyone ought to be modest." Seeing someone acting the way that Kang Youwei did, self-important and arrogant, always assuming that he was superior to everybody else, one knows that he was fundamentally no good.

Alitto: So in the realm of thought there was no...

Liang: His thought had its elements of creativeness. One of his books was *A Study of the False Classics of the Xin Period.* And there was that other book...[34] Both of these works are extremely famous. But experts know that the things in these two books were stolen from another man, a Sichuanese named Liao Ping. Quite a bit of Kang Youwei's thought, his opinions, and especially his analysis of the classics, were plagiarized from Liao Ping. Others have all said this. He stole Liao Ping's stuff and published it under his own name.

Kang Youwei's works also have their value, those of the early period. But the older he got, the worse he got. I heard that in the later period he forged and plagiarized things. There were other affairs that I know about... For example, there were two cases. In the south side of the city of Xi'an in Shaanxi there was a monastery. I seem to remember it being called the Monastery of the Sleeping Dragon. There was an old edition of a Buddhist sutra, extremely valuable. Kang appropriated it for himself. At

梁：不算是反对。因为中国的古书里头，特别是《礼记》里头《礼运》那篇，它都讲到了，“人不独亲其亲，不独子其子”，“天下为公”，那个是人类社会发展的前途、未来，会走到那一步的。我的意思就是说，人呢不要老怀抱着一个希望未来，好像把一切希望都寄托在未来，反而把当前的事情啊，看轻了，忽略了，不能够好好地在当下用心。

艾：您以前说很讨厌康有为，那可不可以比较详细地说原因在哪里呢?

梁：康有为他后来总是欺骗人，开头是很了不起嘛，倡导维新，他是维新运动的领袖，那很了不起，很了不起。在当时呢，可以算得先知先行，那我们当然佩服、恭敬他。不过后来他老骗人，他尽说假话啊，一方面尽说假话，一方面自高自大，简直可以说要不得。我们应当说一句话，人人都应当谦虚；自高自大，总把自己摆在众人之上，这个根本上就看出这个人不行啊。

艾：那在思想方面有没有……

梁：思想方面他有创新，他有著作，他有一本书叫做《新学伪经考》，还有一部什么书，两部书都是很出名。可是内行人、懂得的人，知道他这两部书从旁人那儿偷来的。有一个四川人廖平，康有为的许多思想见解和特别是对古书的看法吧，他都是从这儿来的，从廖平来的，旁人都是这么说，他是窃取了廖平的东西发表。

康有为他有他的价值，不过他的价值是在他比较早的时候，比较年轻的时候，他越到后来他越是不行了，后来他有造假的事情，还有我所知道的……比如我知道两件事。一件事，是在陕西西安，城南有一个庙，好像叫卧龙寺，那个庙里头有古代版本的佛经，很有价值，他就把它据为己有。那个时候

that time, transportation was very inconvenient. There was no railroad, only mule and horse carts. He loaded the valuable edition of the Buddhist Canon—many volumes, extremely heavy—into a cart, intending to take it away. He had already gone out of the East Gate of Xi'an and was on the highway when Xi'an natives who had discovered the theft overtook him. They took the sutra from him and returned it to its place in the temple. How do I know about this incident? When I was nineteen or so, I went to Xi'an, and as I liked to visit that temple, I got to learn about it.

There was another incident. In the early years of the Republic, there was a national assemblyman who was a big capitalist. In the late Qing, there was a kind of national bank called the Great Qing Bank. After the Qing court abdication, in the Republic of China, the bank's name was changed to the Bank of China. There was a director and a deputy director. The deputy director's name was Yu Fancheng. I was very friendly with Yu, and it was he who reported to me his encounters. Yu Fancheng was the deputy director of the Bank of China. Later he left the Bank of China, but he became a "private" banker capitalist. When a person wanted to borrow a relatively large amount of money from the bank, he must first put up collateral to guarantee the loan. What was used for collateral? Some valuable object that was universally recognized as having great value, such as a famous great painting. Only after the old painting was deposited in the bank as collateral would the bank lend him the money, for instance 2000 silver dollars.

Kang Youwei knew that there was a certain famous painting securing a loan in the bank, and asked Mr. Yu to take it out so that he could view it. Of course, as Kang was such a celebrity, Yu took the painting out and hung it up for viewing. Kang praised it non-stop, sighing and exclaiming how excellent it was and so on. Then he asked Mr. Yu Fancheng if he could take it home to enjoy it carefully. Because Kang was such a well-known person, Mr. Yu felt that if he made such a request, he had no choice but to agree to let him take the painting home. He thought that perhaps Kang would enjoy it for two or three days and then bring it back. After three days, he went to Kang and asked for the painting back but Kang didn't give it back. After several more days he again went to Kang and asked for the painting, but he still refused to give it to him, saying that he wanted to appreciate it for some more time. How many days had

啊，交通不便，没有铁路，是骡马车。他就把卧龙寺那个好版本的藏经——数量很多，并且很重——装在骡马车上要弄走，已经出了西安的东门，已经走在大路上，西安本地人发觉了，追上去，不答应，把书弄回来，有这么一次事情。这事我为什么能知道呢？因为我 19 岁、20 岁的时候，我到了西安，我喜欢到那个庙里头去，知道这件事情。

再一件事情。有一个民国初年的国会议员，是一个资本家。在清朝末了有一个国家银行叫“大清银行”，后来清朝退位了，就称为中华民国了，就改为“中国银行”。中国银行的第一个主事人叫做总裁，还有一个副总裁，姓余，叫余凡澄（音同）。余凡澄跟我相熟，余凡澄把他遇见的事情告诉我。余凡澄他是中国银行的副总裁，后来他离开中国银行了，但是他是一个私家银行的资本家。有人来向银行借钱、借款，或者借比较多一点的钱，就要抵押，才能保证银行借钱。拿什么来抵押呢？用一幅很贵重的、有名的画，人人公认这个是价值很大，古代的画，古画就作抵押品在银行里头，银行就贷给他比如说是 2000 块钱。

康有为就知道了这个有名的画在这个银行里头，他就去找到余凡澄，他说：“听说这个画在你们这个行里头，你拿出来我们看一看，可以不可以？”那么当然他康有为是个大名人啦，这个余先生就从行里头把那个画拿出来，挂在那儿看，这个康有为非常地赞扬：“啊呀，这个画多么好啊”，在那儿叹息，在那儿看。末了，他说：“可不可以我拿回家去，我慢慢再多看看呢？”这个余凡澄因为他是大名人嘛，一定要这样要求嘛，只好答应他，让他拿走了。他拿走的时候，他也不说在家里头仔细看看，多看两天、三天这样子就送回来了。过了两三天去要，他不给，再过几天去要，还不给：“我还要多看一看。”好多天啊！这个不行

passed! This wouldn't do. Yu Fancheng thought to himself, "You want to take possession of it yourself?" So he went to Kang Youwei's house with a lot of people, and forcefully took the painting back. Yu himself told me about this incident.

So I knew about these two incidents, one in Xi'an, and one in Shanghai. In his later life his behavior was bad, especially [in the case of] his disciple, a student named Chen Huanzhang, who established a "Confucian Church." He needed money (donations) to build a church on Xidan Street [in Beijing]. He set certain regulations. If you contributed five thousand silver dollars, you were so forth and so on, and if you contributed ten thousand, you were so forth and so on, so as to wheedle contributions out of people. That sort of thing was just awful! This was the worst kind of sordid vulgarity and ignoble philistinism that was utterly devoid of noble, lofty thought! So this was what Kang's student Chen Huanzhang was like.

● A few words on representatives of Neo-Confucianism

Alitto: Aside from you, who else in the modern period is a representative Confucian personage?

Liang: I can't say, but I will address a few words to the issue. There's someone named Feng Youlan. When I was teaching at Peking University, he was a student in my class. He studied in America. While in America, he often sent letters to me, corresponding with me. After he returned from America he became a university professor, a very famous one. He authored three books, especially [well-known] is the one titled *History of Chinese Philosophy*. This man—each person has his own disposition and individual personalities are different—he appears to be a Confucian and to have developed and elaborated upon traditional Chinese thought. It appears that way, but in reality, he behaves more like a follower of Laozi and Zhuangzi. The Laozi school is not like the Confucian in that a follower does not have a commitment to one's own integrity and to honesty. He isn't that way. He is more like what, like cynical and frivolous. He is not like [a Confucian] who loyally follows and acts according to the principles he believes in, who does not bend with the prevailing wind. No, he is more cynical and frivolous.

Alitto: Actually we Westerners who study China generally acknowledged this.

Liang: Later, didn't that Jiang Qing think highly of him and go to Peking University to see him? He even gave some poems to Jiang Qing. Later Jiang

了，这个余凡澄就想："怎么你想霸占这个东西啦？"那么就带了很多人强迫地到康有为的家里头把这个东西取回来了。这个余告诉我的。

我知道的这么两件事，一个在西安，一个在上海。他后来他品行很不好。特别是他有一个弟子，一个门人、学生，叫陈焕章，办"孔教会"，在北京西单修房子，需要款，叫"劝募款"，定一个条例，如果捐5万块钱就怎么样，捐10万块钱怎么样，引诱人捐款。这个简直要不得，完全是一种名利的俗心，俗得不得了，一点高尚的意思都没有。这是他的学生，康有为的学生陈焕章。

• 点评"新儒家"代表人物

艾： 除了您自己以外，在现代最具有代表性的儒家人物是谁？

梁： 我说不上来。说不上来我还要说几句话。有一个人叫冯友兰，我在北京大学教书的时候，他是我班上的学生，他是留美，在美国。他留美的时候还常常从美国写信给我。从美国回来就做大学教授，很出名，写了三本书，特别是他有一部《中国哲学史》。这个人呢——一个人有一个人的性情，个性不同了——他好像是儒家，好像是发挥中国传统思想，可其实呢，他的为人是老庄的吧。老子一派，就是不像那个儒家，好像忠于自己，一定要很正直，他不是那样，他是有点……有点玩世不恭，他不是那么本着自己的相信的道理、很忠实、不随风转舵，不，他有点像玩世不恭。

艾： 其实这一点我们西方研究中国的人都是公认的。

梁： 后来不是那个江青很赏识他，到北京大学去看他？他还把诗词送给江青，后来江青失败了，所以他的名气也就不好了。这个

Qing was defeated, so his reputation withered. He is still alive, still at Peking University, but he doesn't have any work responsibilities. All he has now is a good salary, that is, a professor's salary. His health has not been good either. He has cataracts, and someone supports him when walking.

Alitto: No one is representative [of Confucianism]?

Liang: No. There is another philosopher. He cannot really be considered as representing Confucianism. Someone named He Lin. He is better [than Feng], not so willful and wanton. He teaches mostly German philosophy, Hegel. There is another philosopher named Shen Youding. They all play an important role in the Institute of Philosophy at the Chinese Academy of Sciences. There is another philosopher in Beijing; he studied in the U.S., his name...it's on the tip of my tongue.

Alitto: Do you think that the Hong Kong Confucian thinkers like Mou Zongsan and Tang Junyi have made a contribution to the elucidation and development of modern Confucianism?

Liang: They have made a contribution.

Alitto: Have you read their publications?

Liang: I have here six volumes by Tang Junyi. I haven't read Mou's.

Alitto: What about Tang Junyi?

Liang: He's good. I think that what he has to say about Confucianism is all accurate. Mou is a Shandongese, Tang a Sichuanese. I have been sent Tang's works. I have six big volumes of his. Right now I have only two volumes left of the six. Someone took four away. It's a pity that Tang has already passed away. Mou is still alive.

Alitto: Yes, Mou is still alive. Are they considered Xiong Shili's students?

Liang: Mou is. It seems that Tang has no connection with Xiong. Mou has been on intimate terms with Xiong. He addressed him as teacher. It seems Tang did not.

● Contemporaries who influenced me

Alitto: Have any others influenced you?

Liang: If you are referring to my contemporaries, such as my friends and

人还在，还在北京大学，不过不担任什么事情，只有一个好的待遇，教授的待遇。人也不行了，眼睛有白内障，走路也旁人扶着。

艾： 没有一个具有代表性的？

梁： 没有。还有一个哲学家，他也不一定算是代表儒家，有个叫贺麟的，贺麟比较好，比较不是那样随便，不过他是讲德国哲学，讲授黑格尔的。还有一个哲学家，叫沈有鼎，姓沈，沈有鼎。这都是中国科学院哲学研究所的重要角色。还有一个也是在北京的哲学家，留美的，叫什么名字……口里头说不出来，心里头有。

艾： 您觉得牟宗三、唐君毅，在香港的儒家思想家对现代的孔孟之道的发展和阐明有没有贡献？

梁： 有贡献。

艾： 他们的著作，您看过没有？

梁： 我这里有的就是还是唐君毅的，有六本，没有看见牟的。

艾： 唐君毅的怎么样呢？

梁： 他还好，对儒家所见还正确。牟宗三是山东人，唐君毅是四川人。唐君毅的一些著作他们都送给我，有六大本。现在没在这里，可能还有两本，有四本让旁人拿去了。可惜唐已经故去了，牟还在。

艾： 是，牟还在。他们算是熊十力的学生吧？

梁： 牟算是，唐好像跟熊没有什么关系。牟是亲近过熊先生，他称熊先生为老师，好像唐没有。

· 同代中对我有影响的人

艾： 也有别人影响过您的生活或者是思想吧？

梁： 如果不说古人，说跟我同时代的人，说我的朋友、老师，那是

teachers, there are two people. One was a Fujianese. Mr. Lin, someone I very much admired. In thought and in his actions as a man, I revered and admired him, and he was also someone who influenced me greatly.

Alitto: Who is this Mr. Lin?

Liang: Perhaps some people don't pay him much attention, but in fact he was someone of much worth. His name was Lin Zhijun, and his sobriquet was Zaiping.[35]

Alitto: I didn't pay attention to him either. How is it that you knew him? Was he your teacher or your friend?

Liang: First I'll say something about Mr. Lin. He was of extraordinarily noble character. It seems that people didn't pay much attention to him, that he was not all that famous. In fact, he was the person who Liang Qichao most admired. When Mr. Liang was about to die, he sent a great box of his writings—manuscripts (some finished, some not), poems, essays (some dealing with politics, some with academic matters)—a great big box, with the injunction to his children—to give the box to Mr. Lin, wanting Mr. Lin to examine them and decide which were wanted and which were not necessary to keep, and to decide on his collected works after his death. So this book of Mr. Liang Rengong (Qichao) published after death—generally these are called "collected works," sometimes titled "complete works"—was titled "collected works" for publication. When he was still alive, many bookstores published many of his works for him, so the *Works of the Ice Drinkers Studio* is extensive. [Before he died] he gave the great box filled with his published works, his unpublished works, and unfinished manuscripts to Mr. Lin, to have Mr. Lin examine and approve them. The final result was the *Collected Works from the Ice Drinkers Studio*. I mention this to prove Mr. Lin's erudition, and even more to prove his moral character. His moral character was excellent, the highest.

There is another matter I want to mention. Mr. Liang Rengong was very active in politics. He had a political party that he led. The name of this political party changed through time. He wanted to have Mr. Lin join his political party, and for a time Mr. Lin did participate, but after a short time, he withdrew. Even though Mr. Lin was a very good friend of Mr. Liang, he would not engage in this business of his with him. Why? Because in seeing Mr. Liang in politics, he saw that Mr. Liang was

有两个人。一个是福建人林先生，林先生是我很佩服的，在思想上，乃至为人都是我很恭敬、很佩服，也是对我有影响的一个人。

艾： 这位林先生是谁啊？

梁： 也许有些人不大注意他，可是实际上这个人是很有价值的。他名字叫林志钧，号叫宰平（*应是字宰平*），他是福建人。

艾： 我也没有注意他了。怎么认识他的？算是您的一位老师啊，或者朋友啊，或者……

梁： 我就先说一说这个林先生。林先生这个人，人品最高了。他好像是人不大留意，好像不大出名似的，其实呢，他最为梁启超所佩服。（*梁启超*）临死，把自己一大箱著作、手稿，有写完的，有没有写完的，有诗，有文，有论政治的，有论学术的，一大箱，嘱咐自己的儿女交给林先生，要林先生审定，哪个要的，哪个不必要的，殁后出我的文集都由林先生决定。所以梁任公先生的……殁后出来的这部书——普通叫“文集”，有时候说完全的“全集”，梁任公先生的著作用“文集”的名义出版的，在我在的时候，很多书店给他出了，所以《饮冰室文集》是好多好多了。可是他把所有的东西，以及没有出版的东西，乃至未写完的东西，一大箱都交给林先生，由林先生审定，最后出了《饮冰室合集》。我说这个话，证明林先生的学问，更证明林先生的人品，他人品最高了。

还要说一件事，梁任公在政治上很活动的了，他有他领导的政党，政党的名称也前后有些变化，他要拉林先生到他的党里头，林先生也一度参加，但是时间很短，他就脱离了，尽管跟梁任公还是很好的朋友。他说你这个搞法啊，我不行，我不跟你一块搞。为什么这样子呢？为什么他不跟梁任公一块搞？

politically ambitious and that he wanted to do a lot politically. But Mr. Lin had no such ambition. Mr. Lin found fault with Liang Rengong, disliked Liang's moral disorder. Mr. Lin truly refused to be corrupted by bad influences. You could say that he was as clean as a whistle in all aspects—politically, socially, or whatever—throughout his life. So it was because of his character that Liang Rengong admired and respected him so, and that he left his affairs in Lin's hands after his death—to examine and finalize his writings, to decide which to keep and publish. So, from this incident you can see Mr. Lin's great worth. His merit was truly tremendous. He was 14 years older than I. I'm now 88. If he were still living, he would be over a hundred now. I truly admire him. I can't be considered his student, but I should call myself his later generation. He was very good to me and looked after me. I often introduced my friends to him, for example, Wu Guanqi and Xiong Shili. They both met him through me, because I was so close to him. Mr. Lin used to call Xiong Shili "Old Xiong." They all developed deep friendships. Later, Mr. Xiong would always give his manuscripts to Mr. Lin for inspection.

Alitto: How did you get to know him?

Liang: They were all of the older generation. Mr. Lin was 14 years older than I, Liang Qichao 20 years, and Mr. Cai Yuanpei 30 years. I was really fortunate. The older generation of scholars all thought highly of me very early on. They didn't wait for me to seek them out; they sought me out, protected and took care of me before I had really done anything. Mr. Lin was also like that. So it was with Liang Qichao, and also with Cai Yuanpei. They patronized me and appreciated my abilities, and looked out for me while I was still very young. I wasn't even 30, just 28 years old when Mr. Liang Qichao came to see me at my home. He was such a celebrity, and I wasn't at all famous. At that time, the older generation of scholars were modest and humble, and looked out for young people of promise, and wanted to help them. Their desires were admirable. Mr. Lin,

Mr. Liang and Mr. Cai were all like this. If Mr. Cai hadn't thought highly of me, I would never have been able to teach at Peking University. I was very young.

Alitto: Did Mr. Lin also seek you out?

Liang: Yes, I'll tell you of my experience. When I was 24 years old, I took

梁任公是在政治上有野心的，他要大有所作为的，可是这一点林先生没有，林先生就嫌梁任公、讨厌梁任公有点乱七八糟。林先生是这样一个人，洁身自好，他一生干净极了，在政治上、在社会上他是这样一个人。所以梁任公佩服他、敬重他，把身后的事情交给林先生：我这个著作都请你来审定，哪个要的、哪个不要的，你定了之后出版。从这个地方可以看出来林先生的价值，这个价值了不起。他大我 14 岁，我现在 88，所以他如果还活着，那就超过 100 了。我很佩服他，我很佩服林先生。我不能算是他的学生，但是我应当是对他自称后学。他对我也很好、很爱护，我的朋友我常常介绍给他，比如伍先生，他也跟林先生好，刚才我说的熊先生，都是因为我的关系与林先生相好——林先生管熊先生叫“老熊”，他们感情都很好。熊先生后来有什么著作都要请林先生看。这是说林先生。

艾： 林先生您是怎么认识他的?

梁： 这个是好几位前辈，林先生是我的前辈，大我 14 岁，梁任公先生也是我的前辈，大我 20 岁，蔡元培先生大我 30 岁。我很幸运，这些个前辈、老先生他们很早看重我，没有等我去求他们，他们就对我表示一种爱护。都是这样，林先生也是如此，梁任公先生也是如此，蔡元培先生也如此，我都是受他们的知遇、爱护。年纪很小的时候，我还不够 30 岁，28 岁，梁任公先生就到我家里来看我，他是个大有名的人，我还没有出名那个时候。他们老前辈虚心，爱护有前途的青年，帮助青年，他们的意思好得很。林先生如此，梁先生如此，蔡先生更是如此。没有蔡元培先生对我的赏识，我不能进北大，我还年纪轻得很。

艾： 那林先生也是去找您了?

梁： 对。就我的过去的经过说吧。我是在 24 岁的时候就参加当时

an unimportant position in the central government of the time. It was as a secretary in the Ministry of Justice. Right before I took the position, my article "On Tracing the Origins and Solving Doubts" came out. In the Ministry there was a man named Yu [Shaosong] whose rank was slightly higher than mine. I can't think of his name right now. He was a friend of Mr. Lin's. Mr. Lin read my article "On Tracing the Origins and Solving Doubts," and so asked Mr. Yu to introduce us. (He had heard that I was working there.) He told me that he wanted to get to know me. So, that person who was my friend, who was working in the Ministry of Justice with me, introduced us and we became friends. Didn't I say just now that when I was 28, Mr. Liang Qichao came to see me and introduced himself? That time, Mr. Lin came with him. Mr. Liang also brought his son, Liang Sicheng, the architect. There was another person of some repute with them, Mr. Jiang Fangzhen. The four of them—Liang Qichao, Jiang Fangzhen, Lin Zaiping and Liang Sicheng—came in the same car to my home to see me; at that time I was 28 years old.

Next is Mr. Wu Guanqi. Mr. Wu was also a person of great merit. If someone were to ask me, which person whom you personally have seen in your entire life you most admire, my answer would be him. He was a good friend of Mr. Lin's, but different from him. Mr. Lin was an erudite, learned man. He very much liked to write poetry. But this Mr. Wu did not. He was a down-to-earth and practical-minded man. Didn't I just say that the most important thing I've done in my scholarly life was my book, *The Human Heart/Mind and Human Life*? I have felt that I have a very heavy, great responsibility, that is, to propagate Mr. Wu's own learning and his character to the world. Mr. Wu was an unadulterated Confucian, a practical-minded, pragmatic Confucian. He manifested this throughout his life...

I'll give you an example. When I was 36 years old, I had two friends, one surnamed Wang and the other Huang. We three friends went to see Mr. Wu. At that time, Mr. Wu had a very heavy responsibility. The Nationalist Party had a Nationalist Revolutionary Army, which had a general headquarters. Its commander-in-chief was Chiang Kai-shek. The Chief of Staff was Li Jishen. Chiang Kai-shek, as commander-in-chief, set out on the Northern Expedition. Li Jishen, as Chief of Staff, remained

的政府，做一个小事情，做司法部的秘书。后来，就在我在司法部做秘书的时候，《究元决疑论》在那个之前发表了。在司法部跟秘书在官位上差不多、稍高一点的，那个人叫什么名字来的？那个名字叫余什么……，我一时说不上来那个名字了（应为时任司法部参事的余绍宋）。那个人跟林先生相熟，林先生就对那个人说——因为林先生看见我那个《究元决疑论》了——说请你介绍，请那个朋友，那个朋友在司法部跟我一块，你跟梁表示，我想跟他做朋友。这样经那个人介绍，跟林先生就成了朋友。刚才我不是说我 28 岁那年，梁任公到我家看我吗？就是林先生同他来的。同他来的时候梁先生还带着他的儿子，他儿子叫梁思成，是建筑学家，还有一位有名的人，叫蒋方震。那一次，他们——梁任公、蒋方震、林宰平跟梁思成，他们四个人坐一辆汽车来我家看我的，那个时候我 28 岁。

其次再说一下伍先生（伍观淇，字庸伯。可参阅《伍庸伯先生传略》一文，见《梁漱溟全集》卷四）。伍先生的价值很高。假如有人问我：你一生所亲自见到的、最佩服的人是谁？那我就回答是这个（人）。他跟林先生相好，可是跟林先生不相同。林先生学问很丰富，他很喜欢作诗词，可是这个伍先生不作，他是一个脚踏实地做人的一个人。我不是说，假定说在学术方面我最重要的就是写《人生与人心》（应为《人心与人生》）吗？可是我自己认为我有一个很重大的责任，很重大的责任是什么呢？就是替伍先生，把他的学问、为人，我要介绍给世界、给后人。伍先生这个人，就我来看，我认为是一个纯正的儒家，脚踏实地的儒家。这个纯正的、脚踏实地的儒家表现在什么地方？表现在他的生活，在生活上能够“自主自如”。

比如我，特别是我从前的时候，我很早的时候，举个例吧，我 36 岁的时候，我同两个朋友，一个姓王，一个姓黄，我们三个人去看伍先生。这时候伍先生正在负一个很重要的责任，负一个什么责任呢？国民党啊，叫做国民革命军，国民革命军有总司令部，总司令是蒋介石，总参谋长是李济深，蒋作为总司令就出师北伐，从广东出来军队要北伐，李济深就作为

in Guangdong. Mr. Wu and Mr. Li were very good friends. Mr. Li regarded Mr. Wu as his teacher. So, when Li had the responsibility of administering the rear area, he appointed Mr. Wu to be the Director of the Office of the Chief of Staff. The three of us went to Guangdong. I was 36 years old at the time. We went to see Li Jishen, and also went to see Mr. Wu in Wu's office. Noontime came, and he invited us for lunch. After lunch, he said, "Make yourselves at home. Talk together freely. I have to rest a bit. I'll nap for fifteen minutes." He sat down on a chair, closed his eyes and fell asleep. After he had slept for fifteen minutes, he woke up. I admired this greatly and was greatly astonished. Why? It was right at that time that I was suffering from insomnia. So when I wanted to sleep I could not. When I didn't want to sleep... He said he would sleep and he fell asleep right away. He said he would wake, and fifteen minutes later he woke up. My Goodness! I was truly astonished, and admired it! This is indicative of how he was serenely inner-directed. He actually was able to keep the body and the spirit united, really able to be inner-directed, quite an achievement.

Alitto: I admire people like that too. Speaking of influence, how did Messrs. Wu and Lin influence your life, or your thought?

Liang: I admired Mr. Lin very much. However, he did not influence me as much as Mr. Wu did. If I was to emulate someone, I would emulate him.[36]

Alitto: That is, the influence is... Mr. Wu was your model. Is that what you mean?

Liang: Right. I should add a word about Mr. Wu. He was an authentic military man. At the end of the Qing, he already had been engaged in training the new style armies that were modeled on foreign armies. He was training the New Armies, and commanded troops. Later he participated in the 1911 Revolution, and even after that, he went to Infantry University and graduated from it. After graduation, he remained at Infantry University as an instructor. He was originally a student there, but because he made excellent grades, he later was an instructor there. He diligently put into practice the two old sayings... (Mr. Liang writes them down for Alitto. According to Liang's "A Brief Biography of Mr. Wu Yongbo,"[37] these two old sayings should be "Be true to your words; in your

总参谋长留守广东。伍先生跟李济深他们是很好的朋友，差不多李济深都把他当老师。这个时候，他担任留守后方的职务的时候，他就请伍先生给他做总参议办公厅主任，负一个很重要的责任。我同两个朋友，……我们三个人，那时候我36岁，去广东，主要是看李济深，也是看伍先生。伍先生正在那负责做总参议办公厅主任，我们三个人就到他办公的地方同他谈话。到了中午了，他留我们吃饭，吃完饭，他就对我们三个人说：你们随便坐，随便谈话，我要休息，我睡15分钟。他就坐在一个椅子上，闭起眼睛来就睡着了，睡了15分钟就醒了。我非常地佩服，非常地惊讶，为什么呢？因为这个时候我经常闹失眠，失眠的人想睡睡不着，不想睡的时候又……他说睡就睡了，说醒，15分钟说醒就醒。哎呀，我真是惊讶、佩服！这就是表明他生活自主自如。他是真正能够把他的身体、精神很统一，很能够自主，很能够自如，这个是很了不起。

艾：我也很佩服这种人。那说到影响，林先生跟伍先生这两位是怎样影响您的生活，或者影响您的思想的？

梁：林先生是我很佩服的了，尽管我很佩服，可是给我的影响不如伍先生。如果说我愿意学，那我愿意学伍先生。

艾：那就是说影响是，伍先生当过您的榜样，是这个意思吧？

梁：对。我补充一句话，这个伍先生是一个地道的军人。清朝末年开始模仿外国练新式军队，他是练新军里头的人。练新军带兵，然后参加辛亥革命，然后又到陆军大学，在陆军大学毕业，毕业之后留在陆军大学做教官，他原来是学生，因为成绩好做教官。他力行两句中国的古话（梁先生写给艾）（据《伍庸伯先生传略》，这两句古话应是“言忠信，行笃敬”）。他在陆军大学毕

conduct be sincere and respectful."[38]) This was the kind of man he was. After he graduated, at that time he went to be a section head in the Third Bureau of the Chief of Staff Headquarters. Responding to Yuan Shikai's attempt to become emperor, all of the Beijing officialdom—from high officials down to their underlings—was pandering to Yuan Shikai, sending memorials and petitions urging him to become emperor, expressing their support. Officials high and low in every government office had to sign. Wasn't he the section head in the Third Bureau of the Chief of Staff Headquarters? They wanted him to sign, but he was unwilling to. He said, "When I put my name to something, I must be certain that it is right. I am presently thinking over whether I should sign, and have not made a decision, and have not affirmed that I should sign. So, I cannot sign." Everyone said, "All else signed, but you don't sign; isn't this matter dangerous or bad?" That can't be helped.[39] Later it turned out fine.

The War of Resistance to Japan started up; the Japanese were invading China. Mr. Wu commanded guerillas, about 2000 men, in Guangdong. He was a guerilla commander dealing with the enemy. From the time that the Japanese first occupied Guangdong, to the time when the Japanese withdrew from China, Mr. Wu went through eight solid years as a guerilla commander. But his area of activity was not the entire province, but rather only a four-county area.

There's an incident that happened during this period that I should mention. He was always able to predict the enemy's actions. Once he was leading a part of his troops—the 2000 men were split up, not [all] with him. He had not more than a few hundred, something like 300 men, so there were 300 men with him, and the 2000 were distributed in several places. There was an intelligence officer sent out to spy out a certain area. That intelligence agent returned to report, saying that there was a body of the enemy, possibly 300 men—about the same number of troops that he [Wu] had with him—coming north from the south, coming to their location. Possibly they were coming to attack? Mr. Wu thought for a moment, and said that the enemy was not tracking them to attack and that he reckoned that the enemy's target was such and such a place. Everyone half believed him, thought his reckonings [might be] correct, but weren't completely sure. He then said to everyone, "You keep watch. I want to rest," because he was not too strong [physically]. In the countryside outside the county town there was a high platform which was

业了，他就到那个时候的参谋本部第三局做一个科长。赶上袁世凯要做皇帝，北京各官府，从长官到下属，都迎合袁世凯，上书"劝进"，劝袁世凯做皇帝，表示拥护，各衙门大大小小的官吏都要签名。他这个时候不是做参谋本部第三局的科长吗？要他签名，不肯签名，他说："我一定要认为我签的是对的，我才能签名。我现在考虑我应不应该签名，我还没有决定，还没有点头认为这是应该签的，所以我不能签名。"大家说人人都签名，你不签名，这个事情怕危险吧？不好吧？那也没有办法，他就是这样。后来也没有事。

抗日战争起来了，日本人侵略中国，伍先生带着游击队，大约两千多人，在广东，做游击司令，跟敌人周旋。从广东被日本人占领，一直到日本人失败、退出中国，他始终担任游击司令，在广东。不过，他这个游击司令是一个范围的，叫第几区的司令，那个区是管四个县，不是全省的，有四个县是他的范围，一直抗战 8 年，他就担任 8 年的游击司令。

他在当游击司令的时候，还有这样的故事：他料想敌人呢，"料敌如神"。有一次他带一部分军队——有 2000 人，2000 人是分开的，没有都跟在他身边，他身边不过几百人，比如 300 人的样子，身边带着 300 人，2000 人分布在几个地方、几个点上，还有谍报的人——出去侦探的。到了某一个地方，那个谍报的人来报告，说是现在有一部分敌人，可能比如说是 300 人，跟他自己身边的人数差不多，从南往北来了，就要到我们这个地方，可能就是来打我们吧？伍先生想一想，他说不是，他不是来跟踪我们、打我们，我推想他的目的地是在哪个地方。大家也就半信半疑，也以为他料想得对，也不敢完全把握。他就对大家说：你们警戒着，我要休息休息。因为他身体不是太强。乡间啊，在县城外边有一个高的台子，是预备过春

a stage for opera performances for the lunar New Year. He had a chair, said that he was going to rest, and so he rested. At this time everyone on the one hand was afraid that the enemy was coming, because the spy had reported that over 200 of them were coming in this direction, and on the other had believed the commander's words—that the enemy was not pursuing them but had another target, but no one dared make predictions about this matter. Probably the commander was just resting, and didn't necessarily fall asleep. Someone went onto the stage to look at him and he had fallen asleep after all, and was sleeping very soundly. That is to say, he was able to "pick it up, and put it down." Ordinary people cannot pick it up or put it down. He was truly serenely self-directed. This kind of learning is not book learning, and isn't the kind of learning that is casually chattered about. This is Confucius' life learning.

Don't I often mention what Confucius had said, "At fifteen, I set my heart upon learning." What kind of learning was that "learning"? After that he said, "At thirty, I established myself." We don't know either what this "establishment" is, and how he established himself. Age by age he was speaking about life and being, and didn't speak about anything outside it. The disciple he valued and loved the most was Yanzi (Yan Hui). What was Yanzi's strength? One was that he did not take his anger out on others, and that he did not repeat the same mistake. How does one not take anger out on others? How does one not repeat the same mistake? It's not to be guessed at wildly. But we see clearly that he didn't speak about anything else except for his life and being. So Mr. Wu's learning and skill is authentically and thoroughly Confucian. He walked the Confucian road most correctly. I've never seen another person like this. He did not talk philosophy.

● The ones I admire most

Alitto: Who is the Chinese you most admire, either in the past or at present?

Liang: Very early, when I was young I admired Zhang Shizhao. His sobriquet was Xingyan. His nom de plume was "Qiutong" ("Autumn Tong tree"). When I was still young, in middle school, between 14 and 19 years old—during this time I read Mr. Zhang Xingyan's articles. I didn't know the [real] name of this person. I just saw his nom de plume Qiutong.

节过年演戏的戏台，他就有一个椅子，他说我要休息一下，他就休息了。大家这个时候，一方面是害怕敌人来，因为谍报说两百多人往这个方向来，一方面也相信司令员的话，他不是来追我们，他是另外有目的。不过这个事情，谁也不敢断定，恐怕司令在上面休息，也不过休息休息吧，未必睡着。有人到戏台上去看他，居然睡着了，睡得很熟。就是说，他提得起，放得下，普通人提不起，放不下。他是真正能够在他的生命上自主自如。这个学问不是书本上的学问，不是随便讲一讲、说一说的学问，这就是孔子的生活之学。

我不是常常讲，孔子所谓"十有五而志于学"，那个学是什么学呢？底下他说"三十而立"，三十而立我们也不知道是什么，怎么一个立法啊？一层一层地都是在说他的生命、生活，没有说到外头去。他所最欣赏、最心爱的徒弟是颜子，颜子的长处是什么呢？一个是"不迁怒"，一个"不贰过"。怎么样"不迁怒"，怎么样"不贰过"，我们也不好乱猜，不过看得很清楚，他没有说旁的，他说的是他自己的生命、生活。所以伍先生的学问功夫是真正的、彻底的儒家，他把儒家的路子走得最正确，我没有看见第二个人这样。他不谈哲学。

• 我所佩服的人

艾： 您最佩服的中国人，无论是过去的或者是现在的中国人是谁啊？

梁： 我很早、就是我年轻的时候很佩服的，是章士钊，他号叫章行严先生（*应是字行严*）。他写文章的笔名有时候写"秋桐"——"秋天"的"秋"，"梧桐"的"桐"。我年纪小的时候，我在中学读书，14 岁到 19 岁毕业了，十四五六七八，这个时候我就看见章行严先生——章士钊了——他的文章，不知道他这个人的名字，姓名不知道，就是看见他的笔名叫秋桐。

One form that his articles took was as European dispatches. He wrote articles at Europe for newspapers. I read them with great interest. I especially liked his discussions of political systems. Because at that time China had started to copy Western political institutions, there was the issue of a national parliament, so there was much discussion over whether to adopt a bicameral or unicameral assembly. Other matters that he wrote on were the English system of a cabinet responsible to the parliament, a party cabinet. I was extremely interested in these essays. At that time in my life, I was fanatical about government reform in China and most admired the English-style government. So, just then he was writing on those things and discussing them—such as in learning from foreign countries, whether China should adopt a bicameral system or a unicameral system. I liked to read these essays of his very much, although I didn't know who the writer was. I was in my teens, in middle school in Beijing, and after reading his articles in newspapers, I admired this person and his writings very much.

Later, I started reading the *Minlibao* of Shanghai. Most of its articles were also on politics. He wrote for it too—called himself Xingyan. I said to myself, "This Xingyan must be the Qiutong I have read before." I still didn't know his real name, but I judged them to be the same person. Later, Liang Qichao established a publication *Guofengbao* in Japan. It also mostly featured articles on politics and government. Once, there was an article on translation of Western scholarship or academic things into Chinese. Yan Fu [Yan Jidao] had in the past also discussed this problem of translation. He had three criteria: fidelity or faithfulness, ability to convey, and elegance. Yan was very particular about it. So in translating foreign writings, he would adhere to these three criteria and always translated them into literary Chinese, very elegant. He did not use colloquial style. This is the problem of translation. So, in the *Guofengbao*, I read an article on the translation problem. It was signed Mingzhi. The topic was very different from his other writings on politics. It was not signed Qiutong, or Xingyan, but a new pen name, Mingzhi. However, I believed the three must have been one and the same. Later it proved to be accurate.

他写的文章，一种是欧洲通讯，他人在欧洲，写给报纸，把欧洲情况，叫做欧洲通讯、留欧通讯，我看得很有趣味。特别是呢，他有些个论政治制度的文章，因为那个时候中国要学外国，政治上学外国，那么就有开国会的问题，有议院。议院有一个问题，就是还是两院制呢，还是一院制？议院跟政府的关系，像英国，政府是对国会负责，对众议院负责，责任内阁，政党内阁。他写文章讨论这个问题，我非常有兴趣。因为那个时候我们都是热心中国的政治改造，最欣赏的、最觉得好的是英国式的政治，他刚好是介绍这个东西，讨论这个东西，中国要学外国，就是学两院制呢，还是一院制就可以了呢？有没有必要两院呢？他这些个文章我都爱读，可是我不知道他是谁，只留个笔名。这是在我年纪轻的时候，年纪只有十几岁的时候，而且在北京中学读书的时候，看报纸、看文章看到这个，我就欣赏这个人，欣赏这个人的议论、文章。

后来呢，就看见上海有一个叫《民立报》,《民立报》发表的文章也多半是论政的居多，这个文章笔名就写“行严”。我还是不知道他到底姓什么，可是我看见行严的文章，就想这个人的文章恐怕跟秋桐是一个人，真的姓名我还不知道，我判断他恐怕是一个人。后来呢，在日本，梁启超——梁任公出了一个刊物叫《国风报》。《国风报》上偶然登了一篇文章——《国风报》多半都是论政的——偶然登了一篇文章，是讲把西文、西洋学问的名词翻译成中文，翻译、译名的问题，怎么样的译名算是译得好。因为过去严复——严几道先生他就讨论过译名的问题，他有三个标准：一个是要信；还有一个达，表达出来；第三个还要雅，文雅。严先生论翻译讲究这个，他翻译外国东西要遵守这三个标准，所以他翻译出来外国的东西，都是文言的，都是很文雅的，没有白话。这个问题就叫做译名问题、翻译名词的问题。在《国风报》上看见有一篇文章，是讨论译名、讨论翻译问题，署名叫“名质”——“人名”的“名”，“物质”的“质”，讨论的问题不是论政，跟我看到的文章不相合。这个名质用的人名、笔名，既不是秋桐，也不是行严，而是用一个很新鲜的“名质”两个字，但是我一看，这三个名字实在是一个人，我的判断是这样，后来证明果然是一个人。

At that time he was in Japan publishing a journal called *The Tiger* (*Jiayin*). It was at that time that I corresponded with him and only after that did I know his name was Zhang Shizhao. Later he came to Beijing. I liked being with him very much, and admired him. After that, however, I was greatly disappointed. Why? The revered Mr. Zhang, older than I by quite a bit, was a very talented and able person, so his desires were also powerful. So his personal life was corrupt. He smoked opium, gambled, visited prostitutes, and had concubines, altogether three. I was most disappointed. But although I was disgusted with his personal character, up to the time he was 90, I still associated with him.

Alitto: He passed away in Hong Kong in 1973.

Liang: Right, at age 93.

Alitto: Look, this isn't bad. Although his life was this way, he still lived to 93. It seems it didn't have any influence on his health!

Liang: Yes, it would seem that way.

Alitto: Others whom you admired were...

Liang: This was someone who I admired when I was young. There's another Zhang, that is, Zhang Binglin (Zhang Taiyan). I think his scholarship was good. I think that he was still a layman [in Buddhism], that he knew very little about [true Buddhism]. Wasn't he an important revolutionary figure in his youth? At that time, he was critical of Confucius. Later he changed, and then revered Confucius in his old age.

Alitto: Before the 1911 Revolution he was an advocate of the "National Essence." He didn't want Confucius, but wanted to retain Mozi and Xunzi. What aspect of him did you most admire?

Liang: His erudition was very profound, and his personality was independent, original. He never went along with everybody else in his opinions. He was of strong character.

Alitto: Anyone else? You have spoken of... (Liang: Two Zhangs.) Later in the 1930s, 1940s and 1950s, was there any change in the people you admired?

Liang: Speaking of famous people of the time, didn't famous figures in China include Kang Youwei and Liang Qichao? I much disliked Kang

这个时候，他在日本出版一个刊物，叫做《甲寅》，这个时候我给他通信，从书信上有来往，我才清楚他的名字是章士钊。后来到北京，我就很喜欢跟他亲近，很佩服他。可是佩服他之后，我又失望，怎么失望呢？因为这位章老先生，他比我岁数大了很多，他是一个很有才的人，多才，多才嘛他就多欲，欲望多，所以他的生活很腐烂——吃鸦片，赌博，赌钱，嫖妓女，娶姨太，娶妾，一个、两个、三个，我很失望，我很不喜欢。虽然很不喜欢，我还是一直到他 90 岁的时候我还跟他往来。

艾： 在香港 1973 年逝世的。

梁： 对了，93 岁。

艾： 您看这个也不错，虽然生活上这个样子，一样活到 93 岁，好像没有影响他的身体。

梁： 好像是那样。

艾： 别人呢，您佩服的就是……

梁： 这是我年轻的时候很佩服的。再一个我佩服的也是姓章，就是章炳麟——章太炎先生。我觉得他的学问好。……我认为他是外行，隔膜的，他比较年轻的时候也算是革命的重要人物，他那个时候是有点批评孔子、反驳孔子，可后来又变了，晚年他又佩服孔子。

艾： 辛亥革命以前，国粹的道理，孔子不要，墨子、荀子还是要，那您对章太炎最佩服的是哪一方面的？

梁： 学问很深造，人品也个性很强，不是一个很随便的人。

艾： 有没有别人了？您讲的……（梁：两个章。）后来您到了 30 年代、40 年代、50 年代，您佩服的人有没有变？

梁： 如果说那个时候，在中国的名人里头不是有康、梁吗？我是很

Youwei, but admired Liang Qichao very much. It also so happened that I was close friends with Liang Qichao, had a lot of contact with him. This was quite extraordinary: as he was of the older generation, he made an overture to me first, when I was still very young, a beginning student. I very much admired this in him. He was twenty years older than I. This was very modest, self-effacing on his part. I was first acquainted with him through his writings in his *New Citizen Journal*, which I liked very much. Later, we got to know each other. In 1920, as I said, he came to see me at my home. He was of the older generation, and he was famous. I was not yet famous at the time. I admired him in my heart. Why did he come to see me? At that time, he was interested in Buddhism. Someone told him that I was teaching Buddhism, so he came to see me. In the area of Buddhism, he was quite modest; even though I was of the younger generation, he was quite deferential. Alas, I lost all of the many letters he wrote me; they were not preserved [referring to them being destroyed during the Cultural Revolution].

Alitto: So you had some contact with him until...

Liang: Until the spring of 1929, when he died. In 1929, I returned to Beijing from Guangdong; he had already died by the time I arrived. When I was in Guangdong, we still corresponded.

...I forgot to mention this person I greatly admire. (Liang writes the name.)

Alitto: Yes, Ma Yifu. I know of him.

Liang: Talking about the old Chinese learning, he was extremely well read, especially in the old Chinese books. He had seen much, a person of great understanding. He seemed to have great understanding of all Eastern learning—Confucianism, Daoism and Buddhism. Mr. Ma could be regarded as someone I very much admired.[40]

Alitto: What was your relationship with him?

Liang: [Our relationship was] only that I admired him, and asked for his advice. He had always lived in Hangzhou. I also went to Hangzhou to see him and ask for his advice, more than once. When the War of Resistance to Japan began, he also withdrew to the southwest, to Sichuan. His friend asked him to teach, and founded a Revival Academy. At the Revival Academy he accepted students and taught and at the same

不喜欢康。我佩服梁任公，喜欢梁任公，刚好跟梁任公也有来往、亲近，并且这个亲近呢是……我嘛比他是后辈啦，小学生啊，他来我家先看我，很虚心，这点我很佩服他。他大我 20 岁，他从办《新民丛报》那个时候，我就爱读他的文章，后来就跟他认识了。像刚才所说的，民国九年（1920 年），他居然一个老前辈，很有名望的，先到我家里来看我，我那时候还没有名，我心里头很佩服他。那么他为什么来看我呢？原来他这个时候注意佛学，人家告诉他，说我讲佛学，所以他来看我。在佛学方面他很虚心，尽管我们是后辈，他很虚心。可惜他给我很多信，我都损失了，没有保留。（指在“文革”中被毁。）

艾：您跟他有往来一直到……

梁：一直到后来，到后来民国十八年春（1929 年）他故去了。民国十八年我从广东往北方回来，到的时候他已经故去了，在广东的时候，他还跟我通信。

……我就想起来一个人，我忘记说了，这个人是一个我很佩服的。（梁先生给艾写姓名。）

艾：是，马一浮，他我是知道的。

梁：讲中国的老学问，读书非常地多，特别是中国的老书，他见得多，并且熟悉，很通达，并且他对东方的学术，儒家啦、道家啦、佛家啦，他好像都很通。马先生可以说是我很佩服的一个人。

艾：您和他有什么关系呢？

梁：我仅仅是佩服他，向他请教。他一直住杭州，我也去到杭州去见他，向他领教，不止一次。抗日战争起来了，他也是撤退到西南，到四川，他的朋友请他讲学，成立一个叫做“复性书院”（的学校）。他在复性书院里头一方面收学生，他讲；

time carved words on a woodblock for printing. Chinese people liked to use woodblock to carve and print books. He carved several books of Confucian works that he held to be important. These included collected works of Luo Rufang (Luo Jinxi), and of Yang Cihu (Yang Jian). This old gentleman's knowledge was abundant. He knew and understood quite a lot, especially in the old scholarship of China. He has died.

...Didn't you ask me whom I most admired among the ancients? I just thought of Zhuge Liang. Zhuge Liang was of noble moral character! There are sayings about him, "Be direct and open." He really was that way, very good! He told his subordinates, "Constantly criticize my faults" —if you see any faults or mistakes you must regularly point them out. He was modest, circumspect and fair. That kind of character is very good. I should say that of all the ancients, I admire him the most. I made a gift for you, a piece of calligraphy with words of Zhuge Liang's.

Alitto: Did you admire him since you were a child, or...

Liang: I have always admired him. The first time I went into Sichuan, to Chengdu, where there was a shrine to him, I went there and performed the bows. I said, "In my heart I have always wanted to pay obeisance to you. Now having come to your shrine, I must kowtow and pay obeisance to you." The temple had a registry book. I wrote the date that I had come and knelt down to pay respects.

Alitto: His native place was in western Henan.

Liang: Right, he was born there. Didn't he take charge of Sichuan's... The shrine had a written sign "Temple to Zhuge, Marquis of Wu." The shrine was primarily to him, but Liu Bei's tomb was in the back of it. But everyone calls it the Marquis of Wu Shrine, not including Liu Bei. That is, everyone reveres, loves and respects Zhuge Liang. Sichuanese all commemorate him. They like to wear white turbans. Why white? They say that they are "wearing mourning for Zhuge." When the Chinese have a funeral, they wear mourning.

After Zhuge died, many of the people in the area wanted to sacrifice to him. Liu Bei's successor emperor Liu Chan didn't like the idea, but it wouldn't work. If you didn't erect a shrine to Zhuge, the people's shrines to him would be even more numerous, so the government built a proper shrine.

Alitto: Another separate question: Who is the foreigner whom you most admire? That is to say, among those you have heard about, or have read about, who do you most admire?

一方面就是刻书。中国喜欢用木板刻书，他刻了几种他认为是儒家的要紧的书，其中包括我刚才提到的罗汝芳——罗近溪的书，罗近溪的文集，杨慈湖——杨简的文集。这个老先生学问很丰富，知道的东西太多了，懂的东西太多了，特别中国的老学问。他故去了。

……你不是问过我：古人佩服谁？我就想起来诸葛亮。诸葛亮品格高啊。（关于）他有两句话："开诚心，布公道"，他真是那样，好得很哪！他对部下说"勤攻吾过"——你看我哪里有不对的、有错处，你要勤着指出来。谦虚、谨慎、公道，那个品格，好得很。应当说，对古人的佩服，我佩服他。我写了一张字，要送给你的，就是写了他的话，写了诸葛亮的话。

艾：您是从小就很佩服他，还是……

梁：一直很佩服他。我第一次入川的时候，到成都的时候，成都有他的庙，到他庙里头我就下拜，我说我心里总想拜你，现在到了你的庙里头，我一定要磕头，拜。庙里头有个本子，我就写上某年某月某日我来了，我拜了，我下拜。

艾：他的故乡还是豫西那个地区……

梁：对，他在那里出生的。他不是主持四川的……？那个庙写着"诸葛武侯祠"，庙是以他为主，可是刘备的坟墓就在庙后边，可是现在庙大家都叫武侯祠，把刘备没有算上。就是大家都恭敬、爱戴诸葛亮。四川人都纪念他，四川人头上喜欢缠一个白布，为什么缠白布？他们说是"戴诸葛孝"，中国人有丧事要戴孝。诸葛死了之后，乡间都要祭祀他。后主刘禅不喜欢，可是不行，你不给诸葛立庙，民间的庙更多，还是由政府来搞一个好的庙。

艾：另外一个问题，您最佩服的外国人是谁？就是说您听说有、或是书本里认识的外国人，您觉得最佩服的外国人是谁啊？

Liang: Well, at least about philosophical thinkers, the person I like the most and revere most is Henri Bergson.

Alitto: So, to the present it's still him. I remember that when you were writing *Eastern and Western Cultures and Their Philosophies*, you said this. You said that the first time you read Bergson's writings, you felt that it was a matter of great joy in your life. So you still feel that as far as foreign thinkers are concerned...

Liang: Of course I also admire the profundity of Germany's Kant.

Alitto: What about foreigners in the area of politics?

Liang: I'm not really so clear on who the great people are in politics or in military matters. In general, those great people who are often mentioned, like Napoleon.... Well, I just go along with everyone else, and don't have any particular opinion of my own.

● I'm afraid the greatest Chinese is Mao Zedong.

Alitto: If I ask who you think the greatest Chinese is, would your answer be different? Is there a difference between who you admire and who you think great?

Liang: There is a difference.

Alitto: So, who do you feel is the greatest Chinese, no matter whether a historical figure or someone still alive?

Liang: I feel that it's not in the too distant past, nor the present. I'm afraid that it is Mao Zedong. He was really formidable. He is a world-class great historical figure. When he became old, however, he was no good. He made a lot of mistakes in his dotage.

Alitto: What was Mao Zedong's greatest achievement?

Liang: It was that he created the Communist Party. If there were no

Chinese Communist Party, there would be no New China. This is absolute, 100% fact. But in his later years, he became muddle-headed, and made a lot of mistakes. Now, Zhou Enlai on the other hand did not fail in his later years. Zhou Enlai was what we used to call a paragon. You cannot find any failures, or any mistakes in him; they are practically absent. He was truly a paragon. But, as it happens, he was innately a

梁：我在哲学思想上最喜欢的，也算是崇拜吧，是法国的柏格森。

艾：到现在还是。我记得您当年写《东西文化及其哲学》的时候，您也这么说，您说第一次阅读柏格森的著作，觉得是一生中非常愉快的事。所以您还是觉得外国思想家来说……

梁：当然，德国的康德，我也很佩服他的思想上的深刻。

艾：那么政治界的外国人，您有没有觉得伟大的?

梁：我就不大清楚了，政治家、军事家，我不大清楚。一般地，常常说出来的伟人，像拿破仑啊，一般地大家所说的，那么我也就随着大家吧，自己没有特别的看法。

• 最伟大的中国人物恐怕还是毛泽东

艾：假如问您觉得最伟大的中国人是谁，回答会不会有不同? 佩服与觉得伟大有分别吗?

梁：有分别。

艾：您觉得最伟大的中国人物——无论历史上的人物还是在人世的，是谁?

梁：我觉得也不是太过去，也不是现在的，恐怕还是毛泽东。毛泽东实在了不起，恐怕历史上都少有，在世界上恐怕都是世界性的伟大人物，不过他晚年就不行了，晚年就糊涂了，有很多的错误。

艾：那毛泽东最伟大的成就是什么?

梁：创造了共产党，没有共产党没有新中国，这个是百分之百的事实。不过他这个人到晚年就糊涂了，有很多做错的事情。这个错的事情、失败的事情，在周恩来没有。周恩来是中国从前叫做“完人”——完全的人，你指不出来他的不好的、做错的事情，几乎没有，非常地完全他这个人。不过，很巧地，他是

second fiddle. He was born to be Mao Zedong's assistant. As a man, however, he was the best, the very best. (Alitto: I actually also think that you are right in this statement.) Everyone honors Zhou Enlai's memory. On the other hand, some people were and are dissatisfied with Mao, or with certain things he did.

Alitto: Comparing Mao with other figures in Chinese history, which figure in Chinese history does Mao most resemble? In a hundred years from now, when studying China of this age, with what figure in Chinese history will future historians compare his historical role to?

Liang: Most people see him as a Han Gaozu or as a Tang Taizong in the Chinese history of the past several thousand years, but Mao himself thought that these dynastic founding emperors were run of the mill, nothing special.

天生的第二把手，天生地给毛泽东做助手的这么一个人。论人可是最好了，周恩来人最好了，最好。（艾：我也倒是觉得您这个说得很对。）人人都纪念周，可是对毛，有人就不满意，某一件事情不满意。

艾：毛主席同中国历史上的人物来比，您觉得他比较像历史上的什么人物？再过 100 年，100 年以后的历史学家研究这个时代的中国历史，他们会不会把毛的角色和过去的什么人的角色来作一个比较？

梁：中国过去几千年的历史，一般的说法都说汉高、唐太——汉高祖、唐太宗，一般大概都是说这样子。可是毛看这些人，不那样，好像他看得平常。

● I approve Colloquial Literature Movement and I'm not conservative.

Alitto: ...Colloquial language vs. literary language can be said to have been a debate in bygone days. You never advocated the use of the literary language, right?

Liang: Right. I think that the Colloquial Literature Movement launched by Hu Shi and Chen Duxiu in Beijing greatly liberated intellectual and academic circles. Liberation was good. So if we stuck with convention again using the literary language to communicate thought and knowledge, that would be too passive. So liberation was good. The Colloquial Literature Movement developed. No matter in what field of learning, everyone used the colloquial language. Now it is called "prose written in the vernacular," that is, a colloquial style of the written language used in all fields of academic learning. I very much approve. This is progress. This is a kind of liberation.

There were two figures who opposed the Colloquial Literature Movement. One was Lin Shu (Lin Qinnan). The other was Zhang Shizhao (Zhang Xingyan). They didn't approve of colloquial literature. Their reasons were that there were some profound scholarship and thought that couldn't be communicated in the colloquial language. This is not totally wrong. So how could this problem be solved? The solution is for literary men to write in the colloquial, but to quote the old books in literary Chinese, and then add explanation in the colloquial language. That way, the profound knowledge in the old books could still be communicated in a simple, straightforward way.

Alitto: But the average young person cannot understand literary Chinese now. (Liang: Right.) A large part of China's cultural heritage is literary and historical works. One could say that, aside from the colloquial novels, the modern generation of young people are estranged from all literary works before May Fourth; a language barrier separates them. What should be done about this?

Liang: There is probably no solution to this problem. The only thing to do is to just let literary Chinese become a kind of special knowledge,

贰 我对世界的看法

· 我赞成白话文运动·我不保守

艾：……白话、文言文可以说是当年的辩论啊，您一直都没有主张用文言吧？

梁：对。我觉得，胡适、陈独秀在北京发动一种白话文的运动，是给知识界、学术界一个大解放。解放是好的，所以如果还是拘守再用文言文表达思想、表达学问，那个太被动了，所以解放好。开展白话文运动，无论任何的学问都用白话文，现在就叫做语体文——“言语”的“语”，像是跟说话一样，用语体文来发表学问，这个我是非常赞成的，这个是一种进步，是一种解放。

有两个人反对白话文。一个就是林纾——林琴南，一个就是章士钊——章行严，嘿嘿，都不赞成白话文。他们的理由呀，就是说有一些学问深的地方、思想深的地方，白话文表达不出来。这话也有一点道理，那么就怎么解决这个问题呢？就是我们写东西、发表东西还是白话文，要引用古书、文言文也可以引用，再用白话文来解释一下，还是可以介绍这种很简要的古书的文言文，还是应当介绍。

艾：不过，一般的年轻人现在根本看不懂文言了。（梁：对。）那么中国的文化遗产的一大部分，就是以前的文学呀、史学什么的，一些著作啦，可以说是五四以前，除了这些白话小说以外的，所有的文学作品都跟现代的青年人之间有隔阂，有个语言隔阂，那这个怎么办啊？

梁：这个恐怕没有什么好办法。只能够搞某种学问，这种某一种学问是要看古书的，是要借这个文言文的，那就是成为一种

necessary for some scholarship. It becomes a specialty, with a small number of people specializing in it. Most people don't necessarily need to use it; it can only be this way.

...This tidal current, the colloquial language couldn't be stopped. This current met the requirements of the majority of people, especially the requirements of the young.

Alitto: To return to the second question, which is that good scholarship can be considered conservative. (Liang: Right.) The term "conservative" is extremely difficult to define. What, after all, can be considered conservative? In this book [of mine], I also discussed this question. My important question is: do you willingly accept or oppose the designation "conservative" that some Chinese and foreigners have applied to you?

Liang: Of course I'm not conservative.[41] From what I just said a moment ago, you can see that I'm not conservative.

● Comments on the May Fourth Movement

Alitto: What is your view of the May Fourth Movement?

Liang: We have already talked about Chen Duxiu, Hu Shi and the Colloquial Literature Movement. Naturally, the influence of the May Fourth Movement on the following periods was tremendous. It created new historical currents, a whole new way of thought, and new ways of life. No longer were things confined to the old Chinese philosophy of life. Confucius began to be the object of criticism. Wasn't there a slogan "Overthrow Confucius and Sons"? This was unavoidable, because although Confucius wasn't really a religious leader, succeeding generations of emperors had regarded him as a religious leader. So there were Confucian temples, and all the literati worshipped him. And so Confucius, who was not originally a religious figure, became [regarded as] one. They made him up to look like a religious figure. Especially in the later times, there was a term—"rules of propriety and status." It was important to abide by the rules of propriety. It was important to have a hierarchical order according to social position and age. There were a great many rules. These rules and regulations helped the ruling classes maintain themselves. The ruling classes made use of these rules of propriety and status. After much time had passed, at the time of the May Fourth Movement, a general repugnance arose against these

专业，少数人专搞那个东西，多数人就不一定这样搞了，只好如此。

……他还是挡不住这个潮流，挡不住白话文、语体文。还是这个潮流迎合了多数人的要求，特别是年轻人的要求。

艾： 那您刚提到的第二个问题，就是说学问好还可以算是保守，（梁：对。）那“保守”这个词在有些时代很难下个定义，到底什么算是保守啊？那我这书里前面呢，也是讨论过这个问题。我主要的就是说，您对一些中国人、一些外国人，把保守主义者或者保守加在梁老师头上了，那您是甘心地承认呢，还是反对呀？

梁： 我当然是……，我不保守，从刚才的话里头可以看出来我不保守。

• 对五四运动的评价

艾： 梁老师对五四运动、五四时代的评价是什么？

梁： 我们已经谈到了陈独秀、胡适、白话文运动。五四运动当然是很影响到后来的，它开出来一个新的潮流、新的思想、新的人生，不再拘守老中国对人生的那个看法，对孔子开始怀疑、批判。不是有“打倒孔家店”的口号吗？这是不可免的。因为孔子虽然不是宗教，可是历代的皇帝都把他好像当作宗教一样，所以有孔庙，所谓念书人都要拜孔子，本来不是宗教的孔子，都把他装扮成孔教。特别是后来，有一个名词叫“礼教”，礼教就是很重要守礼啦，很有尊卑长幼啦，有很多规矩啦。这种规矩嘛，很能够帮助统治阶级，统治阶级就很利用礼教。那么日子久了之后嘛，就是到五四运动的时候，当然就对日子太久

old behavioral codes that helped the ruling class, and Confucius was involved. In actuality, the problems and responsibilities of society did not rest with Confucius. Society at large needed a code of behavior, and the ruling classes needed such codes even more. They [ruling classes] relied on these codes to support their rule. After much time had passed, the codes became ossified and rigid. People developed antipathy toward these ossified things. During the May Fourth era, when there was repugnance toward the ossified rules of propriety and status, Confucius was blamed for them.

Alitto: During the May Fourth era, many people blindly worshipped everything Western and wanted wholesale Westernization. Now to look at the last year or two, there was also a bit... Especially among the younger generation...it smacks of this [wholesale Westernization].[42] What do you think of this?

Liang: This is a kind of natural tendency, right? Things have developed naturally into the situation today. There's nothing to be surprised about. There is no need for rebuke. Actually, you could say that the foundations [of Chinese culture] cannot be shaken.[43]

● Why I opposed the Buddhism of the time

Alitto: You yourself opposed the idea of a "Confucian religion"?

Liang: Right! Confucianism is not a religion.

Alitto: Also in your book *Eastern and Western Cultures and Their Philosophies*, you opposed Buddhism of the time, saying, first, those people who were propagating Buddhism at the time were not good people, and second, what our China needed at present was not Buddhism. In the book you also brought up a point—that since the problems of the first and second paths had not yet been solved, Buddhism was out of the question. Yet you yourself throughout were a Buddhist. Your problems of the first and second paths had not yet been solved either. Isn't this a contradiction?

Liang: It was not only me as an individual. As far as I myself was concerned, I was inclined toward Buddhism, and wanted to study Buddhism. This was OK. If someone else as a private individual was this way, I would also approve. I probably, moreover, could help him. But as far as broader society and China's requirements were concerned, this thing was not needed.

了的、帮助统治阶级的礼教有反感、反对和破除，那么这样子就把孔子牵涉进去了。其实，问题、责任不在孔子。是为了广大的社会，广大的社会它需要一种礼教，统治阶级更为需要，借着这个它便于统治，日子久了，它就很僵化、僵硬。人们对僵化的东西都有反感，到了五四运动的时候，就是对僵化的这个礼教反感的时候，就归罪于孔子。

艾：五四时代也有很多人是盲目地崇拜西洋的一切，要全盘西化。那您看现在最近一两年，也有一点，尤其是年轻一代的也有一点这个味道了。您对这种现象有没有意见呢？

梁：这个也是一个自然之势吧。事情发展到今天，自然如此。这个不足怪，也不必责备。实际上，可以说是动摇不了根本。

• 我为什么反对当年的佛教

艾：您自己很反对"孔教"这个观念的？

梁：对，孔子不是宗教。

艾：在写《东西文化及其哲学》那本书的时候，您很反对当时的佛教。说现在搞佛教的人第一不是好人的，第二我们中国现在所需要的也不是佛教的。书里提到一点，第一条路和第二条路的问题还没有解决的时候，还谈不到什么佛教。不过您自己啊，还一直是佛教徒，您第一条路、第二条路的问题也还没有解决，这有没有矛盾啊？

梁：不但是我一个人，就我自己说，我倾向佛教，想学佛，可以；假如另外一个人，他作为一个人，他这个这样子，我也赞成，我并且也许还可以帮助他；可是就着广大的社会、就着当时的中国的需要说，不需要这个东西。

Alitto: Oh, this notion is that the individual and the whole of society were not the same.

Liang: They weren't the same. I would add one more point. At the time this kind of view was a bit extreme and one-sided. Why was it one-sided? It emphasized only the escapist religion side of Buddhism. Actually, it's not necessary to emphasize that aspect which negates and denies human life in order to propagate Buddhism. One can emphasize another aspect in developing it, and that is "compassion and mercy." In Buddhism there is a four-character phrase: "compassion, mercy and joyful giving." "Joyful" sometimes refers to "rejoicing in the welfare of others." "Giving" refers to the state of renunciation of everything, the opposite of covetousness. "Joyful giving" is to help people with their good desire, or good behavior. So, Buddhism can be developed from this compassion and joyful giving aspect. You don't have to "leave the world" to be Buddhist. This way is fine too.

At the time, I was looking at Buddhism too inflexibly. That is to say, if China at that time had internal disorders and civil war, and each person closeted themselves in their houses to chant sutras all day, the chaos would become even worse. [My meaning at the time was] don't be negative, don't renounce the world. Rather, bring "compassion, mercy and joyful giving" into play. [I wanted everybody to] go out and do something. To use Chairman Mao Zedong's terminology, I wanted everyone to "struggle." Struggle was necessary in order to turn the situation around and prevent the warlords from acting foolishly. The more everyone let things take their course and did nothing—that is, closing their doors—the worse the chaos would become. So, that was my meaning at the time.

Alitto: You proposed one of the Confucian virtues—resoluteness or firmness. Is this similar to the spirit of struggle?

Liang: Yes, they are similar in one way.

- **Chinese moral: the standards for right and wrong should not be sought in the external world.**

Alitto: ...Take China as an example. Before the Opium War, of course, China had a lot of weaknesses, but at least there was a standard for morality. Later, as you yourself said, regarding the Republican era, you wrote that in the 1920s and 1930s, the intellectuals ("scholars") had no shame. Previously at least in traditional society, they would not dare to struggle openly and

艾： 哦！这种观点是个人和整个社会不一样。

梁： 不一样。并且还可以再说一点。当时这种所见不免有点偏，偏什么呢？片面地看佛家是一种出世的宗教。其实呢，也可以不必这样看，就是，把佛教看成不必从出世宗教、否定人生那面去发扬它，而从另一面，就是慈悲。佛经里有这么四个字——"慈悲喜舍"，"喜"有时候叫做随喜，"舍"嘛就是舍弃了，跟贪取是反面的，随喜就是人家有一点好的心愿或者好的行为，就帮助他。所以从这个"慈悲喜舍"这面来发扬佛教，不必拘定要出世，那么样也很好。

我当时的意思就是看得呆板一点，就是说，如果中国那个时候正是内乱、内战，每一个人都要关起门来念佛，那个乱就更乱。不要消极，不要想出世，要发挥慈悲的意思，要出头，按现在的毛主席的话说，要斗争，要斗争才能够转移这个局面，不能够让那个军阀乱来。如果大家越是听天由命，越是关门，那更乱了，当时那个意思是那个意思。

艾： 您用的一个字，是孔子的一个美德，就是"刚"。那"刚"跟斗争、斗强，您现在说是一样的意思？

梁： 有相同的一面。

- **中国的道德：是非的标准不要向外找**

艾： ……拿中国来说吧，就是鸦片战争以前，当然有很多别的缺点，不过起码道德标准是有的。以后您自己也说，就是这个民国时代啊，您自己在书里也写过啊，20 年代的、30 年代的知识分子——"士"——是无耻的。他们起码以前在传统的社会里不敢公开地、张胆明目地为了自己的自私的理由而争执，

brazenly for their own selfish reasons. Now, the surface standards no longer exist. So, I say that the biggest difference from the previous situation is that moral standards are no longer pure and absolute. Rather, they are relative... [China's is not regarded] as the only moral standard in the world. Previously we felt that the difference between foreigners or Westerns and ourselves was that we could be considered comparatively human while they [foreigners] were not sufficiently "mature," and still hadn't become real humans. They had no morals, but we had morals. That is to say, humans had morals. In the Republican era, this already began to change. So, how can it be said that "the proper nature of the mind/heart" is what all human societies have in common?

Liang: I feel that the standards for right and wrong should not be sought in the external world. In *The Mencius*, he called it pursuing righteousness and benevolence and "walking the path of righteousness and benevolence."[44] These two are different. The pursuing of righteousness and benevolence refers to what the ordinary social conventions and mores hold as benevolence and righteousness, and what is good. Observing social conventions is pursuing righteousness and benevolence. Mencius held that that was not worth doing. He did not want people to pursue righteousness and benevolence. He wanted people to walk the path of righteousness and benevolence, that is, to go back to one's self, to return to one's own proper nature of the mind/heart. The more you seek it in the external world, the more bewildered and dazzled you become. Don't look to the external world, look to yourself, ask it of yourself. In *The Mencius*, in particular, he said, "the calm air of the morning," and "the restorative influence of the night is not sufficient to preserve the proper nature of the mind/heart."[45] A Chinese proverb says, "Examine one's conscience in the stillness of night." When, in the stillness of night, in the middle of the night you wake up, you examine your conscience in the quiet. That is, you yourself ask questions of yourself. At this time it's clear [what's right and wrong].

Alitto: Ask oneself. The problem is that each person's answer to the questions asked of oneself is the same or different. Or does the proper nature of the mind/heart have a common...

Liang: That is to say, when in the stillness of night you awaken, you are not subject to external influences. So examine one's conscience in the stillness of night, asking yourself: Is this right? At this time, in Chinese it's called the "recovery of conscience." Chinese farmers have a saying...these two sentences are marvelous: "If you don't owe taxes, you do not fear officials.

现在呢，表面上的标准已经没有了。所以说跟以前最大的不同，就是说道德的标准已经不是纯粹的、绝对的，而是相对的，……不是全世界唯一的道德标准。以前我们觉得外国人、洋人他们和我们的不同就是，我们是比较算是人，他们还没有"熟"，还没有成为真正的人，他们没有道德，我们是有道德，那就是说人是有道德的。在民国已经就开始了这么一个变化了，所以，"本心"应该怎么说才能说是人类社会的共同之处?

梁： 我觉得，是非的标准不要向外找。《孟子》上头有个话，他叫做"行仁义"和"由仁义行"，这两样不同。所谓"行仁义"嘛就是一般的社会习俗上认为那样是仁义、是好，按照着那样子去做就是"行仁义"。孟子认为那不足取，不要"行仁义"，要"由仁义行"，就是还是回到自己身上来，返回到自己本心，越向外找越迷乱、越眼花缭乱，不要向外看，要自己问自己。特别是，在《孟子》他也说，"平旦之气"，"夜气不足以存"。中国人的俗话常这么说，叫"清夜扪心"，你清夜、半夜里头醒来的时候，清静，"扪心"就是自己问问自己，这个时候清楚。

艾： 问自己啊。问题是每一个人的自己回答的答复一样不一样，或者"本心"有没有共同的……

梁： 这个就是说，清夜醒来的时候，比较不受外边的影响，"清夜扪心"，问问自己，这样对不对啊? 这个时候啊，按中国话说叫"良心发现"。中国农民有这样的话，这两句话很了不起："不欠钱粮不怕官，不昧良心不怕天。"这个话我觉得很了不起。

If you have not ignored your conscience, you do not fear Heaven." I think this saying is great. If I haven't ignored my conscience and done anything bad, I do not fear Heaven. The first line, "If you don't owe taxes, you do not fear officials." Everyone must pay taxes. I've already paid my taxes, and so I don't fear officials at all. This kind of society existed only in the old society of China; there is no such society outside of China. So, this thing conscience, the more you look externally, the less it exists.

● Chinese society is disorganized and liable to peace.

Alitto: I agree. In all of your works, you emphasize this point. No matter whether you use the term "benevolence" or "conscience," or "rationality," they are all one thing. So in this book [referring to *The Human Mind/ Heart and Human Life*] you still have a similar thing. You call it "spirituality" or something like that. Actually the meaning is the same, right? Either the term you just used, conscience, or the term benevolence, or if you call it rationality, it's the same. As you just said that saying among the common folk existed only in Chinese society. It didn't exist in other societies. So, if benevolence, rationality, and conscience are things that humanity shares, why is it that historically they appear comparatively commonly in Chinese society?

Liang: This is because Chinese society is a loosely organized society.

Alitto: I understand that. You mean that originally Western society, because of religion, was used to group organization.

Liang: Western society organized groups. People in general lived in a group. Previously, during the Middle Ages, the group overly constrained and repressed the individual. In modern society, capitalist society, the individual awakened to resist the group's excessive intervention and repression. This is the kind of change from ancient times to modern times. But this transformation didn't take place in Chinese society.

China's old society lacked group organizations. At most it was family and lineage. In the past the emperors and rulers' best method was not to interfere with the affairs of the common people, the so-called "Laissez Faire" and "governance by non-interference." The more the government allowed people, the more it let people live their own lives, the better.

我不昧良心，我没有做一点坏事，“不昧良心不怕天”；前头一句话“不欠钱粮不怕官”，每一个人嘛都要交钱粮，钱粮我已经交了，我官都不怕。这样一个社会啊，只有中国老社会有啊，外国没有这个社会。所以“良心”这个东西啊，你越向外看、向外去找越没有。

- **中国是散漫而容易和平的社会**

艾：我同意。您著作无论是哪一本，都是注重这一点，无论您说“仁”——原来您说的是“仁”，或者“良心”，或者“理性”都是一个东西，那您这本书也是同样地说有这么一个东西，说是灵性或者怎么样，其实基本的意思是一样的，是不是？您刚才用的是“良心”这个词也好，或者用“仁”这个词也好，或者用“理性”这个词也好，您也刚说了，就是民间的那个说法了，只有中国社会有的，别的社会也没有的。那么假如“仁”、“理性”、“良心”，是人类共同具有的一种东西，为什么历史上中国的社会是比较会有的？

梁：这是因为中国的社会是一个松散的社会。

艾：这个我明白。您的意思就是西方社会本来因为宗教的关系有团体的习惯了。

梁：西洋的社会啊，它有集团，人呢一般是生活于集团中，那么过去的、中世纪的社会，是集团拘束了、压迫了个人多一些；那么近代的社会——到了资本主义的社会，转入近代社会，个人的觉醒反抗这个集团的过分的干涉压迫，有这样一个古今的变化，就是中古跟近代的变化。可是这个变化在中国的社会是没有的。中国的老社会它是缺乏集团的，它尽是家庭、家族，过去的皇帝、统治者他最好的道路是不干涉老百姓的事儿，所谓“端拱无为”、“无为而治”，你越是不干涉老百姓的事，越是随他去、随他自己去生活，越好。

In China for several thousand years, life was lived like this, a passive "live and let live" state, without any active governance. Society followed custom and convention, with the people living unorganized peaceful lives. Disorganization is more liable to lead to peace. Peace is more liable to lead to disorganization. To put it in another way, struggle is liable to lead to organization, and group organization is more likely to lead to struggle. So, old Chinese society lived disorganized and peaceful days, days that were passive and peaceful. So, the Chinese didn't know what a nation was. He only knew "Peace in All under Heaven." The "All under Heaven" had no boundaries. Nation had parameters. Relations between nations are adversarial, but there was no relationship with "All under Heaven." The Chinese always dreamed of "Peace in All under Heaven." They wanted to live a passive, peaceful life, and hoped that the imperial court and the government would not quite interfere with their affairs. These circumstances did not exist in Europe.

● Chinese society began to differ from Western society.

Alitto: In modern European society these kinds of circumstances didn't exist, but in the Middle Ages, there was a Church—a Catholic Church. So although society had the habit of organization, the organizations were church organizations. But you can't say that it was struggles between organizations. Only in the 17th and 18th centuries were there nationalities, and only with nationalities came nations.

Liang: In a modern nation... Before, the aristocracy ruled the peasants [serfs]. The peasants were attached to the land. This is different from the Chinese peasantry of the past.

Alitto: Yes, these two societies were different. In general, I agree completely with the historical explanation you just articulated. I agree. My question is, your theory has always had a contradiction. If there is something that humanity possesses in common, how could it be a special product of China? I know, you just explained this from the background of societal development. I have felt always that this is a contradiction. As mentioned in my book, I think that the contradiction is: In the 1920s and 1930s, you advocated the restoration of China's inherent "rationality" and "benevolence." Only by this restoration could the entire country be revived, be modernized and be able to absorb Western

中国的过去的几千年，过日子就是这么样子过日子，消极地彼此相安，而没有一种积极的统治。它就是本着习俗，过着一种散漫的、和平的生活，散漫嘛就容易和平，和平嘛也就容易散漫，换句话说，斗争嘛就容易造成团体，而有了集团就更容易斗争。所以中国的这个老社会啊，它都是过一种散漫和平的日子，一种消极相安的日子。所以中国人他也不晓得什么叫“国家”，他只晓得“天下太平”。什么叫“天下”啊，天下是没有边的，“国”嘛就是有个范围的，国与国有对抗性，对天下没有啊。中国人啊，他总是梦想天下太平，他就是要过一种消极相安的日子，希望朝廷啊、官府啊不要多干涉我，不要多管我们的事，这个情况在欧洲是没有的。

• 中西社会分歧的开始

艾： 可以说在欧洲的、现代的社会没有这种情况，可是中古时代啊，国外的地方都是一个教会——天主教，所以虽然组织的习惯，组织都是教堂的组织，可是也不能说是组织对组织的战斗。现在到了 17、18 世纪才开始有民族的情形，才有了国家。

梁： 在近代国家，……之前，贵族对农民统治，农民常常是随着土地的，这个跟中国的过去的农民不同。

艾： 是，这两个社会是有不同的。一般地来说，我完全同意您刚说的历史方面的解释，我都同意。我问的问题就是，您的说法一直有个矛盾：假如某一个东西是人类的共同有的，这个东西怎么会是中国的特产呢？我知道，您刚才是从社会发展背景来解释，我一直觉得是个矛盾，我书里提到的、我所觉得的矛盾的地方是：您 20 年代、30 年代提倡把中国固有的“理性”或者“仁”复兴起来，这样中国才能全国复兴，

science and technology. Group organization could develop the things that China inherently possessed. Where is the contradiction? If we say the fundamental reason why China originally wasn't modernized, hadn't developed science and technology, and didn't have group organizations was because China had developed "rationality," how suddenly could this rationality, originally an obstacle to modernization, no longer be an obstacle, but become a...?

Liang: It wasn't an obstacle. In the past, it wasn't an obstacle either.

Alitto: So in the past it wasn't an obstacle?

Liang: It was that the paths of societal development were different.

Alitto: Alright, then why were the paths different?

Liang: What do the different paths refer to? In remote antiquity a person's life could not be separated from the group. People formed groups. The more ancient it went, the smaller the scope of the group was. Each group had two aspects. One was consanguinity, and one was locality. In brief, beginning in remote antiquity, life was lived in a group. One aspect was family, and the other was a group that transcended family. In China's societal development, the particular emphasis was on the aspect of family. In foreign countries the emphasis was on the group. Initially, these were both group and family. One developed to emphasize this aspect, and the other to emphasize that aspect. Each had its own inclination. It's a religious issue when a group of people go astray and need to be pulled back. Religion helps people form group organizations, and Confucianism helps people emphasize lineages and families, and family ethics. The two are separated in this way.

Kin organizations emphasize the degree of consanguinity and the principle of seniority, paying attention to this concept. Moreover, this concept is extended into society at large. So in the emperor-subject relationship, the emperor is called the "Father-Emperor." The emperor refers to his subjects as "newborn babies" (*chizi*)—this term "*chi*" is the color red—because newborn babies have red skin. So, being influenced by Confucianism, these emotions of familial affection are extended into society. The emperor is "father," the teacher is also "father." Students of the same teacher are "brothers of the same master." Good friends are the equivalent of brothers. Affection was thought highly of. Affection transcends vital interests.

才能现代化，才能吸收西洋的科学技术；团体组织可以发展中国固有的东西。矛盾何在呢？假如原来中国没有现代化，科学技术不发达，没有团体组织，基本的原因是因为中国先发展"理性"，为什么假如原来是现代化的障碍，为什么到了现在这个理性突然不是个障碍反而是个……

梁：它没有障碍，它过去也没有障碍。

艾：过去也没有障碍？

梁：它是社会发展走的路子不同。

艾：好，不过为什么路子不同呢？

梁：所谓路不同是指什么说呢？在远古，人的生活都是离不开人群的，都是成群的。这个群的范围越古的时候越小。每一个群都有两面，一面是血缘的关系、血统的关系，还有一面是地域的关系。总而言之，开始远古的时候生活是集体的，一方面是家庭，一方面也是超乎家庭的集团。中国的社会发展、演进是侧重家庭这一面，外国是偏重在集团一面。最初的这些它又是集团、又是家族，这个偏到这面走了，那个偏到那面走了，那么各有所偏了。让这个各有所偏的帮助那个各走一偏的路子的，就是宗教问题。宗教帮助人走集团的一面，儒家的东西帮助人走家族、家庭、家庭伦理这一面，这样就分开了。

在家庭、家族上它就讲一个"亲疏长幼"，注意"亲疏长幼"这个观念，并且把这个观念从家庭向社会上去推广。所以管君臣的君叫"君父"，为"君"的对于自己的百姓称为"赤子"——"赤"就是红颜色——就是小孩子。所以受了儒家的影响啊，它总是把这个家庭的这种亲爱之情推广到社会上去。君是"父"，老师也是"父"，同一个老师的，我们是"师兄弟"，好朋友也是等于兄弟一样，它特别是重情谊，情谊嘛，它就超过了利害关系。

Alitto: I still want to ask why this division occurred in remote antiquity. In the final analysis, what was the cause?

Liang: I don't know. There were respective inclinations [in the two societies] to develop this or that aspect. Why was it? There were conditions that supported in this or that direction. The conditions [in the two societies] were different.

Alitto: This seems to be different from the way you put it in *The Essence of Chinese Culture*. In that book, you wrote that it was the Confucian viewpoint. That is, China originally did have a religion. China was originally a clan society, in the Shang Dynasty. After the Zhou, Confucianism destroyed it. The scholars awoke. In accordance with Confucian thought, it substituted pure ethics for religion. The old religion could be said to no longer exist. Of course, among the common folk there were still relatively superstitious religions, but [formal] religion no longer existed. From what I understood, it was only at this time in the religious realm that the two societies had their respective inclinations... You now locate this phenomenon earlier in time, but you still don't know the reason.

Liang: That is to say, each society developed on its own path, and each had its respective inclination.

Alitto: What's the reason? You said that certain conditions were a reason. What were these conditions?

Liang: We can't say at present. But there were in any case reasons that can be looked into and studied. Our knowledge is limited.

Alitto: Did not you discuss this question in your several books? That is, the question of Chinese and Western societies developing in different directions.

Liang: Probably I did.

● Intellect, rationality and spirituality

Liang: If we want to describe and explain the mind/heart, first we must explain its subjective initiative or its self-conscious autonomy, its consciousness. They are equally the same. This is a property of humanity, its most important property.

艾： 我还要说，为什么在最远的古代，原来的这个分别，归根结底的原因是什么？

梁： 不知道。它就是一个偏成这面走了，一个是偏成那面走了，它原来最初是集团，集团包含着两面，一个偏这面走了，一个是偏那面走了，那么，为什么各有所偏呢？应当是，帮助向这方面发展的，有些个条件，帮助向那方面发展的，有些个它的条件，彼此的条件不同。

艾： 那好像跟《中国文化要义》里您的说法有点不同了的。《中国文化要义》（中）您说，还是儒家的观点，就是说到宗教的问题，中国原来的这个宗教，中国原来的宗族社会，就是说商朝那个社会，到了周朝后面是给儒家算打破了，"士"醒了。按儒家的意思呢，来把纯粹的伦理代替宗教，那宗教可以说没有了。当然民间有一些比较迷信的宗教，不过，宗教没有了。依我所了解，这时候宗教的问题才各有偏……那您现在说还有一个更在前面、说不出来的原因，还不知道。

梁： 就是说啊，各走一路，各有所偏。

艾： 原因呢？您说条件，那条件是什么？

梁： 我们现在说不上来，但是总还是有，可以研究，可以去探讨。因为我们距离知识还是很有限，知识上有限。

艾： 您几本书里有没有讨论这个问题啊？就是中西社会的不同方向的发展的问题。

梁： 恐怕有吧。

· 理性、理智与灵性

梁： 我们要描述要说明这个人心，先要说它的主动性。主动性又可以称作自觉，自己觉悟，自觉能动性。主动性就完全等于自觉能动性。这是人类的特征，顶重要的特征。

Alitto: Does this concept of autonomy or self-activeness have something to do with the will?

Liang: Of course the will is included within it. It has subjective initiative, flexibility, and lastly, the ability to plan. So, in order to explain the ability to plan, I had to use all this verbiage.

Alitto: In your book *The Essence of Chinese Culture*, you made a basic distinction between intellect and rationality. Now [in this book] you have expanded into three elements: subjective initiative, flexibility, and the ability to plan. The first two probably are subsumed under rationality. The ability to plan is probably part of intellect. Is there this distinction? Probably the ability to plan is in reference to relatively abstract calculations for the future...

Liang: You just now used two terms, rationality and intellect. How would you distinguish between the two?

Alitto: I would still use the same distinction you made in your book *The Essence of Chinese Culture*. For example, when a man does a mathematical problem, the part of his mind that does the calculating is his intellect. The technique is intellect. And the part of him that wants to get the right answer or not—the moral aspect—is rationality.

Liang: Yes, that's about right.

Alitto: So I thought that you would have developed the concept you used before and asked this question. Now [in this new book] you have divided it into three basic aspects: subjective initiative, flexibility, and the ability to plan, the last of which is the most complex. I also know that in this book it seems you use quite a bit of material on the most recent scientific research. In this section in which you analyze the mind/heart, you also make use of the most recent science, and psychology too. Which psychological school do you think is the most correct?

Liang: In foreign psychology, for example, I remember one psychologist named McDougall, who liked to talk about instinct.

Alitto: That was someone quite popular when you were writing *Eastern and Western Cultures and Their Philosophies*. Later, he wasn't as popular.

Liang: He enumerated a great many kinds of instinct. The Englishman Russell wrote a book called, as I recall, *Construction*... [referring to Russell's *Principles of Social Reconstruction*], right? He divided humanity

艾： 是不是跟意志有关系啊?

梁： 当然意志包含在内了。主动性、灵活性，最后是计划性。为了说明计划性，要用这么多话来说明。

艾： 按照《中国文化要义》的说法，您分的还是理智跟理性的基本分别了。那么现在您好像进一步又分了三部分——主动、灵活、计划。那头两个也许是属于理性，计划性是属于理智，有没有这个分别啊? 那么也许计划是指的比较抽象的，为了未来而计算的……

梁： 刚才，你用了一个理性、理智，你这两个怎么分?

艾： 那还是您的《中国文化要义》里的分别。就是举一个具体的例子啊，就是一个人在算一个数学的问题，那么算得正确不正确还算是理智啊，就是说计数方面是理智啊，不过道德方面，要不要算、正确不正确那是理性。

梁： 对，差不多。

艾： 所以我以为您又是按照当年写的这本书的关于基本观念而继续发展而问的这个问题。现在分了三个基本方面——主动、灵活、计划，而计划是最复杂的。我也知道您的这本书好像有不少的最近科学方面的研究资料。您在分析人心的这部分，也是在利用最近科学，那心理学也是一部分内容，那您觉得心理学哪一种派别是比较对?

梁： 外国的心理学，比如有个喜欢谈本能的，叫麦克迪科。

艾： 这是您当年写《东西文化及其哲学》的时候最流行的，以后就不流行了。

梁： 他列举了好多样的本能。英国的罗素写过一本书，好像叫《创造……》(*疑为罗素的《社会改造原理》*) 是不是? 那本书是讲，

into three kinds, one was called the possessive impulse and another the creative impulse. But there is a third kind, called spirituality. I originally quoted this in *Eastern and Western Cultures and Their Philosophies*, but disagreed with his three-way division. I said...one was intellectual, one was instinct. Originally I saw it this way. I only understood later after the publication of "Trend toward Diversification"[46] that his third entity called spirituality actually referred to something; it wasn't just empty talk. I accepted his trichotomy, not the dichotomy [of intellect and instinct].

I'll explain another point. Originally I also had this dichotomy. I didn't understand the spirituality. I felt that it wasn't necessary; I felt that an intellect and an instinct were sufficient. Why? Because I subsumed morality into instinct. Later I understood that this was not so, not correct. Why? Because instinct is also an instrument for life; it is a backup instrument. Now, intellect is also an instrument, a backup instrument. The entity of spirituality is higher than these two. So at that point I understood Russell's trichotomy and thought it correct. Religion, for instance. You can't explain it as intellect or as instinct. Religion and morality are something higher than either instinct or intellect. That is what Russell called spirituality. Later I accepted Russell's statement.

● Customs and truth

Alitto: Could you give a very brief summary of what your ideas are on this relationship between the mind and body?

Liang: The mind/heart transcends the body. From the standpoint of physical existence, your body and my body are separate and not in communication. When I eat, your hunger is not satisfied. But the mind/heart transcends the body. So the relationship between minds/hearts can be described with these eight characters: the fist four are *haowuxiangyu* (mutual communication of likes and dislikes). [The other four characters are *tongyangxiangguan* (sufferings are interrelated).] What I like, what you like—likes and dislikes can be communicated. Likes and dislikes include moral judgment. So, I think that this kind of action or this kind of person is good. You also recognize it as good. So likes and dislikes can be communicated, meaning mutual understanding.

Alitto: "Mutual communication of likes and dislikes." Does this mean that there is an absolute, objective standard in people's psychology? Can it be stated that way? Telepathy between human minds/hearts? So, are you

他把人类分成三样，一样叫做占有冲动，还有一样叫做创造冲动，但是还有一个第三，它叫灵性。我起初在《东西文化及其哲学》里头，引了他的话。我不同意他的三分法，我说是……一个是理智，一个是本能。起初我是这样，后来在《多元化趋势》出版之后，我才明白，明白他的第三个叫灵性的这个，也是有所指，不是一句空话。我承认他的三分法，不是二分法。

再说明白一点，原来我是二分法，我对他这个灵性不大懂，觉得也不必要，觉得二分法就够了，一个理智，一个本能就够了。为什么？因为我把道德归到本能里头去。后来我明白不是，不对。为什么不对呢？本能还是我们在生活中，为了生活，为了做生活我们的一种工具，是个备用的东西。那么理智也是一个工具，备用的工具，那个主体高于这两个。所以呀，那么我才明白罗素的三分法有道理。比如他说吧，宗教单用理智来说，说不了，用本能也说不了，宗教道德高于这个东西，那个东西是灵性。后来承认罗素的这个话。

• 习俗与真理：极高明而道中庸

艾： 身体与心理之间的关系，可不可以扼要地讲一讲？

梁： 心是超过身的。从身来说，你的身体跟我的身体不相通，我吃饭，你不饱。可是从心来说，心高于身，心超过了身。所以心跟心的关系，它可以说八个字，头一个就是“好恶相喻”（*另四个字应是“痛痒相关”*），我喜欢什么，你喜欢什么，“好恶相喻”。这个“好恶”包含着是非心，我觉得这样的行为、这样的人是好人，你也承认是好人，好恶可以相喻，“相喻”就是彼此了解，“好恶相喻”。

艾：“好恶相喻”，您的意思是有个绝对的、人的心里有的一种客观的标准了，可以这么说吧？就是说“心心相印”，就是无论什么

saying that no matter in what era and in what culture, humans' reactions to a certain phenomenon are the same? That is to say, this behavior is bad, that behavior is good. Right?

Liang: People, as far as the fundamental definition goes...

Alitto: Which is the most fundamental?

Liang: There are differences in the social customs and habits of each society, and differences in time and place. In terms of space, that society and this society are far apart. There's also a difference in time. Societies in different ages are also different. Societies in different places and times differ; they have their own social customs and usages. An individual person is often influenced by the customs, habits and social usages of his society. And so because of this, the situation that "I am right and you are wrong" occurs. But there are certain fundamentals that are the same. Very basic ones. For example, every society dislikes and loathes lying, right? For a lot of things, due to their different social customs and habits, what this particular place or society recognizes as good is not so regarded in that place or society; or, today it is regarded as good, but the ancients held it to be bad.

Alitto: As you just said, there are temporal and spacial differences among all societies' social customs and habits. The goals of purposefulness will also be different. So doesn't that count as moral behavior being different?

Liang: Of course, they are different. There are different moralities in different eras and different societies. Each society has its own morality. Therefore, in reality this isn't true morality; they are just customs and usages.

Alitto: They are just customs and usages? What is the source of true morality?

Liang: True morality is conscious awareness and self-discipline. Usually, the majority of people in society follow others; they just follow the society's social customs and habits. Those whose vital force is great may not follow customs. He is capable of great conscious awareness and self-discipline. So he may choose to act in a certain way following his own self-conscious decision regardless of the opposition, and the ridicule and taunts of others. Revolutionaries are able to do this. The ordinary person does not make revolution. Revolution is always foresighted.

社会、什么文化的人，他们对某一现象会有同样的反应了？就是说这个行为不好，那个行为好，是不是？

梁： 人从一个很基本的定义说……

艾： 最基本的是哪一种？

梁： 就是有些个它是由于各个地方的风俗习惯不同，也有的是古今不同，有地方的不同——那个社会跟这个社会，属于从空间上说，相离很远，这是一种不同。还有一种古今时代不同，它的社会也不同。不同时代的社会，不同地方的社会，都有它的风俗习惯。一个人常常为他自己所生存的社会习惯所影响，因此就搞得我说的对，你说的不对了。可是在某些个很基本的上头，还是相同的。很基本的，比方说吧，说假话，每一个社会都不喜欢，都讨厌，是吧？比如这样的。可以有许多事情，它还是由于社会风俗习惯不同，这个地方、这个社会认为好，那个地方就不认为好。或者今天以为好，古人认为不好。

艾： 每一个社会的风俗习惯，您刚才说的，时间的分别、地方的分别都是有的。有所为的目的也会不同，那什么算是不道德的行为也不同了？

梁： 那当然了，不同的，是古今的不同，地方空间的不同，各有各的道德。因为各有各的道德，实际上不是真道德，实际上是礼俗。

艾： 实际上是礼俗啊？那么真道德的来源是什么？

梁： 真道德啊，是自觉自律。通常社会上多数人是随着人走，随着社会的风俗习惯走。生命力很强的人，他可以不随俗，他能够自觉自律，不随俗，所以不管旁人的诽笑、反对，本着自己的自觉自律来行动。革命家能够这样，普通人不革命，革命都是先知先觉。

Alitto: This revolution is what Marx discusses as a revolution. The masses take action out of their own self-interest, out of their own material interests.

Liang: But revolutions don't happen often. Of course those revolutionary leaders who take the lead cannot separate from the masses, but they can transcend and lead the masses. They have foresight. Their creative power is great. The average person...

Alitto: There is still a fundamental problem. What in the end is the goal of society's evolution? What path does it follow? According to what principles does it develop? You say that revolutionaries are foresighted. Where does their understanding of their standards and goals come from?

Liang: We can't lay down a general rule because it is different at different time, places and environments.

Alitto: I mean, if there was an eternal unchanging truth...

Liang: No. There is no objectively existing eternal unchanging truth.

Alitto: But you stated that although each individual person's body is independent and unconnected, as [the example you gave previously] "when you eat, my hunger is not satisfied." You say that the mind is still...

Liang: Likes and dislikes mutually communicate.

Alitto: Why do they mutually communicate?

Liang: Mutual communication means that I understand you, and you understand me. This is called mutual communication.

Alitto: But why? Why does mutual communication exist? That is to say, human nature has aspects that are shared. Each individual person has...

Liang: It is what Mencius said: Human minds/hearts are the same.[47]

Alitto: But humans have developed through evolution. Humans of today and humans of ten thousand years ago are different. Humans today will also be different from humans ten thousand years from now. But where is the common property [the basis of humanity]? Where does it come from?

Liang: The common property is that they are living things. All have life; if they have life, they all have likes and dislikes. The closer dislikes and likes are to the corporeal, the easier it is for them to be different. Take smoking

艾： 这个革命就是马克思的意思论革命，群众为了他们自己的利益而行动，为了他们物质上的利益才行动。

梁： 可是革命不是常常有，先出头领导的革命领导人当然离开群众不行，可是他超出群众、领导群众。他是先知先觉，他的创造力大，一般人……

艾： 还有一个更基本的问题啊，您说到底人的社会演变有什么目的啊？按照什么途径、什么原则发展的？您说革命者是先知先觉，他的标准、目的的了解是哪儿来的？

梁： 它是看不同的时代、不同的地方、不同的环境，我们不能够笼统地说。

艾： 我的意思就是说假如有一个永久不变的真理……

梁： 没有，永久不变的真理没有，客观存在的永久不变的真理没有。

艾： 您刚才说的人跟人的身体当然有区别、不同，您吃饭，我不饱，心灵您说还是……

梁： 好恶相喻。

艾： 为什么相喻？

梁： 相喻就是我懂得你，你懂得我，这叫相喻。

艾： 不过为什么？有什么原因相喻存在？就是说人性有共同的地方，大家每一个人都有的……

梁： 就是孟子所说的人心有“同然”。

艾： 不过人是演变而发展出来的，现在的人与一万年前的不同，现在的人又跟未来一万年后的人不同，可是共同的地方在哪里？共同地方的来源在哪里啊？

梁： 共同的都是活的东西，都是生命，有生命就有所谓好恶。离身体越近的好恶很容易不同，如你喜欢抽烟，我不喜欢抽烟，

as an example. You like to smoke and I do not. That is, those likes and dislikes that are close to the corporal (physiology) are easy to differ. An individual person...

Alitto: Which likes and dislikes are comparatively similar?

Liang: Those transcending the corporeal.[48]

Alitto: Those in the mind?

Liang: Transcending the corporeal, transcending the corporeal. Just like the example of lying that I just mentioned. Lying is an example.

Alitto: Possibly there are societies in which lying is not considered wrong.

Liang: That is a question of social customs and habits. I admit that there is that kind of society, but that [acceptance of lying] is part of the social customs and habits of society. Social customs and habits are different from conscience. Social customs and habits make the humans of different ages and different places differ from one another. Social customs and habits are this way.

Alitto: For example, in the West, quite a few people feel that fundamentally conscience doesn't exist. Then what are humans? They are created by society. Human nature is society's creation. Especially in the Women's Liberation Movement, they feel that there is no basic difference between men and women. In fact, there is a distinction, but that is because men control society, with the result that females are raised specifically to become what they are. Males are raised differently. But there is no distinction between consciences. This is one way of explaining the difference.

Liang: This is a difference between the innate and the acquired.

Alitto: They mean that there are no innate differences, aside from the differences of corpulence, height—naturally the genitals are different, the reproductive system is different—they say that aside from that there is no great difference. That is to say, there are no inherent qualities. I don't agree. You don't agree. But the reasons are that there is no [common universal] conscience. Sooner or later modern societies...will have no standard. The process of rationalization breaks down the basis upon which standards rest. What you have just articulated and what you held previously are about the same. But in the current situation of the Western society, and especially in the future situation, standards of morality—standards for good and bad—are disappearing. Starting from the 18th

就是离身体太近，离身体太近的好恶那很难相同。个人……

艾： 那哪一种好恶比较相同?

梁： 超过身体的。

艾： 心理的?

梁： 超过身体的，超过身体的。说假话是一个例子。

艾： 可能有一种社会是说假话不一定是坏事。

梁： 那个是习俗不同。我承认有那样的社会，但是那个是归在习俗上，习俗跟本心不同。习俗容易让不同时代、不同地方的人彼此不一样，习俗是这样的。

艾： 那比如在西方，不少的人觉得根本没有本心。就是人是什么?就是由社会创造出来的，人性是社会的创造品。尤其是妇女解放运动，她们觉得男女根本没有分别，事实上是有分别的，那是因为社会是由男的控制的，而结果女的从小就养成这个样子，男的养成另外一个样子，不过本心没有分别，有这么一个说法。

梁： 就是一个是先天的，一个是后天的。

艾： 他们的意思就是说先天的分别是没有的，除了长得胖、长得矮的、长得瘦这些分别以外——当然生殖器也不同，生殖系统不同——他们说这以外没有什么大的分别了。就是说没有本心，我也不同意，您也不同意。不过道理就是说，没有本心……现代社会迟早……就是没有标准了，理智化过程好像把所有的标准的基础啊，打破了、坏了。您说的道理跟您以前的基本的道理是一样的，不过现在西方的社会的情况，尤其是将来的情况，道德的标准、好坏的标准越来越没有了。自从 18 世纪

century Enlightenment to the present, our standards become fewer and fewer, more and more relativised; relativised moral standards are the equivalent of being absent.

Liang: This is all peripheral, not fundamental. It still comes back to that statement by Mencius, that people's minds/hearts are the same. The sage knows beforehand the similitude of our minds/hearts.

Some sixty years ago, when I was only in my twenties, I published *Eastern and Western Cultures and Their Philosophies*. In that book, I explained Confucius according to my understanding of him at the time. Now, doesn't Confucius often speak about Perfect Virtue (*ren*)? What did I say in that book? I said that Confucian *ren* is a kind of extremely sensitive, acute intuition. Didn't Mencius like to use the terms "intuitive understanding of the good" (conscience), which was what we call "instinct." *Zhijue* in Chinese is called "intuition" in English. *Benneng* is called "instinct" in English. So in this way, I used these modern terms to explain Confucius' and Mencius' thought.

Now, I know I was wrong. These modern terms are close to the meanings I meant to convey; they are close, but they are not very direct equivalents. It was not really correct, nor completely incorrect, because Confucius' Perfect Virtue can be very deep and profound, so much so that it becomes abstruse. As in *The Analects*, the master said, "Is Perfect Virtue a thing remote? I wish for it, and then virtue is at hand." If you explain *ren* in too abstruse a fashion, it is too one-sided, too narrow. *Ren* does not necessarily have to be explained in profound, abstruse ways. *Ren* is both shallow and profound, both simple and complex. If you only understand its superficial, shallow, easy aspects, that is not real understanding. So my mistake in that book was to stress its simple, shallow aspects too much. Mencius is also that way. When you go to understand Mencius' intuitive understanding of the good, it can be understood both on a shallow level and on a profound level. For example, intuitive understanding of the good, that is, conscience—who doesn't have a conscience? Everyone does. Is this saying right or wrong? Can you put it this way? You can certainly put it this [simple] way. But, on the other hand, you can't understand it too simplistically, too shallowly either.

Why can't it be too simplistic, too shallow? Because we humans live within society, and cannot depart from society. It is likely that humans will follow the mores and usages of their society. If the mores of a society take

启蒙运动开始到现在，我们这个标准越来越少了，越来越相对化了，道德标准一相对化就等于没有了。

梁： 这个都是末梢，不是根本。还是孟子那个话，孟子说，人心有同然，圣人是先得我心的同然。

在 60 年前，60 年前的时候我才二十几岁，那个时候发表《东西文化及其哲学》，那里边我就对孔子有一些解说，按照我当时的理解、我所能懂得的，来说明孔子。为了说明孔子——孔子不是喜欢讲那个“仁”吗？——我当时那个书里头，我说：“孔子说的‘仁’是什么呢？是一种很敏锐的直觉。”孟子不是喜欢说“良知良能”？那个就是现在所说的本能。直觉嘛，英文就是 intuition，本能就是 instinct。我就是这样子来把孔孟之学，用现在的名词来介绍给人。

现在我知道错了。它只是近似，好像是那样，只是近似，不对，不很对，不真对。这个不真对，可也没有全错啊，也不能算全错。因为孔子所说的“仁”，它可以很深，可以很高深。孔子不是有那个话：“仁远乎哉？我欲仁，斯仁至矣。”所以你把“仁”说得太高深，也就偏了，不必一定说得很高深。一方面是可以这么说，可浅可深。如果你就是从浅的一方面来懂它，那是不够的。所以我在当初的书里头，就是太从浅的方面来说。孟子也是那样，孟子的“良知良能”，你去懂得它，你去了解它，也是可浅可深。比如说“良知良能”，就是良心，谁没有良心呢？都有良心。这样说对不对呢？可以不可以这样说？完全可以这样说。可是又转过来说呢，不能看得太简单，不能理解得太浅。

为什么不能太简单、不能太浅呢？因为我们这个人啊，人总是生活在社会里头，他离不开社会，所以他容易随着社会走，社会习俗上这个算对，他也就对，习俗上以为这个不好，

[this] to be right, the individual considers it right. If the morals and mores of a society take it to be wrong, so does the individual human. It is easy for people to do this. But societies and their mores and morals are different. There are differences in both time and space. East and West are different. The modern and the ancient are different. People tend to follow their social norms. So, what is considered wrong in one society is considered right in another. This is very common, unless it is an inherently extremely gifted person, or an extraordinarily wise person, who possibly won't follow conventions—he often would lead a revolution. Exceptionally gifted people are this way, and so it is hard to say if these words apply to them.

Alitto: Each society has its own customs and mores. Each society has its own value judgments. If we say that each society is different, then does humanity have a universal truth, a universal standard for value judgments?

Liang: The answer is yes and no. Let's first address its non-existence. This life of ours must be lived in a society, so we must go along with the values of our respective societies. If you oppose society, you will not be accepted by society. So the values can be taken as "customs" or "etiquette." Probably on the one side of the issue, we can admit that each age, each place—that is to say, each society—has different customs, mores and morals. Probably it is natural to be in accord with different societies' values. The "rules of propriety" are for that time and place reasonable and true.

On the other hand, however, there is also a kind of truth, which is not the principle of a particular time and place, bound by customs and mores. Rather, it is an absolute truth. This truth does exist, but only very few enlightened brilliant people are conscious of it, or realize it. They can rise above and see further than the average people. On the one hand, there are few of these pelple. On the other hand, there is an old Chinese saying that "Something something...great height and brilliancy, so as to pursue the course of the Mean." This kind of person is himself very brilliant and wise, but he does not want to divorce himself from the society of his time. So the path he takes is still the middle path. I don't know if you are aware that I never studied the Four Books and Five Classics? (Alitto: Yes, I am.) So the quotation I just used is not complete. "Something something...great height and brilliancy, so as to pursue the course of the Mean." This is because I never memorized the Classics, and so I'm not all that familiar with them. [The original phrase is: To raise it to its greatest height and brilliancy, so as to pursue the course of the Mean.]

他也就跟着走，人很容易这样。可是所跟着走的这个社会，东西南北，在这个国家，在那个国家，在这个洲，在那个洲，在西洋，在东洋，社会很多不同，古今也是很多不同，在空间上、时间上很多不同。人多半都是随着社会走，所以在这个社会认为是不对的事，在那个社会认为是对的，这是常有的。除非天资很高的人，智慧很高，他可能不随俗，他常常是领头革命，天资高的人常常是这样，所以有些话就很难说了。

艾：每一个社会有每一个社会的习俗，有它的风俗习惯，也有每一个社会的价值判断。假如说每一个社会有不同，人类有没有一个普遍的真理，一个普遍的价值判断的标准？

梁：一方面说有，一方面说没有。先说没有吧。没有就是说人生就是得在社会里生活，你就得随俗，你一定反对社会，会不见容于社会，所以我们把这个俗或者叫“风俗”，或者叫“礼俗”。我们可以承认不同的时代，不同的地方，这就是说不同的社会吧，随着不同的社会走，也是理所当然。不同的时代、不同的地方的所谓“礼”，就是理。一方面可以这样说。

当然，还有一面，可以说是一种真理吧，不是世俗之理，而是真理。真理是有的，不过是只能在很少的高明人才意识得到，很少的高明人才能够超过众人，他看得高，看得远。这种高明人那是很少了，并且一方面是很少，还有一方面好像中国古话有一个叫“什么高明而道中庸”一句话，他自己是很高明，可是他不跟当时的社会……不愿意脱离社会，他走的路还是走中庸的路。这个地方我补一句，我不知道你知道不知道我是没有念过“四书五经”？（艾:知道。）所以刚才引的话，“什么高明而道中庸”，这句话所以我说不完全，因为古书没有背过，不熟。（原句为“极高明而道中庸”。）

Alitto: It's OK. I know. I haven't memorized ancient books but I know this sentence. These enlightened ones understand and are conscious of the truth. It's all one truth, right? It's one standard for all value judgments. That is to say, no matter where the enlightened ones are from, their conscious truth is the same.

Liang: We should say that there is only one absolute truth, but I usually say that there is a "material physical truth" and "a human truth." The reason used in natural sciences and social sciences, especially the former, is this material physical truth. This truth exists objectively, and does not follow man's will. It doesn't make any difference whether you like this truth or not, it still is ever there. The other kind of truth, "human truth," exists subjectively. When encountering this kind of truth, everyone nods his head, and says "Right" or "Yes." This truth (or reason) has some element of subjectivity. When encountering this kind of truth, people have a favorable impression of it, and are well disposed toward it. Let's say it is a matter of justice, for example. A person will say that he has "a sense of what is right." Justice resides in a sense of what is right. So in my final analysis, there are two truths—a physical truth and a human truth.

Master Zhu (Zhu Xi) of the Song Dynasty never made a distinction between these two truths. He had a paragragh, which I cannot recite. Anyway, he never separated these two kinds of truth or reason. I can give you another example, concerning biological evolution. That is, in natural selection, the weak are eaten by the strong. This is a phenomenon that has an objective existence, a truth or a reason of the natural world. But we humans all dislike and oppose it. We feel that...

Alitto: Do you mean that people, no matter when they live or what place they are from, all dislike it? This "we" is in reference to humankind, no matter where one is from?

Liang: In what stands to reason with humans, the phenomenon of the weak being oppressed, being bullied gives a feeling of unfairness to the onlooker, and the onlooker does not like it. This feeling of dislike is reason, a kind of human truth. The strong eating the weak has an objective existence and that objective existence is material physical truth.[49]

艾： 这没有关系，我知道，我也没有背过古书，我知道这句话。这些高明的人，所了解、所意识的真理，都是一个真理，对不对？都是一个价值判断的标准。就是说，无论是什么地方的高明的人、超众的人，所意识的真理是一致的。

梁： 应当说真理只有一个，不过普通我总是说，有一种是"物理"，有一种是"情理"。这个科学——自然科学、社会科学，特别是自然科学，自然科学所发明、所讲出来的道理就叫"物理"。物理存在于客观，不随着人的意志，不能够说我喜欢它，我不喜欢它，那不成。无论你喜欢不喜欢它，它一定是那样的。可是另外有一种叫"情理"，情理是存于主观的，合于情理，人人都点头，人人都说对、是这样，情理是在主观这一面。合于情理，就好办，比如说是正义的事情，不是有人就说它是"正义感"吗？正义就存于正义感上。这我归结下来，一种叫"物理"，一种叫"情理"，不要把它混了。

从前宋朝朱子——朱熹，他就是没有分开这两个。他有一段话，我也背不上来了，朱子说的，他就没有把这两种理分开。我可以再举一个例子，讲那个生物进化，有自然淘汰，有一句话叫做"弱肉强食"，弱的肉被强的人吃了，弱肉强食是一个客观存在的现象，一个自然之理，可是我们都不喜欢它，对弱肉强食我们都反对，觉得……

艾： 无论是什么时候的、什么地方的人，都不喜欢，是这个意思？"我们"的意思是人类，无论是什么地方的？

梁： 按常情来说，对小的、弱的被欺负，站在旁边，都有一种不平，不喜欢那个样子。这个不喜欢是一个理，这个理有，这个理是个"情理"。那个弱肉强食客观存在，那是个"物理"。

● Western culture, Chinese culture and Indian culture

Alitto: Does the essence of Chinese culture, its core substance, still exist?

Liang: There are still some remnants of Confucian culture. It is, of course, not possible to sweep away all traditional cultural lock, stock and barrel. Something still remains, in the area of family ethics.

Alitto: In your book *The Essence of Chinese Culture*, you mention a definition of the essence of Chinese culture; you defined it as what makes humans human. The early Chinese sages discovered what made humans human prematurely, before the minimal primal material demands of humans were met. Do you still think that what makes humans human is the most important in Chinese culture?

Liang: What, in my view, to my knowledge, is the difference between Chinese culture and Western culture, and Indian culture? It is that Chinese culture knows of human rationality.[50] Chinese culture believes in the human; it does not believe in God, as with Western culture or in Allah as in Islamic culture. Chinese culture is built upon and trusts the human. The distinguishing characteristic of Confucianism is that it relies on, and is built upon humans, not some other being. This is what Mencius later pointed out—that "human nature is good." Confucius himself said no such thing, but Mencius mentioned it specifically. So the distinguishing characteristic of Confucianism is that it believes in, and is confident in, humans. Humans can make mistakes, or sink into degeneracy. But how can you correct the human who makes mistakes? How can you keep him from moral degeneracy, from doing evil? What do you rely on to do this? Aside from the human himself, there is nothing else that is dependable. So I feel that the distinguishing feature of Confucianism is that it has faith in man.

In foreign countries, in Christianity, it is said that Adam ate some fruit. There is such wording? There is such a theory. This is in the West. In India there is something different still. India is very strange indeed.

From ancient times [the tradition of] India was to deny human life, to negate it. It held that human life itself was a mistake. This was the common attitude and convention in ancient India. Were there any exceptions to this attitude? Yes. In Buddhist writing there is the saying "to act in accord with the world, its ways and customs, and with non-Buddhist doctrines." Act in Accord with the World was a non-Buddhist sect, and was held as a heretical, outside path. A lot of other religions, aside from Buddhism, also

• 西方文化、中国文化与印度文化

艾： 中国文化的要义、核心的实质，还存在吗?

梁： 残余的还是有，不能说一扫而光啊，还是有些个遗留。所留下的还就是那个家庭伦理那方面。

艾：《中国文化要义》那本书里，您提到了“中国文化要义”的定义，下了个定义就是“人之所以为人”，说中国的圣人很早以前，物质生活还没有达到可以满足一切起码的要求以前，中国的圣人就了解到“人之所以为人”了。那您还是这么想的，就是说中国文化的最重要的是“人之所以为人”?

梁： 在我的看法、我的认识，就是这个中国文化不同于西洋，不同于印度，在什么地方呢? 就在它认识了人的理性。它相信人，它不相信上帝，也不相信像回教什么真宰、真主。它信赖——依赖、依靠的意思——它信赖人，儒家的特色它是信赖人，不信赖旁的。这个就是后来孟子点出来的“人性善”，“人性善”这个话在孔子倒没有说，可是孟子点明了。这个儒家的一个特色，它是很信赖人。人嘛当然也可能错误，可能也有走入一种下流，可是，你怎么样子能够矫正它，让它不趋于下流、不去为恶呢? 你靠什么呢? 除了靠人，没有别的可靠。我觉得儒家的特色在这个地方。

好像在外国，在基督教，好像是说亚当怎么吃了什么果子，有那个话? 这是在西洋。在印度它也跟中国不相同。印度很奇怪，它是从很古的时候就否定人生，它认为人生就是错误，这个是在古印度普遍的风气。有没有例外呢? 有一个例外，就是在佛书里头所称为“顺世外道”的——顺着来，“世界”的“世”，“顺世外道”——佛家认为是个外道，佛家以外很多旁的宗教，也都排斥它，也认为是外道，它是在古印度

excluded it and considered it cult. This was the one and only affirmation of life in ancient Indian thought. Aside from this, all others held that human life was bafflement. The ancient traditions of India were quite different from everywhere else. This is very strange.

Alitto: What is the greatest threat to Chinese culture, in the present situation?

Liang: I think that there is no threat. Even if some of the old customs, practices and usages are now destroyed, I think that the future is bright (for Chinese culture). Sixty years ago in the last chapter of my book *Eastern and Western Cultures and Their Philosophies,* I said that the future culture of the world would be a revived Chinese culture. I am explicitly not pessimistic about the future of Chinese culture.

Alitto: Mr. Liang, you still hold that the future world culture will be...

Liang: A revival of Chinese culture.

Alitto: Why did I ask? Because in *Eastern and Western Cultures and Their Philosophies*, you made this kind of prediction, but in your books written after that, you seldom mention this. You have just said that those old social customs and habits no longer exist. (Liang: They were undermined.) In that case, what in Chinese traditional culture must be preserved? What things?

Liang: Of course I want to answer this question. I want to explain why I'm so optimistic about the future of Chinese culture. Very early I made an analysis of human life, and concluded that it had three great problems.[51] The first is the problem of humans versus the natural world. This is the first and foremost problem. Before humankind had created cultures and civilizations, humans suffered from floods, wild animals, earthquakes, and so on. So later Western culture developed. The development of Western culture can be encapsulated in two phrases: the conquest of nature and the utilization of nature. It adopts an attitude of conquest toward nature, an attitude of utilization. In this Western culture has always been very successful, right down to the present. Its successes continue to be higher and higher through time. It can now go into space and circle the earth; it can go to the moon. In its conquest and utilization of nature, Western culture has achieved great victories. This is a characteristic of Western culture. It is a problem of man versus matter [nature]. As soon as man opened his eyes and looked around, what he saw was matter. He extended

唯一无二的肯定人生的。除它以外，都认为人生是一种迷惑，这是印度的古风气，跟旁的地方很不同，这很奇怪。

艾：在现在的情况来看，对中国文化最大的威胁，您认为是什么？

梁：我看没有什么威胁。近来尽管有点对旧的风俗习惯有些个破坏，但是前途并不悲观。我不是在 60 年前有一本书《东西文化及其哲学》？那个书里头的末一章我就说：在世界未来，将是中国文化的复兴。所以我刚好不悲观。

艾：那，梁先生，您还是认为将来世界文化，还是……

梁：中国文化复兴。

艾：我为什么问呢？因为您《东西文化及其哲学》这本书是有这种预测，可是后来写的书，很少提到未来的事，那未来的事嘛，您刚提到这些旧的风俗习惯已经没有了，（梁：被破坏了。）那么中国传统文化必须保留的，是哪一些？是什么？

梁：这个问题当然要答了。我要说明为什么我对未来那样乐观。就是我在过去，很早有一个分析，这个分析就说是人生有三大问题。第一个大问题就是人对大自然界的这个问题，这个是第一个问题，这个是最先的问题。人类还没有创造出来文化、文明的时候，非常地受大自然的洪水、猛兽、地震种种的压迫，所以后来有西洋文化的发达起来。西洋文化的发达，主要是两句话，就是“征服自然，利用自然”。对大自然界，它取一个征服的态度、利用的态度，并且很成功，一直到现在还是成功的时候，成功越来越高了，它可以跑到天空上去围着地球转，可以到月亮上去。它是在这个问题上，在征服自然、利用自然上取得了伟大的成功、胜利。这是西洋文化的特色。这个呢，我就说是人对物的问题。人一睁开眼睛看见的，那就是物，都是

his hand and what he touched was matter, what he was standing on was matter. So, man versus matter was the first problem encountered by man, and Western culture solved this problem. Aren't the solutions to this problem highly developed?

Following on this path, I think that it is quite natural that human society should advance into socialism; capitalism will evolve into socialism. The so-called capitalism is a society in which the individual is the basic unit. Capitalism can be encapsulated into eight characters: *gerenbenwei, ziwozhongxin* (Individual based Egocentrism, and Self Centeredness). These characterize European and American modern societies. It is obvious that these societies (all human societies) will undergo a transformation to socialism in the future. Socialism is unavoidable. Capitalism will become a relic of the past. That is to say, the means of production and the materials of production definitely will be publicly owned. At present property is nominally individually owned. In fact, the economic production of a society is the whole society's production, not just the big capitalists'. Later society will become socialistic. This is inevitable. Society based on the individual as the unit will become based on society as the unit. When this has taken place, man comes to confront what I call the second problem, the problem of man versus man. That is, how to make it so that men can get along together, live in peace together. To do this, the relationship between man and man must be straightened out. That is, create a situation whereby I show consideration for you, and you show consideration for me. An old Chinese term describing this is "to give precedence to the other out of courtesy" (*lirang*), and "to govern a state with courtesy" (*lirangweiguo*). At that time, the problem of man versus man will become the primary one, while the problem of man versus nature will not have totally disappeared, but it will have receded to second place in importance.

...That is to say, science and industry will continue to advance, but the major problem will be the problem of man versus man. This is the way in the future. In the future, when this problem must be solved, that will be the time of Chinese culture, because Chinese culture is based on the family. The old term for this is "filial piety and fraternal duty": the father is benevolent and the child is filial. I only use four words: *xiao* (filial piety), *ti* (fraternal duty), *ci* (kindness), and *he* (peace-harmony). So, in my

物，人伸手一摸的，都是物，脚踩的也是物，所以人对物的问题是第一个问题，头一个问题，而西洋文化就是在这个问题上的胜利。这个问题，到现在不是已经达到很高的程度了吗?

再往前走，顺着这个路再往前走，我认为很自然地要走入社会主义，资本主义要转入社会主义。所谓资本主义就是个人本位的主义，可以说八个字："个人本位，自我中心"，我自己，以自我为中心。"个人本位，自我中心"，这八个字就是说的近代的欧美社会。可是它底下走到后来，它要转变，要转变到社会主义，社会主义不可避免，资本主义要成为过去。这个就是说生产工具或者生产资料一定要归公，现在名义上是归个人、大资本家，而事实上社会的生产已经是社会性的生产，底下它要转入社会主义，这个是不可避免的。那么，个人本位变为社会本位，以社会为本位。到了社会本位，人生问题就转入了第二问题。刚才说第一个问题是人对自然的问题、人对物的问题，第二个问题就是人对人的问题，就是人对人怎么样子能够彼此相安、彼此处得很好。要把人与人的关系搞好，就得你照顾我、我照顾你，中国老话叫做"礼让"，"礼让为国"。总而言之吧，人跟人彼此相安相处，处得很好，在这个时候成为头一个问题；人对自然的问题，退居第二位，不是没有了，不过退居第二位。

也就是说自然科学、工业还是要进步的，不过人对物的问题不是头一个问题了，它是退居到第二个问题。第一个问题是人与人怎么样子彼此相安、共处，这个是未来的，未来的事情要这个样子，这个样子就是到了"中国文化"，这个就是中国文化。中国文化原来是起于家庭，老话嘛就是孝悌，或者说是父慈子孝，或者说四个字，四个字是什么呢？它就是"孝悌慈和"。孝、悌、慈，还有一个字叫"和"——"和"就是和平、

view, when human society reaches the stage of socialism, then probably all people will have to strive for filial piety, fraternal duty, kindness and peace-harmony, to strive for respect for age, for treating children and the young with kindness, for harmony and good relations between brothers, and so go create good relations generally throughout society. This is the problem that takes place within a socialist society. Again, I say, at this stage the problem of man versus nature still exists, but is in second place, not the most pressing problem. And so this stage I call the revival of Chinese culture.

I do want to say more about this now. After the revival of Chinese culture will come the revival of Indian culture. I estimate, just off the cuff, that this revival of Chinese culture will probably last a very long time. Probably humanity will be in this kind of atmosphere and circumstances—this kind of customs, conventions, and social practices—for a long time. But society will still change; it won't be forever this way. It will change and transform, in my view, into a revival of Indian culture.

What was ancient Indian culture like? What would it look like? I just inadvertently mentioned "acting in accord with the world, its ways and customs, and with non-buddhist doctrines." That is, that particular sect affirmed human life. Its influence was quite small. Broader ancient Indian society, however, denied life, saying that human life had no value, even to the extent that life was deluding and confusing. Human life takes place in delusion and confusion. This attitude was common in ancient India, aside from the one small sect that I mentioned before. There were many religions in India aside from Buddhism, which arose later. Buddhism was not the earliest school of thought in India. Yet Buddhism pushed these attitudes of negation to their natural conclusion most completely. So, in my view, in the far distant future of mankind, this attitude and atmosphere of ancient India will arise. People will feel that their own life has no value. In Buddhist terms, the person will want to seek release or deliverance or liberation from worldly cares (*mukti*). This is the ultimate liberation. So, the above is my own deduction, my own logic.

Alitto: Actually, this reckoning is similar to that expressed in *Eastern and Western Cultures and Their Philosophies*. I myself am persuaded by your theory. According to logical inference of developments in the future, it should be like this. But I still have a theory. I think that this process of modernization, or you could say the process of rationalization, is in conflict with, in contradiction with "what makes humans human"—

和好、很和气。我这么看，我这么推想，到了社会主义，恐怕就要大家都来讲究孝悌慈和，推讲敬老啦、抚幼啦、兄弟和好啦，把人与人之间的关系搞好，这是未来社会主义里头的问题。自然，人对自然的问题还是有，可是退居第二位了。这个我就谓之"中国文化复兴"。

那么还要再多说一点，就是中国文化复兴之后，将是印度文化的复兴。中国文化复兴，我这么遐想吧，随便说吧，会要很长，时间恐怕很长，恐怕有……人类要在这种空气中、在这种习俗中、风俗中，可能时间很长。时间很长之后，它还是会变的，不会永远是一个样子，它会变，会转变，转变出来的，依我看就是印度古文化的复兴。

那么印度古文化是什么文化？什么样子呢？刚才无意中说了一下，就是在古印度除了顺世外道它肯定人生——那一派势力很小，广大的印度古社会都是否定人生，说人生没有价值，它甚至于说人生是迷妄——"迷"就是糊涂，"妄"就是"狂妄"的"妄"，人生是在迷妄中。这些是古印度的普遍的风气，除了顺世外道之外，印度宗派很多，并且佛教还是后起，佛教在印度不是最早的，佛教否定人生算是最到家了吧。所以我的推想，人类很远的未来，古印度的这种风气就来了。人对于自己的生命、生活，感觉到没什么价值……还要按着佛家的意思解脱、解放。人嘛，就是常常地在求解放，这个就是最后的解放。这是我的这么一种推想，我的一种逻辑。

艾： 其实您的这个推想，跟当年《东西文化及其哲学》那本书，所表示的差不多了。我自己还是信服您这个说法是对的，按逻辑推出将来的发展，是应该如此。不过我还有一个想法，我觉得现代化这个过程，或者说是理智化这个过程，跟"人之所以为

be it the "human" in Indian culture or in Chinese culture. Does the present Four Modernizations Movement hold any harm for Chinese culture?

Liang: China exists in this present world, and cannot go against the current. It can only advance forward and develop material culture, which is necessary. But the important thing is that in the past, the development of Western material culture was based upon capitalism. Ever since the overwhelming power of the West reached China, China has had no opportunity to develop capitalism. So China had to take the socialist road. It could only seek individual welfare within the context of the welfare of the whole society. It could not allow the welfare of the individual to prevail over that of society. So the appearance and success of the Communist Party in China is very reasonable, and not peculiar or strange at all.

Alitto: In the future, Western culture and Western society will evolve into [the way of] China. In the present phase of history, what should Western society learn from the East, from China?

Liang: A human being, immediately upon being born, is related to other humans. At the least, he is related to his parents, and siblings. As he grows up, he has friends, teachers and so on. These relationships are called *renlun* (human ethical relationships) in Chinese. Human beings always live in the interpersonal relationships. One cannot be detached from other people, so how to foster the relationships becomes a major question. And those relationships, as the Chinese old term goes, are called *renlun*.

The distinguishing feature of Chinese culture lies in this. Chinese culture puts importance on human relationships. It expands the familial relationships into broader society beyond the family. For example, a teacher is called "teacher-father" (*shifu*), a schoolmate is called a "school brother" (*shixiongdi*). In ways like this, a person always has the close, family-like, intimate feelings. Applying such relationships to society, it seems to bring distant people closer together, to bring outsiders inside. This is the distinguishing feature of China and Chinese culture. To put this feature into a few words, it is the opposite of the individual-centered, egocentric way. What is that, then? The essence of the matter is mutually to value and respect the other party.

人"，就是无论是印度文化或是中国文化的"人"，是有冲突的、有矛盾的。您觉得四个现代化这个计划对中国文化有无什么害处?

梁：中国生活在现在的世界上，它不能够违反潮流，它只能往前走，把物质文明发达起来，那是需要的。不过要紧的就是，过去的西洋物质文明发达是靠资本主义发达起来的，中国是自从西洋强大的势力过来，中国已经没有走资本主义的路的余地了，不可能走资本主义，所以它不能不走社会主义的道路。只能在谋社会福利的里边，有了个人的福利，不能让个人的福利压倒社会福利，不可能。所以共产党在中国的出现并且成功，那是很合理的，不特别、不奇怪的。

艾：将来西方文化、西方的社会还是演变成中国，以现在历史阶段来说，西方社会应该向东方、应该向中国学习一些什么?

梁：人啊，一生下来就有与他相关系的人，至少他要有父母，或者还有兄弟，长大了之后到社会上还要有朋友、有老师、有什么，这个就叫做人伦，叫做伦理。人始终要在与人相关系中生活，人不能脱离人而生活，人不能离开人而生活。所以怎么把人与人的关系搞好，是个重要的问题，这个叫做伦理、人伦，中国古话叫人伦。

中国文化的特色在这个地方，中国文化的特色就是重视人与人的关系，它把家庭关系推广用到家庭以外去，比如说它管老师叫师父，管同学叫师兄弟，如此之类。它总是把家庭那种彼此亲密的味道，应用到社会上去，好像把那个离得远的人也要拉近，把外边的人归到里头来，这个就是中国的特色，中国文化的特色。这个特色一句话说，它跟那个"个人本位，自我中心"相反。那么它是怎么样子呢? 它是互以对方为重。

For example, since Confucius in *The Analects* liked to talk about filial piety and fraternal duty, we should ask what they are. They are respect for and obedience to the older generation on the part of the young. There is also the virtue of kindness, which means affection and kindness for the younger generation on the part of the older generation. So, to sum up in a word, these virtues are mutual respect. For example, a guest arrives. The host shows respect for the guest. In all things, the host thinks of and is considerate to the guest. The best seat is given to the guest. Tea is made for the guest. Now, a good guest will also turn this around, and respect his host. He will take the host into consideration in everything. And so, in Chinese society there exists the custom of *lirang*. What is this *lirang*? *Rang* is regarding the other person as important. *Li* is to respect the other. China, under Confucian influence, has always told people to respect others. Afterwards, when capitalism has passed away, and socialism has arrived, probably this *lirang* as a social convention will also arrive [on a worldwide scale]. With everyone living together, mutual respect is very important. So, that's why I say that the future of the world will be a revival of Chinese culture. I will say, in conclusion, that I have always felt that Marxism is quite good. It is superior to Utopian (Fantasy) Socialism. Owen of England, and Fourier. There were three men. Utopian Socialists. Their hearts were in the right place, but they didn't understand that the natural development of society and history would produce socialism. So Marxism is called Scientific Socialism, which means that objective development of history will be in that direction.

● Development is always good.

Alitto: Can humans have a life without disputes and fighting? How do you think we can decrease disputes and fighting?

Liang: Disputes and fighting are facts of the biological world. Not only is humanity like this. In speaking of the struggle for survival, isn't there the saying that "the bigger fish eat the smaller fish"? Dog eats dog. So, this is an undeniable fact. Everyone in the biological world can be seen engaged in these kinds of mutual struggle, murder, and fights to the death. But humanity should be more elevated than animals, and in fact, it already is. This is one aspect of humanity. There is another aspect that

比如说，中国人从孔子、从古书《论语》上，它老是爱讲"孝悌"，孝悌是什么？是说儿子或者幼辈，对父母、对长辈的尊重、顺从，这就叫孝悌。不是还有个"孝悌慈"吗？什么叫"慈"呢？慈就是父母那边慈爱子女，慈爱幼辈。一句话，归总一句话，就是"互以对方为重"，我以你为重，你以我为重。比如说客人来了，在主人这一面就以客人为重，什么事情都替客人设想，给客人好的位置坐，给客人倒茶喝；一个好的客人又转过来了，又是尊重主人，事事为主人设想。所以中国社会礼俗，刚才提到礼让，什么叫礼让呢？"让"就是看重别人，"礼"就是尊重旁人。中国在儒家一直就是叫人礼让，这个礼让也就是刚才我说的，到了未来，资本主义过去了，社会主义来了，恐怕这个礼让的风气会要来了。大家在一块生活，互相尊重是很必要的，所以我就说，世界的未来是中国文化的复兴。我再说一句话、结束的话，我是乐观的，我觉得那个马克思主义很好，它比那个空想的社会主义高明。欧文啊，英国的欧文、傅立叶，他们有三个人。空想的社会主义，他们的心是很好，不过他们没有想到，没有清楚社会的发展、历史的发展，自然会到那一步，自然会要到社会主义。马克思主义所以叫科学的社会主义，它是认为客观的发展就要走到那里。

- **发展总是好的**

艾：人类是不是可以过没有争执、斗争的生活？您认为怎样才能减少争执、斗争？

梁：争执、斗争是事实，是生物界有的，不单是人类如此。生存竞争，不是有"大鱼吃小鱼"这话吗？弱肉强食，所以这个是一个不可否认的事实，生物界处处可以看出来这种彼此之间的斗争啊、残杀啊、你死我活。不过人类应当高于动物，事实上人类也已经高于这个东西，这是一面。还有一面，就

in the situation of competition, struggle and mutual slaughter, there is already looking after one another, and helping the weak and small. The history of societal development marches forward, ever decreasing mutual estrangement and mutual discrimination [between people]; minds broaden and become generous and tolerant; people look after others. I think that this probably develops through time; it becomes more and more developed through time. The overall trajectory of this development is this way.

When humanity had no culture at all, it led a collective life, but the collectives were not large. Gradually the collective bodies increased in size. At first there were struggles between small collective bodies causing great estrangement and misunderstanding. The more things progressed, the more they evolved, the more they became civilized, the easier it became for people to have emotional communication with one another, and the easier it was for mutual understanding to be enhanced. In the future, in socialism after capitalism, it will probably be even more this way. So in looking at mankind's future, we should be optimistic. What question were we discussing just now?

Alitto: I just asked you if there was any [possibility] of a conflict-free, struggle-free life, and what had to happen before it was possible to decrease disputes and struggles.

Liang: I think that this matter is one of natural development. People's demands are like this; the natural course of development is in this direction. The natural future [course] is in this direction. In the immediate present, wars still can't be avoided, but this is only the present. In the distant future, capitalist society will certainly become a thing of the past. After capitalism comes socialism; it should be socialism. The sight of capitalist society is fixed on production and pursuit of production, but after the transformation into socialist society, production will be always advancing, so people's sight will be fixed on life; it will be fixed on how to live life and on how to have peaceful coexistence; the way to do that is through small collectives. The situation of struggle between small collectives will change. The scope of the collective will be expanded, and simultaneously there won't be that kind of hostility and estrangement between collectives. It seems there was a saying, "one world, one man"—one world, maybe not, but everyone will be in peaceful coexistence. The future definitely will be this way. Because no one would dare

是还是在这个里头，还是在竞争啊、斗争啊、彼此残杀里头，已经能够彼此照顾、帮助弱小，这一面也有，已经有。社会发展史越往前去，这种要减少——彼此的隔阂、歧视要减少，心胸要开阔，照顾旁人。这方面恐怕是要发展，应当是越来越发展，它的趋势是如此。

当人类还没有什么文化的时候，都是集体生活，可是集体不大，慢慢地集体要扩大。起初小集体与小集体彼此斗争，彼此很大的隔阂，不了解。越进步、越进化，越文明，人彼此情感上容易相通，容易增进彼此的了解。将来在资本主义之后出现了社会主义，恐怕更是这样。所以往人类的前途看，应当是乐观的。刚才是我们想谈一个什么问题来的？

艾： 刚才我问的是没有争执、没有斗争的生活，您认为怎么样才能减少争执和斗争？

梁： 我认为这个事情是一个自然的发展，人有这方面的要求，自然的发展也是往这个方向去，自然前途就是往这方面走。就眼前说，战争还是不可避免，然而这是眼前。远的未来，资本主义社会一定要成为过去，资本主义之后的社会呢，就是社会主义，应当是社会主义。资本主义社会人的眼光注意在生产上，追求生产，可是转为社会主义社会之后，生产还是要随时进步，可是人的注意，在怎么样生活，注意生活，注意彼此相安共处。也可以说小集团、集团与集团的斗争，那个情况要变，集团的范围也要放大，同时集团与集团之间也不是那样子仇视、隔阂，恐怕也要变了，过去了。好像有那么一句话，叫“one world，one man”，一个世界，或者没有，大家和平共处，未来一定是那样，

use lethal weapons, everyone will coexist peacefully. Gradually, the prejudices, distinctions and hostilities between races and continents will recede. People will not dare to have destructive wars.

...There are many tragic things. We don't want to look at them, but they will still happen. But I myself say, I think that human history is uninterruptedly developing. It naturally will go ahead and develop, and not stop. Since it will develop naturally with nothing that can obstruct it, at the same time development is good. In development unavoidably there will be destruction; unavoidably there is some great destruction. On one hand, it's unavoidable; on the other, we seek to avoid it. We at least try hard to reduce and to narrow the unavoidable. This is still something that we should strive for. But one need not be pessimistic toward the future. Since things are going to develop in this way anyway, what use is being pessimistic? Things will develop. Development is always good. I think that development is always good.

Alitto: Such statement as "Development is always good" really is the opposite of conservatism. Your "Development is always good" is precisely the diametrical opposite of many conservative points of view.

Liang: Isn't there a term "optimist"?

Alitto: Yes, optimist.

Liang: It seems that I am an optimist.

● Crisis of modernization is not very severe.

Alitto: ...Another definition is more abstract, that is the process of rationalization.[52] That is, all social organizations and processes take efficiency as their standard of value. As the process of modernization proceeds, morality is less and less capable of functioning and serving as a norm because the only norm is efficiency. [All other values are based upon it.] This is also one of the definitions of modernization. There is another definition of modernization that has to do with economic growth and the GNP. But this is more difficult to discuss, because it is in the realm of economics. As I previously discussed with you, I feel my own viewpoint and standpoint are more pessimistic than yours. I myself think that modernization is a process whereby human nature is gradually lost.

因为杀人的武器，大家都不敢用了，大家彼此还是相安共处吧。慢慢地，地球上，不同的种族之间、不同的洲土之间，那种成见、分别、仇视，都退后了，不敢有毁灭性的战争了。

……不少的惨事，我们所不愿意看见的事情，它还是要来，还是要有。不过就我自己说，我是认为人类历史都是在不断发展，它自然地要发展，不会停步的。既然它自然会发展，停不住、拦不住，同时呢，发展就是好，在发展中不可避免地有破坏，不可避免地有些重大的破坏。不可避免是一面，我们求着避免又是一面，总还是要求着避免的，不可避免我们至少力求减少吧、缩小吧，这还是应当努力的。但是不必悲观，对前途不必悲观，既然事实发展要如此，你悲观有什么用呢？事实要发展，发展总是好的，我认为发展总是好的。

艾："发展总是好的"，这样的话，您真是跟保守主义者相反。您（说）"发展总是好的"，跟保守的很多观点正好恰恰相反。

梁：不是有个名词叫"乐天派"？

艾：是啊，乐天派。

梁：我好像是一个乐天派。

• 现代化的危机不会很大

艾：……另外一个定义是比较抽象的，就是理智化的程度，就是一个社会里一切的组织或各种事物、过程，都是以效率为价值判断的准绳。那么现代化的过程中，道德已经越来越不起作用，越来越不是一个准则，因为唯一的准则就是效率。那也是现代化的一种定义。还有一种，是跟经济成长有关系，就是和国民生产总和有关的，不过，这个是比较难讨论的，因为这是经济学方面的。我以前跟您讨论过的，我自己觉得，我的观点、立场比您的悲观一点，我自己认为现代化就是一个逐渐失去人性的一种过程。

Liang: What is modernization?

Alitto: It is a process that makes humanity lose its human nature.

Liang: Oh my!

Alitto: Yesterday and the day before we did speak about this. First, because morality is relativised, the morality of any society, no matter what society, is different from those of other societies; there is no absolute morality. No absolute morality is the equivalent of no morality, because morality has been relativised. During these past three hundred years in the West, moral norms have been disappearing. The only norm is efficiency. Or, as far as an individual life is concerned, the demands that emanate from corporeal needs: these are the demands that are common to all societies. The only shared universal aspects are those that emanate from their corporeal needs. On the other hand, shared moral standards are disappearing.

Of course, the historical background of Chinese society is different. Throughout history, the Chinese governmental and moral authorities have often been integrated, Buddhism included... The most recent European, American and Japanese societies can also prove this. They will continue to pay a price for modernization. This price is part of a human's nature. No advancement comes without a price. All of the conveniences of material life, the capacities for high efficiency, control, and the conquest of nature also bring with them some disadvantages. In general terms, it is moral loss. Let's take the family as an example. The concept of family in the West has become weaker and weaker, more and more... If kin relations are one kind of moral relationship, then this kind of relationship has become weaker and weaker through time.

The only relationship left is that of the society's fundamental unit, the individual—the individual and the state, the individual and government. This kind of process is not limited to Europe and America. You can also see it in Japan. Many parts of Japan's original culture have already died out, or soon will... For example, traditional Japanese theatre is called

"*Neng*" (Noh). It still exists, but it exists because the state protects it. *Neng* has become "museumified"; it is no longer alive. So, although there are many things that still seem to live, they have already been made into "museum pieces."[53] Now, the Chinese developmental path is different because of its unique position in history as a culture that has continuously existed for over four thousand years. This is something that exists only

梁：现代化是什么?

艾：现代化是一种使人类失去他们本性的过程。

梁：哎哟!

艾：我们昨天、前天谈到一些道理，第一，道德因为都是相对化的，所有无论什么社会的道德啊，都与别的社会不同，没有绝对的道德了。那没有绝对的道德嘛，那是等于没有道德了，因为是相对化了。所以这 300 年来在西洋啊，这个道德的准则，越来越没有的，唯一的准则、唯一的就是效率。或者以个人的生活来说呢，身体所发出来的要求，那是我们人类无论什么社会共有的要求，别的道德方面的，不是共同有的标准，那就越来越没有了。

当然中国的社会历史背景不同，中国政教常常是合一的，佛教包括……。看最近欧美、日本的社会也可以证明这个道理。他们讲现代化的目的还要继续付出代价，这个代价就是人的本性的一部分。没有一个利不带一个弊，所有现代化的物质生活的方便、高效率，控制、征服自然的能力，也带来一些弊，笼统地说是道德上的损失。具体地来说吧，拿家庭来说，西洋的家庭组织啊，好像观念越来越淡啊，越来越……，假如说亲情关系是道德关系的一种，那这种关系就越来越淡了。

而唯一的关系就是社会的基本单位是个人，个人跟国家、个人跟政府。那这种过程呢，不限于在欧美，连在日本也看得出来。日本的固有文化的许多部分也是已经被淘汰了，甚至于快要……比如，日本传统的戏叫做“能”，有还是有，还存在，不过那是因为国家要保护它，是博物馆里面的一个东西，不是活的。所以虽然许多东西表面上还存在，不过已经是放在博物馆里面看的。那中国发展的路程好像不同，因为它历史上独特的地方，是历史这么悠久，文化一直四千多年，那是只有中国

in China. My pessimistic view is that China will follow other countries. In the course of time, there will come a time when it too will pay the price for modernization. What is your reaction to what I have said?

Liang: As you know, I'm comparatively optimistic. I feel that the changes will not be great. If you say there will be change, or destruction, then the change and destruction started long before. It started since the end of the Qing Dynasty, even more so in Beijing after Chairman Mao's founding of the nation. I'll give an example. Before, it was Old China. It liked and maintained the extended family. If the grandfather was still alive, the grandchildren could not start their own households. If one did, everyone would sneer at them. They would be lacking in decorum if they acted that way. But now everything is fragmented. Now it's changed into the nuclear family. There is no more extended family. Everyone sets up their own households and lives by himself or herself. Before, dividing into separate households included dividing the property. Now the importance of property in New China has reduced greatly. No one has great family property. But everyone can have a salary, especially women who previously willingly stayed at home. Now female comrades are able to participate in society and are able to come out and work, and have their own income. This is a very great change.

Alitto: If one projects this process into the future, then there may be no family, even to the extent that, as I talked about yesterday, the child will not be born of parents, but be born in a factory-like setting using technology. Of course it is not possible now to reach that point, but by logical inference, even if an individual... To put it another way, at present Europe and America—I think, I'm not too clear about the Soviet Union and Eastern Europe—are post-modern societies. The only rules that people respect are the legal ones. We are now in a society that pays attention to law and individual rights. People act solely in their individual self interest, the result of which is that the entire society is fractured. There is no ethical bond between people.

My own opinion—and the one in the book—is that the rural reconstruction plan, which was used even by Mao during the War of Resistance in Yan'an, was aimed partly at preserving morality, and partly at modernization. The situation could be seen as "having one's cake and eating it too"—one keeps the advantages while discarding

有这种情况啊。我悲观的就是，中国跟着别的国家走，久而久之，总有一个时候要付出现代化的代价。不知道您对我这些话有什么反应？

梁：如你所知道的，我是比较乐观。我觉得变化不会很大。如果说是变化，或者说是破坏，早已开始破坏了，早已变化了，从清朝末年已经变化了。在毛主席建国以后的北京，都更加变化。举一个例说，从前都是老中国，喜欢大家庭，保持大家庭，如果祖父在，儿孙都不能分家各自过。如果各自过，那是很遭到大家诽笑的，这样子好像很缺乏礼仪吧。可是现在统统分了，现在都变成小家庭了，没有大家庭了，都是各自过日子，都是分家。从前呢，分家包含分财产，现在新的中国财产的重要性降得很低很低了，谁也没有很大的家财，可是谁也都能够有工资。特别是妇女从前自愿在家庭里头，现在女同志也能够参加社会，能够出来做工，自己有收入，这个变化就很大。

艾：那么这个过程推论到未来，那就不会有家庭了，甚至于昨天讲的这孩子也不是父母生的，是用一种技术在工厂样子的一个地方生的。到那个地步，那当然现在还不可能了，按照逻辑来推论啊，即使个人……换一个说法，现在在欧美，我想苏联、东欧我也还不大清楚，就是现代化以后的社会，人唯一的尊敬的规则，就是法律的规则。现在是讲法律的社会，讲个人权利，那人就是专门为了个人的自私的利益而行动，讲到结果整个一个社会分裂了，没有人跟人之间的一种伦理。

我自己的看法，我这本书里也是这么写，您乡村建设的计划，连毛主席原来抗战的时候、延安的那个时代所用的计划吧，以后还有……就是说也有保存道德的那部分，也有现代化。就是说两者同时，就是"利"要，而"弊"要避免掉，

the disadvantages. Those bad parts would be avoided. The disastrous results that came about by modernization in other societies were to be avoided. The advantages, the good parts were to be retained. That is to say, I myself feel that there is a contradiction involved. One cannot have one's cake and eat it too [getting the good results while avoiding the bad results]. In my view, your plan in the old days, and Mao's own, could be said to have tried to have the cake and eat it too. It tried to avoid the disastrous results of European and American modernization while retaining its advantages. Do you feel that this is possible at present, to have one's cake and eat it too?

Liang: I think it is relatively possible. Assuming that China can be said to have national character and national spirit, the Chinese will still be the Chinese. Even though modernization has already produced great change or great destruction, China will still retain the spirit and flavor of the Chinese people.

Alitto: If we suppose that there is only one standard—efficiency, and all societies are organized for efficiency, no matter which society, e.g., American society, each society in different countries will become increasingly similar. This will happen because efficiency is an objective standard while spirit is a subjective standard. The Tokyo of one hundred years ago and the New York of one hundred years ago were very different. Today's Tokyo and today's New York are quite similar. So, your feeling that Chinese can preserve their original spirit is optimistic.

Liang: As I just said, if a great many Chinese customs and usages and etiquette have been destroyed, they were destroyed long before. Comparing the end of the Qing Dynasty with the early years of the Republic, there had already been a great change. Now there is even more change, and even more destruction. But no matter what destruction, the Chinese are still Chinese. China still has Chinese flavors, Chinese customs and Chinese habits.

Alitto: How can these customs, habits and flavors be preserved?

Liang: Let's put it this way. That they can't be preserved is because from very early on they couldn't be preserved; this is not a phenomenon of the present. But if you mention preservation, what has been preserved has been preserved straight through to the present.

Alitto: So, don't you think that modernization causes people's good nature to disappear, that is, it makes relations between people obdurate and cold? Don't you think that people's desires run wild and morality becomes bankrupt because of the processes that modernization brings with it?

坏的要避免，别的地方的现代化的恶果要避免的，利益还是好处呢，还是要。就是说，我自己觉得这个矛盾啊，不能两者兼得。您的看法，您当年的计划，毛主席自己的，也可以说是两者兼得了，要避免欧美现代化的恶果，而要欧美现代化的好处。现在呢，您觉得还可能吧，还可以两者兼得，就是避免坏处而得到好处啊?

梁： 我想，相对地说是可能的。中国假定能够说有民族性、民族精神，中国人还是中国人，尽管说，他已经变化很大，或者是破坏很大，但是还是有他中国人的精神、中国人的气味。

艾： 假如说，只有一个标准——效率，所有的社会的一切都是为效率而组织的，那么无论什么社会，美国的社会，每一个国家的社会，会越来越一样。因为这个是客观的标准啊，精神是主观的东西，气概是主观的。100 年前的东京，跟 100 年前的纽约很不同，现在的东京和现在的纽约很相同，那您觉得中国人还是能保存原来有的精神，那是乐观的。

梁： 刚才我说过的话，如果说是有许多中国的礼俗、风俗已经破坏，那是早已经破坏了，拿民国初年跟清末比，已经都变化了，现在更变化了，更破坏了。可是尽管破坏，中国人还是中国人，他还有一种中国人的气味吧，中国人的风俗习惯。

艾： 这个风俗习惯、气味啊，怎么能保存呢?

梁： 这样子说，讲不能保存是早已不保存了，并不是今天。可是讲到保存的时候，一直到今天也还是在保存中。

艾： 那您不认为现代化会使人的善良性逐渐地消失了，就是使人与人的关系冷酷无情起来了? 也不觉得人的欲望横流，道德破产了，就是现代化也不一定会带来这一过程?

Liang: As I just said, if it brings on [such costs], it's not just today. It's been bringing these for a long time now. But no matter how much inevitable damage, there is still something not damaged. Even if these things will change in the future, these changes cannot necessarily be called destructive.

Alitto: The mechanization of human life, naturally aside from its conveniences, such as the mechanization of agriculture and technology, has caused people to become half machine, to live in an unbalanced manner. Can this be considered a crisis of modernization?

Liang: A crisis.

Alitto: Oh, you admit this?

Liang: Of course I admit this.

Alitto: So what is the best way of avoiding it? What way is there to avoid these disastrous results?

Liang: Perhaps the state will pay attention to it in education. This education does not necessarily mean formal schooling. Of course schools are included in the education I mentioned. For instance, in primary school, teaching students to be polite, how to help people, how to take care of one another...

Alitto: You feel that the power of education is great?

Liang: Of course, especially primary school education. Education is very useful.

Alitto: Suppose there was a person who, from the time he was small, felt that his life, his everything was for his own sake, not for the group (no matter what kind of group), but for his individual benefit, how would you persuade him to [act] for the benefit of the group...

Liang: Persuasion is not the way.

Alitto: Then what method should we use?

Liang: Persuasion is no good. The way lies in inculcating [good habits and civilized behavior].

● My opinion of Women's Liberation Movement

Alitto: What opinion do you have of the Women's Liberation Movement in the West?

梁： 刚才我已经说过了，如果是带来，已经不是今天的事情了，带来很久了。可是尽管受到一定破坏，但是还是有没有破坏的地方。就是这些点将来有变动，也不一定就叫做破坏。

艾： 那人类的生活的机械化——就是说当然方便的地方以外，农业机械化，技术机械化——我说的是人好像变成半个机械或者活得畸形的样子，这个算不算现代化的一个危险?

梁： 危机。

艾： 哦，您还承认?

梁： 当然我承认。

艾： 那么最好的避免办法是什么? 避免这个恶果的办法是什么?

梁： 或者是国家从教育方面来注意。而所谓教育不一定是学校教育，当然学校也包含在我说的教育里头。比如在小学校里头，对小学生，要他们怎么样子有礼貌啦，怎么样子帮助人啦，怎么样子互相爱护啦……

艾： 您觉得教育的力量还是很大的?

梁： 那当然。特别在小学里头，教育是很有用。

艾： 那假如有一个人，从小就觉得我的生活、我的一切就是为了我自己，不是为了团体，无论什么团体，就是以我个人的利益，您怎么说服他为了团体而……

梁： 办法不在说服……

艾： 那用什么办法?

梁： 办法不是在说服，办法还是在养成。

• 对妇女解放运动的见解

艾： 您对西方的妇女解放运动有没有高见啊?

Liang: I had a foreign friend. His [Chinese] name was Wei Xiqin (Wei Zhong) [Alfred Westharp]. He spoke insightfully on men and women being different. Naturally, this is to say that Heaven gave women the duty, or you could say, the mission, the important one, to bear children. In a woman's life it is the period in the middle when she can bear children. She can't [bear children] too early or too late, when old. When it is too early, a woman is not yet very womanlike. When too old, she is also not very womanlike. In any case, it is in that period in the middle of her life that she is a real woman. In this phase, Heaven has given her the responsibility, the mission, to bear children. This mission lies in the body, not in the brain. A man's mission lies in the brain. So to perform work according to nature is correct. Going against nature and forcing things is not good. So Westharp's argument was that doing scholarship, or even going so far as to be a politician or a military expert, was not suitable [for women]. But possibly being an artist was still suitable. This was his opinion. I agree with him.

It seems that there had been a famous German philosopher—his name was [in Chinese] Shubenhua [Schopenhauer]. He said: What are females? What are women? Women are big children, that is, they are children but they aren't very small children. Big Children. Women are likely to form a group. For example, at a big meeting, the women would get together to talk with one another. The men naturally also gather together into groups, but many will be by themselves. Go to a large meeting and you would see this situation. Women sit together in a group, and speak with one another very happily. In Beijing speech, unlike the men who are able to "keep cool," [women] are a bit flighty. This is all to say that male and female dispositions are different. The importance of this is as I just said, it seems that naturally Heaven gave males the mission to create—no matter academic or political creation, even the creation of military command in combat—it's all creation. This kind of creation should fall to men. Do not look to have this kind of creation fall to women. Because a woman has her assignment; she has her Heaven-given mission. I actually agree with these remarks of Westharp's.[54]

Alitto: Have you changed your notions from what you and Westharp said on the question in the 1920s?

梁： 我有一个外国朋友，他自己叫做卫中——卫西琴，他很深刻地讲男女的不同。自然，也就说是天吧，天给妇女的一个任务或者说是使命，是生孩子，主要的，在妇女的一生中，就是中间的阶段——能够生育的那个阶段，太早了不算，太晚了、老了也不算。太早的时候还不是一个很像女人的女人，太老了也不像一个很像女人的女人，正是中间那一段她是一个真正的女人，这个阶段天给她的责任、任务，是生孩子。她的任务在身体上，不是在头脑，男子的任务是在头脑，所以按照自然的也就是天然的来办、来做事情，才是对的，不按照天然的，勉强地，不大好。所以他——卫西琴，论调是说关于做学问，乃至于或者做政治家、做军事家，（女人）都不合适，不过也可能做艺术家还可以，这是他的见解。我很同意他的见解。

好像是从前有一个有名的哲学家，德国人，叫叔本华，他说过，女子是什么呢？妇女是什么呢？妇女是一个大孩子，是个小孩，可是不是年纪很小的，是个大孩子。妇女跟妇女容易到一块儿，比如一个大的会场，妇女跟妇女就凑在一堆，大家交谈，男人自然也有成堆的，可是有很多是散开的。你到一个大的会场上一看，有这种情况。妇女坐在一起成一个堆，讲话，讲得很高兴，有一个情况，按北京话吧，不像男人那样能够沉住气，有点浮动。这都是说妇女跟男人性格不一样，重要的是像刚才说的话，好像自然、天给男人的任务是创造，无论是学术上的创造或是政治上的创造，乃至军事上指挥作战的创造，都是创造，这种创造都是应当归于男人的。不要把这种创造指望于妇女，因为妇女她有她的任务，她有她的使命，天给她的使命。卫西琴这个话我倒觉得很同意、很承认。

艾： 20 年代，您跟卫先生讲过这个问题，到现在您的观念都没有改变吗？

Liang: As far as my views on the differentiation between men and women are concerned, they are still the same.

Alitto: I don't know, but possibly you don't know about Women's Liberation Movement, especially in the U.S. Europe has it too. The movement demands equal rights for men and women; in the U.S., females even have special treatment. In seeking employment, females should have special treatment. Some have discussed women are already following military careers—but we are presently debating the question whether they should be in combat. Even some of the more radical women's liberationists say that females should not have dealings with males, should not marry them, should not have sexual relations with them; only women together with women are right. It sounds quite strange, especially to a Chinese. First, have you heard about the U.S. Women's Liberation Movement? Second, what is your reaction to or opinion of it?

Liang: I actually agree with the opinions of my foreign friend Westharp that I just mentioned. That friend had also said, "Foreign, especially Western, women are man-like. Chinese men are woman-like."

Alitto: Do you think that this is correct?

Liang: This is a fact. It is this way factually. Is it correct? I think that there is some truth in it. Foreign women are a bit man-like. Moreover, it seems that they are not only already man-like, but in addition, they strive to be men.

● My views of U.S. and U.S.S.R.

Alitto: I have two more questions. Are the present socialist countries based on society in actuality? The violence practiced in socialist countries—Eastern Europe, Cuba, the U.S.S.R., or Cambodia. In Cambodia, for example, millions were killed. Is this an example of mutual respect?

Liang: Of course not. In Russia, it did not evolve naturally because Russia did not have that much of a capitalist stage. Under the Czars there was not that much development of capitalism. Then, suddenly, there was socialism. They did not develop as a capitalist society to the natural terminus, and then move to socialism.[55]

梁：对男女分别的看法，还是那样。

艾：我不知道，可能您不清楚美国，尤其是美国，欧洲也有，妇女解放啊，要求男女平权，甚至于现在在美国，女子无论是什么事情都有优待，找事，女子有优待。有人在讨论女子已经从军了，不过我们正在辩论的是，是不是应该做战士？……甚至于一些妇女解放运动比较激烈的，说我们女子根本不要与男子来往，不要跟他们结婚，不要跟他们有性方面的关系，我们女子跟女子在一起才对。听起来，尤其是中国人，很奇怪啊。第一，您有没有听说美国妇女解放运动情况？第二呢您对此有什么反应、意见？

梁：我倒是同意刚才那个外国朋友卫西琴的见解。那个朋友就说过这样的话，他说：外国人特别是西洋人，外国的女人像男人，中国的男人像女人。

艾：那您以为这个有道理吗？

梁：这是说事实，事实上这样。对不对呢？我觉得说得有几分对。外国的女人呢，有点像男人，并且她好像还要不单已经像男人，而且还要争取做男人。

• 我对美苏的看法

艾：我还是有两个问题：现在的社会主义国家社会会不会是社会本位的？事实上是如此吗？东欧的社会主义国家、苏联、古巴、越南、柬埔寨这些社会主义的国家，尤其是柬埔寨啊，杀人如麻，那怎么能说是彼此尊敬呢？

梁：当然不是。苏联，在俄国这个地方，出现共产党，出现共产主义，不是按照社会自然发展出来的，因为苏联没有经过多少资本主义那条路，没走多少，它在沙皇底下没有多少资本主义，一下就变了。所以，它不是把资本主义走到头，然后转入社会主义，不是那样的。

Alitto: Yes, I know what you mean. Then this is true also of Eastern Europe, of Vietnam, Cuba and Cambodia?

Liang: So in Russia it went from a Czarist dictatorship to a Communist Party dictatorship. If Russia had been allowed to develop under Lenin's leadership, it would have developed later.[56] Unfortunately, Lenin died too early. So it's the old tradition still in the Czarist rule. That tradition still had great power. So after Lenin died, there was a major turning point. Now, especially with Brezhnev...the situation is abnormal. They are still traveling in the same course as the Czars, despotism. The ordinary Russian does not enjoy the freedom and democracy of the Western Europeans, and Russia does not enjoy a really advanced industry, which would have resulted in an affluent society and a high standard of living. So Russian youth look at Western Europe with envy.

So the U.S.S.R., from Khrushchev to Brezhnev, cannot be considered a socialist country.[57] The U.S.S.R. is, in my view, a kind of abnormality, an anomaly, which conforms to the history of Russia. Later on, as it develops, it will possibly, in my own view, reverse itself. That is to say, I think that the party will not be able to maintain their despotism very long. It will undergo a transformation. This kind of rule cannot last for long. When an opportunity arrives, it will change.[58] It won't be like China now. China later will not undergo great changes.

Alitto: Another question. As far as the history of advanced industrial countries by far is concerned, Marx has made misjudgement. He originally predicted that the proletariat would grow more and more numerous, and the capitalists would be fewer and fewer, with the final result that revolution would break out. But in contemporary Japan, Germany, the U.S., Canada and such places, this phenomenon has not occurred; instead there have appeared certain types of what might be called classes that previously no one had thought about. In industry, white-collar workers are more and more numerous; work in the service industry has increased. A capitalist is not as clear-cut and explicit an entity as Marx had said. So, since he was wrong, it is not certain how history in the 21st century will develop.

艾：是。我明白您的意思。东欧的国家、古巴、柬埔寨、越南这些地方也是一样?

梁：在俄国，它还是从沙皇的那种专制转成共产党的专制。共产党专制如果在列宁底下领导，大概会要很好。可是列宁死得很早，所以它那个旧的传统、旧的习惯，还是从沙皇下来的那个东西，那个东西很有力量。列宁死后的斯大林的，特别是现在的勃列日涅夫的，这个情况不是一个正常的情况，还是顺着沙皇的那个老路下来的，顺着那个老路下来的一种专制。而一般的俄国人，他们没有像西欧的国家，享受过自由啊、民主啊，也没有享受过工业很发达，社会很富，人民很有享受。所以现在的青年人，他看到西欧人享受，他很羡慕。

现在的苏联，从赫鲁晓夫到勃列日涅夫，它算不上什么社会主义，在我看起来是一种变态，而这种变态是合于它的历史的，合于俄国的历史的。这种变态往下走，不会这样子稳，我看它是一个变态的，不是一个正常的，所以底下它可能要翻案。我认为这么看，可能要翻案。像是勃列日涅夫他们这种党的专制，恐怕底下不是可以维持很长久的，会要起变化，这种的统治，我想也许它要维持不住了，如果有机会到来的时候，它要变化，它不会很好地维持下去，没有力量维持下去，它要变化。我这么看。不会像中国这样子，中国底下没有大变化。

艾：第二个问题，到现在为止的历史，工业先进国家的历史来说，马克思原来预测无产阶级越来越多，资本家越来越少，结果就爆发了革命。可是现在的日本、德国、美国、加拿大这些地方，也没有这种现象，来了一些以前没想到的好几种可以说是阶级，工业方面的白领工人越来越多，服务事业上的工作越来越多，资本家也没有马克思讲的那么清楚、那么干脆、那么明确。所以呀，他既然错了，21 世纪历史的发展将来说不定……

Liang: He did not expect in his reckoning, his viewpoint and the present situation were not in agreement, not of the sort that he predicted. For the present situation, their interpretation is "the economic substructure, the superstructure." I think that the superstructure in the U.S. is very powerful. This is because the superstructure is not just a question of power alone. It includes culture and learning, which are all tied up with wealth and power. So, it would not be easy to overturn such a superstructure.

● China's future and the future of the world

Alitto: Do you have any predictions about China's future?

Liang: That depends upon the future of the world in general. It is not just a question of China itself. For example, if there was another world war, China would be affected. And another world war is just a matter of time.[59]

Alitto: If this comes to pass, then we humans are finished. Nuclear weapons—if the U.S.S.R. and the U.S. did go to war—even the very soil of the earth would be affected. Even the survival of the next generations would become problematic. Your words are very pessimistic.

Liang: I have only a very shallow, half-formed opinion on the question, but my view is that an eventual war between the U.S.S.R. and the U.S.A. is practically inevitable. But I have another conjecture—that a world war would not last long, but as soon as it broke out, both the U.S.S.R. and the U.S.A. would then have internal problems.

Alitto: If nuclear weapons are used, even social organizations will go. I understand what you mean. I'm saying that if the cities are all blasted flat, all the people killed, radiation would also affect people in the countryside. Of course, one could say that problems would arise in society, and probably at that point, basically there would be no society, while scattered numbers of people would still survive. Probably on this point Chinese and

American views differ. Chairman Mao said that the Atomic Bomb was nothing much, a paper tiger or something, but most Americans feel that once you have this kind of thing, everything is finished.

Liang: Well, my opinion is that the internal problems of both the U.S.A. and the U.S.S.R. would explode as soon as war broke out. I could use a quote

梁： 他没有料到他的估计、他的看法跟现在不合，不像他所料想的那个样。现在的情况，他们的讲法有所谓“经济基础、上层建筑”，现在我看，像美国的上层建筑，很有力量。现在的上层建筑不单是一个掌权的问题，它也是学术文化，学术文化跟有钱、跟有权都连起来了，好像是不容易推翻的。

- **中国的前途、世界的前途**

艾： 根据中国未来前途的展望，您有何见解？

梁： 这是关系到整个世界，它不是中国本身的问题了，中国的前途是看整个世界，譬如说，要有世界大战起来，那么中国是一个情况。世界大战，恐怕迟早要……

艾： 假如真的是这样，那么我们人类就完蛋了。原子弹啊，如果真是苏联、美国打起来了，连土壤也会受影响，将来好几代都还有生存的问题，您说这个话很悲观的。

梁： 我说我粗浅的见解吧。我是这样看，恐怕美苏之间的战争啊、世界性的大战啊很难免。可是我另外一个猜测，这个世界大战不会出场，我想一爆发战争，苏联那边，美国一边，都会内部爆发问题。

艾： 假如是用核子武器，那人类的社会组织也没有了。我了解您的意思，我的意思是说假如城市都已经炸平了，炸得没有人了，乡下的人也受到辐射性污染了，当然也可以说是社会发生问题了，恐怕那个时候根本没有社会了，零散的一些人还是存在的。恐怕这一点我们美国人看法与中国人看法不同，毛主席说过这个原子弹也不怎么样，纸老虎啊什么的，但一般美国人觉得，一有这种东西，什么都完了。

梁： 是那样的。我的意思是这么样，如果一爆发战争，还没有等到多久，各自，就是苏联一边，美国一边，各自内部问题就爆发

from Chairman Mao, who also had a view on the possibility of world war. He said, "Probably war would lead to revolution, or probably a revolution would avert a war." He said this. If the U.S.S.R. had an internal revolution, America too had a revolution, and then there would be no great war. Perhaps the rise of revolution can avert a war, without the two major powers fighting. Or, perhaps a war would bring about revolution. The war would not have to last long to lead to an internal revolution. He had such kind of statement and I think possibly so. Precisely at the time that the world is on the point of a great change, China quite possibly will not have to suffer from another war. When the two superpowers are having their internal revolutions, China will be able to keep stable and steady.

● My expectations for the youth: do what each one can do in this time of hope

Alitto: Can you give the next generation of Chinese youth some inspiration on how to have a more hopeful future, or...

Liang: Toward the youth of China, it is not the same as speaking about outside—I do know about the situation in China. I want to say probably two things. One is directed toward the Chinese domestic situation, including the political situation. Right now is a time of stability and progress, an era of many possibilities, opportunities to make progress, more so than in previous times. It's now been thirty, thirty-one years [since the founding of the nation]. The situation is better than before. Some people envy the U.S. or envy Europe, and they appear to be dissatisfied with the situation within China. I feel that this is a bit blind; it is blind envy of the foreign. This is not right and not good. Of course, to go abroad to take a look, or to study, is good, but this must be done with a well worked out plan in mind that China under the leadership of the Communist Party must proceed toward socialism. This direction is correct. The term now—"the Four Modernizations"—is still for the purpose of having China walk this path and achieve modernization in these four areas, but it cannot ever leave the socialist path of modernization. It is especially important to know that this is a time of better opportunities than before. The political situation is now stable. Hua Guofeng—Chairman Hua is very stable, and Deng Xiaoping is very open-minded—I heard there may be government reorganization this

出来。我可以引用毛泽东的话，他对这个问题他也有一个看法，他曾经说过的话，他是这样说的，他说“也许是战争引起来革命，也许革命避免战争”，他说过这个话。如果俄国内部起了革命，美国也起了革命，反而没有大的战争了，他的话是这样说的——或者是革命起来避免了战争，没有两个大强国打了；也许是战争引发革命，一打，还没有打多久，刚一打内部就出问题了——他有这个话，我觉得好像也就是这样，可能是这样。中国刚好在这个世界起变化的时候，中国可能没有吃什么战争的大亏，倒是在世界上两个大强国都出问题之后，中国还能够稳定。

- **对青年的希望：在这个有希望的时候要各尽所能**

艾： 您能不能给下一代中国青年一些启示，启示他们如何才能获得一个更有希望的将来或是……

梁： 我对国内的青年，我虽然不像对外边一样，我可以知道一些情况，我可以说我想说的话。大概是两样的话：一样的话是就国内大局情况说，包含了政治上的情况，现在正是在一个很平稳而求进步的时候，很有可能、很有机会求进步的时候，比往常都好。现在算是 30 年、31 年了，比过去都比较好。所以有些人都是羡慕美国，或者是羡慕欧洲，好像是不满足中国国内的情况，这个我觉得是有点盲目性，盲目地羡慕外边、盲目地想学外边。这不对、不好。当然出国去看一看，去学习也好，不过要胸中有主，要知道中国在共产党领导下，要往社会主义里头去，这个大方向是对的。现在的名词，叫“四个现代化”，还是为了中国走社会主义这个大道路而要四个现代化，不能离开走社会主义道路的现代化。特别是要知道，现在是一个比过去更好机会的时候。现在政局稳定，华国锋、华主席他人很平稳，很稳定。一方面呢，像邓小平他又很开明，不久的这个 8 月份听说要宣布政府

August. So right now is a time of hope. So, in this time of hope, marching down this correct path, working with what each person can do, what is convenient for them to do, by the sweat of their brow—this should be the path of modern Chinese youth.

● A piece of advice to scholars

Alitto: This question is similar to the one I just asked. Would you give any advice to those scholars in the Chinese cultural domain?

Liang: As far as the present world of thought, the present academic world goes—I do not refer to the various specialized sciences. I know very little about the various specialized sciences; none are my own field. I don't have a specialty. But I do have an opinion, that in China at present, the more famous, the more prominent [scholars] are all mathematicians. Several mathematicians have been invited to go abroad. Mathematics is different from the empirical sciences. Empirical science requires experiments, laboratories, observation and empirical practice. Mathematics can be done behind closed doors. Currently there is a kind of fad, that prominent [scholars] are all mathematicians. If they [academics] move too far in this direction, and not in the other direction, it won't be good. This is a shortcoming. How can we have the general atmosphere not tend in this direction, toward this kind of abstract science? This kind of science, I think, is called "abstract." There's another kind of science called "concrete." It seems that attention should be paid to concrete science. (Alitto: That is, utilitarian science.) Applied science. It [academic work] should not be overly devoted to the abstract. Attention should be placed on reality. But I also feel that there has always been a certain inclination in China, i.e., that of talking about the practical often with insufficient attention paid to impractical, basic scholarship. I think that the point of emphasis should be moved from the practical to the basic. What I can say is this.

改组，听说是这样。所以现在正好是一个有希望的时候，那么，在这个有希望的时候，在这个走一个正确的道路上，来各自就自己所能的、所方便的，来尽一份力量，应当是现代的中国青年的道路。

• 对思想界的劝告

艾：这个问题跟我刚问的有点类似，您愿不愿意给现在中国文化领域中的一些学者一些什么劝告?

梁：现在就思想界来说、就学术界来说，我的意思就是说，不是各自的专门的科学——各自专门的科学我是知道得很少，没有哪一个是我的专门，我没有一种专长。不过我有一点意见，就是中国现在好像比较出名的，很露头角的都是几个数学家，几个数学家都被请到外国去讲学。数学这个东西是一个跟其他的实验的科学不同，实验的科学是一定要实验，一定要实验室，一定要出来考察，要做许多的实践，数学是关起门来也能做。现在有一种风气，就是出头露角的都是数学家，如果太偏于这面了，而那一方面不够，好像是不好、缺欠。怎么样风气不要偏到这面来，不要偏到讲抽象的这种科学，这种科学好像是叫抽象的，abstract，还有一种科学好像叫 concrete，好像是应当注意那边，(艾：就是运用科学。)应用的，应用科学。应当是不要太讲抽象的，应该是注意实际的。可是我又觉得中国从来有一个偏处，偏处就是爱讲实用，对不实用的、根本的学问常常是不够注意，应当是……还是重点要从应用转回到根本上。我可以说的话就是这样。

What kind of person I am

• My hobbies

Alitto: Mr. Liang, do you have any hobbies? Your students all said that you had no hobbies, that you did scholarship or other work from morning to night. I don't know if this was true, or whether...

Liang: I'll tell a little story. I have a friend who had studied in the U.S., specializing in mass education, also called adult education. This person's name was Yu Qingtang,[60] a lady. She was together with friends chatting, and she asked me jokingly what my hobby was. I answered, "I don't know what hobby I have. Eating? I am not that fond of eating. Having fun? I'm not too fond of having fun. Opera? I can take it or leave it. If you ask what in the end I am most fond of, naturally I am fond of using my brain, fond of thinking." "Gosh," Madame Yu said, "that is really frightening."

Alitto: You just mentioned opera, referring to Beijing Opera?

Liang: Beijing Opera.

Alitto: Because you grew up in Beijing, you can appreciate Beijing Opera. But these past thirty years, after Liberation, did you go listen to opera?

Liang: Before, when I was small, I had a certain proclivity, one not too good. One could say that it was a mistake, a fault—that is, I labored at being unconventional and novel. As for the opera, my father, mother, and elder brother—I was second in birth order, I had an elder brother—they were all fond of opera. After finishing dinner in the summertime, they would go outside taking the cool breezes, and they would talk about opera—which opera was best, who sang best, just chatting like that. Just because they were quite fond of this thing, I wanted to be the maverick. I did not talk [opera] names. So if, say, an opera was quite good—if they went, I would not go. I was always fond of deviating from the general rule.

Now that I think of it, when I was in middle school, everyone would have to draw a topic for his or her essay composition; the teacher could [evaluate] your writing style [from it]. Ordinary people, when drawing a paper theme, would develop that theme a bit, and so write a paper

叁 我是一个怎样的人

- **我的嗜好**

艾： 梁先生您有没有嗜好啊？您的学生都说：啊，梁先生什么嗜好都没有啊，一天到晚不是搞学问就是搞别的工作。我也不知道是真的吗，还是……

梁： 我可以说一个，算是一个小故事吧。有一位朋友，是一个在美国留学的，专学民众教育，也叫成人教育，这位是叫俞庆棠先生，是一位妇女。她是在一些朋友的聚会上提出来，随便谈话、说笑话，问我什么是我的嗜好。我说我不知道我有什么嗜好。我说：爱吃嘛，也没什么爱吃；爱玩嘛，也没有怎么样爱玩；爱看戏嘛，我也可以看也可以……。如果说问我到底爱什么？我说我当然是爱用头脑、爱思想。哎呀，俞先生说这个太可怕了。

艾： 您刚才提到戏，说的是京戏？

梁： 京戏。

艾： 您因为在北京长大的，您还能欣赏京戏。但这 30 年来，解放以来，也去听戏吗？

梁： 我从前小的时候，我有一个偏处，有一个不大好，可以说是一个错误、一个毛病吧，标新立异。就是说听戏啊，我的父亲、母亲、哥哥——我是行二，我有个大哥——他们都爱听京戏，夏天吃完晚饭，在外边乘凉、谈话，都是谈哪个戏唱得好，谁唱得好，随便谈。他们因为都爱好这个东西，我就标新立异，名号我不谈。所以本来京戏也很好的，可是他们去，我不去。总是喜欢偏。

我想起来了，我在中学读书，大家要经常抽题目，让你作文章，看看你文笔好不好。普通人都是抽一个题目，在这个题目上发挥一点，写吧，作一个论文吧。我就喜欢标新立异，提到

on it. I, however, was straining to be original and unconventional. In mentioning some ancient historical figure or some event, most would praise the figure. I intentionally would express my dissatisfaction with him, that is, to be a maverick. One of our teachers, a very old man, saw my essay and called it an essay "reversing a previous judgment." People all said this way, but I insisted that way. He was most unhappy. His comments were extremely critical, saying that "As you are always in opposition to common tastes, you are doomed to fail." Another Chinese language teacher was different. His comment used lines from a poem of Du Fu's, "Fight to the death to find words that startle."[61] This is a line from a poem of Du Fu's, which explains how I was in my youth, consciously trying to be different. I had this fault.[62]

I like that kind of opera that they say is "a martial opera sung literarily." It's a martial opera, but the plot and action is still singing, so there is not much fighting. So, a martial opera, but one whose emphasis is on literary singing. I like this kind of opera.

Alitto: Is there any opera that you particularly like?

Liang: Yes. There is an opera with painted-face characters. The major painted-face characters perform warrior roles. One of these characters is called Huang Tianba. I especially like that opera.

Alitto: Before I didn't know that you especially liked the Huang Tianba opera. Aside from opera, of which all Beijing people are fond, are there any other pastimes?

Liang: Of course, there are some novels that I like to read, such as *Dream of Red Chambers*. There's also one called *The Travels of Lao Can*.

Alitto: Do you have a favorite author?

Liang: That should be... There is one novel that is interesting no matter how many times one reads it—*Dream of Red Chambers*, which is profound. You always feel it is of interest. Other novels, well, you read them once, and that's it. So, it's *Dream of Red Chambers*...[63]

Alitto: So, [these are books] "that one never tires of reading." What books have you read after Liberation? I know what you had read before Liberation, but do not know what you have read after it.

Liang: After Liberation, I have read no books especially worth mentioning. Other people ask me that, and I blurt out no answer. After

一个古代的什么人物，或者某一件事情，一般都是称赞这个人，我故意表示我不满意他，就是标新立异。我们的教员老师，有个老的先生，看见我这个文章，叫做"翻案文章"。人家这样说，你偏那样，很不高兴，批语就批得很坏，说你"好恶拂人之性，灾必及于自身"——你将会有灾祸，一位老先生这样批。可另外一位国文教员又不同了，他批语批的说"语不惊人死不休"，"语不惊人死不休"是杜甫的诗——都说明我年纪轻的时候，故意跟人家不一样，有这个毛病。

我喜欢的那种戏，就是他们说的"武戏文唱"，是武戏，可是情节、活动乃是唱出来，并不是打的多，是武戏，可是武戏而着重文唱的，我喜欢这种戏。

艾：那您有没有什么特别心爱的戏啊？

梁：有。有个戏，就是演北京叫花面的，大花脸，演武生，武生就是黄天霸，我喜欢看那个戏。

艾：以前我并不知道您特别喜欢黄天霸的戏。除了听戏以外——北京人都喜欢听戏，小说啊这类的消遣您有没有啊？

梁：当然有，有些个小说书看过，比如像《红楼梦》啊，看过。还有一部叫《老残游记》。

艾：您最喜爱的作家是谁？

梁：那应当是……这一部书意味很深长，什么时候都感觉有意味，那还是《红楼梦》。旁的小说看一遍，知道了就行了。《红楼梦》就是……

艾：百读不厌。解放以来您看过的是什么样的书啊？解放以前您著作里提到的书这些我知道了，解放以后的我还不清楚您读的。

梁：解放以后的书，没有什么特别值得提的书。别人一问，我能够

you asked me, I have to slowly think about it. I remember one book I have read that I liked very much. There is a Japanese, whom I very much admire [Heshang Zhao, Kawakami Hajime]. Later he was a Marxist, and wanted to put it [Marxism] into practice. He was a Communist Party member. But doesn't Marxism say "Religion is opium"? He agreed with Marxism but he didn't agree with this. He said, "Science has scientific truth, religion has religious truth." Moreover, he said that he himself had religious experience.

People probably say that my type of experience was Chan Buddhist; I don't know if it was Chan or not. He wrote a book *Autobiography of Kawakami Hajime.*[64] In Chinese it made two thick volumes. I very much liked it. Moreover, I copied down his experience—his words—in my notebook. He was special. The religious experience he spoke of was not casual, empty talk. He spoke of a true transformation of his own life. When he spoke about this, there was a sentence of this sort: "When I had this experience, it seemed that I had been cast out, to take a look, and I myself took a look. When I had this experience, my body underwent a transformation; I pinched my own flesh with my hand, and it didn't hurt. Moreover, it was like a layer of my skin peeled off." So, this was not only a conscious transformation, a transformation in thought, but it was also a transformation that happened in the concrete. He himself said, "Science has scientific truth; religion has religious truth." So, on the one hand I agree with Marx's statement that religion is people's opium, but on the other, I feel that Marx never had a genuine religious experience.

● How I keep in good health

Liang: Well, my health and age could have something to do with my vegetarian diet; I eat no flesh or animals.

Alitto: And you don't drink or smoke?

Liang: Right. I can drink a little grape wine, but that hardly counts; it's very mild with low alcoholic content.[65] I've been a vegetarian for 69 years. I also eat small quantities. I also have some exercise [regimens] which I learned from others. I'm talking about myself now, not those methods of others. In days of this weather, I wake up at five a.m., and get up. While still in bed I exercise.

马上就脱口而出的没有，你问了之后我还要慢慢想，想不出来。噢，我记得有一本书我很喜欢。一个日本人（*河上肇*），这个人我是很佩服他，这个人是个马克思主义者，后来他是马克思主义者，并且他要实践，他共产党。可是马克思主义不是说"宗教是鸦片烟"？对马克思这个话他也点头，但是他又不同意。他是说，科学有科学的真理，宗教有宗教的真理，并且他自己说，他自己有宗教的经验。

人家也许说我这种经验是禅宗，我不知道是不是禅宗。他有《河上肇自传》，自传中文有两厚本，我很喜欢看，我并且把他的有些经验、他的话，抄下来，抄在我的本子上。他很特别，他说的宗教经验，不是一句随便的空话，他是说自己的生命起一个真的变化。他说到这个地方的时候，有这样的一句话，他说有这个经验的时候，好像我抛出去，看了一下，自己看了一下，有过这个经验。在有这个经验的时候，我的身体起了变化，自己的肉啊，用手掐它，不疼，并且好像肉体上的皮肤，有了这个经验之后脱了一层皮。所以这不单是一种意识上、思想上的变化，而是很实际的起的变化。他自己说，科学有科学的真理，宗教有宗教的真理，所以马克思说宗教是人的鸦片烟，这个话我一方面同意，一方面我觉得马克思缺乏真正的宗教经验。

• 我如何养生

梁： 这个可能跟素食有关系，不吃肉类，什么肉类都不吃，动物都不吃。

艾： 也不喝酒，也不抽烟?

梁： 对，能喝一点葡萄酒，不算什么酒，酒性很淡薄。素食已经69年了，这是一点。再一点就是食量少。再一点就是有一些锻炼身体的（*方法*），就我自己说——我也是跟别人学的，我现在不说人家的，说自己。我每天早晨起床，比如说现在的这种天气，早晨5点钟就醒了，起来了，在床上起来做功夫。

Alitto: What are they like?

Liang: There are many that I do. The most important are like this: the most important is a rubbing of the kidneys with the hands, and then rub the eyes, rub them again, and massage the eyes again. Three times like that, not too much. This kind of exercise is passed on. There are a great variety of exercises. What I just mentioned is just some of many. Rubbing the kidneys is one kind of exercise. Then another important one is rubbing the arch of the foot.

I should explain that there are two major, famous traditions in Chinese learning, two traditions that have been passed down from ancient times. One is the Daoist, the school of Zhuangzi and Laozi. One is the Confucian, the school of Confucius. These two traditions are dissimilar, and are both passed down from antiquity. The Chinese medical tradition is derived from Daoism. It is different from the Western, not only in the medicines it uses. The essential difference is theoretical principle, because the Chinese tradition never developed skills in dissection and anatomy. Well, in far antiquity it did. The *Shiji* talks about Bian Que and Cang Gong. Bian Que sometimes opened up the abdomen, took out the intestines to wash them, and later sewed it up. The ancient books have accounts of this thing. Later, the Chinese didn't dare cut open the body. They relied only on you taking some medicine.

The classical Chinese medical books include *Yellow Emperor's Classic of Internal Medicine* and the *Difficult Classic*. The author of the latter—whoever it was—likes to discuss the Energy Channels of the body.[66] That is, the blood circulation through the veins and arteries. But this discussion is not like that in dissection and anatomical study of the West. It is from the Daoist tradition. Daoism wants the cerebrum to rest. The function of the cerebrum is primarily to cope with the external, the environment. It wants the cerebrum to rest. When the cerebrum is at rest, humans also have an autonomic nervous system. This system is also under the cerebrum, but when the cerebrum rests, it can operate, and function even better. This is because when the cerebrum rests, it can avoid the interference of the cerebrum.

For example, our digestive systems and circulatory systems all belong to the autonomic nervous system. If, when we eat, we are worried about something, or anxious, that eating will not be good; it will influence the digestive process. If you force yourself to eat when worried or nervous, it will influence the digestive process. If you force yourself to eat when angry,

艾：什么样的?

梁：功夫要做很多，有这几样主要的吧：主要的一样就是搓腰肾，搓一搓，揉眼睛；然后再搓一搓，再揉眼睛；再搓一搓，再揉眼睛，这么三次，还不太多。传授这种锻炼身体的，有好多不同的。这不过是好多样中的一样。搓腰肾是一样事情，再一样事情比较重要的是搓脚心、脚掌，要搓一下。

我说一下，中国重要的、著名的学问是两大派，两大派都是从很古的时候传下来的，一个就是道家——老子、庄子这一派，一派是儒家——孔子这派。这两派不大相同，都是传自远古，很古。中国的中医就是从道家来的。中医不单是用药跟西医不同，主要是它的学理就不同，因为它没有多做解剖身体的功夫。在远古的有，在《史记》里讲扁鹊、仓公，他（应指扁鹊）有时侯要开肚子，把肠子拿出来洗，然后缝上，这个事情在古书里头有，后来中医就没有这个了，不敢给开肚子了，就是给你吃点中药。

可是中医的书就是这个《黄帝内经》，还有一种叫《难经》，《内经》之外还有一种《难经》，这种经书内容最喜欢讲人身上的经络，就是讲血脉的流通的。可是它这一方面讲经络、血脉流通，它不是像西方说解剖那样，它是道家，道家要让大脑休息下来——人的大脑主要是应付外面的、应付环境的，它让大脑休息下来。大脑休息下来，人有一种植物性神经系统，这种植物性的神经系统，它也隶属于大脑，可是大脑休息的时候，它就更好活动，因为大脑休息的时候，它就可以避免大脑的干扰。

比如我们吃饭这种消化系统、血液循环系统，都是属于植物性神经系统，如果我们吃饭的时候，心里头还在那儿发愁、忧虑，那个饭吃不好，影响消化，或者你正在发怒，勉强

you get into trouble. If there is no such external stimuli, if you let nature take its course, and the autonomous nervous system very naturally carries out its activities, then digestion is good.

In my view, usually "*qigong*" (the technique of using one's inner strength, such as control of muscle and breathing) requires that the cerebrum rest to allow the autonomic nervous system to function freely, and to utilize the body's own inherent function. Utilizing this inherent function can repair any breakdowns or illness that the body might have. So, in my view, *qigong* operates like this. But I, too, have studied *qigong*. Because I like to think, to ponder, I often have insomnia. Insomnia causes great suffering. So, over twenty years ago, it's now 1980, so it was about 1956, there was a place on the seashore called Beidaihe. It was an excellent spot for relaxation and excursions. Now a *qigong* sanatorium had been established there. I had insomnia, and so went to that *qigong* sanatorium, and stayed there for some time in summer.

There were three kinds of skills used at this sanitarium, each different from the others. Naturally, as soon as you entered you began with meditation. The environment they provided for this was quite good. Each person had a small room. The room was not so big, and was provided for you to rest in and sleep in. The room was designed so as to never have any strong light rays enter. But you were completely free to go out for a walk whenever you felt like it, and to return whenever you wanted. From when you started, for all 24 hours of the day, you were not permitted to see anyone else, to have any contact with others, or to read books or newspapers. You may sit any time you wanted, but only in the prescribed correct posture. You could also lie down—either on your right or left side; that was up to you. The important thing was to allow your cerebrum to rest, to settle down. As soon as you settled down, acting according to instructions, it naturally took effect, and you naturally proceeded down the *qigong* path.

Didn't I just mention that there were three kinds of skills at this sanitarium? For many people who went there, recuperating was quite effective. It was most efficacious and successful for stomach ailments. For example, for ulcers or for gastroptosis. If you practiced *qigong* under their guidance, stomach ulcers would be cured. X-rays showed the ulcer scarred over. Gastroptosis would also be healed. So, this was making use of the vigor of the body itself. No medicines were taken. So those many sick people who went there to recuperate were healed.

吃饭，都不好。就是没有这种外来的刺激，顺其自然地让植物性神经系统很自然地进行它的活动，那就是好。

通常啊，由我的看法，这个气功，在我看都是要大脑休息，给人的身体的植物性的神经，让它活动，利用人身体本有的一种机能，利用这种本有的机能可以把人身上有些毛病，可以把它修理好。依我看呢，气功就是这样。不过我呢，我也曾经去学过气功。我是因为喜欢用思想，所以我就有失眠的病，失眠很痛苦。所以离现在有二十多年了，现在是 1980 年，大概在 1956 年，有一个地方地名叫北戴河，海边上，是一个很好的休息游览的地方，那个地方曾经成立了一个“气功疗养院”。我有失眠的病，我就到那个气功疗养院，住在那个地方疗养，在夏天的时候。

疗养院好像有三种功夫，三种功夫有点分别，不大一样，当然入手就是要静坐。他们布置的环境也很好，每一个人过去都有一间小屋，这个屋子不是太大，给你在里边休息吧，睡啊。这个屋子避免强的光线，不过你喜欢出来散步，完全可以随你意思出去散步，你想回来就回来。一居（音同），包含一昼夜 24 小时，不要见人，不要跟旁人接触，也不要看书、看报。你坐着也可以，不过坐着也有正确的姿势，你愿意躺下来也可以，偏着左侧躺也可以，偏着右侧躺也可以，完全随你。要紧的呢，就是让大脑休息，要静下来。你一静下来，按照他的指点，你就会自然起作用，自然就走上气功的道路了。

刚才我不是说了一下，它好像有三种功夫，很多人到那里去疗养都很有效。最有成效的、有成功的是胃病，比如说有一种胃下垂，还有一种叫做胃溃疡，按照它的指导做气功，胃溃疡就好了。可以透视，溃疡结疤了，胃下垂也好了。它就是借助人身体本有的生命的力量，不要吃药，所以有些个病人到那儿去疗养就都好了。

Now, I went because of my insomnia, and for this, it was also effective. This cure of course was also based upon resting the cerebrum, not using the brain. But I didn't get the way as instructed by the *qigong* sanitarium. It seemed that [my] way was not like that; possibly [my way] was Buddhist. Incidentally, I want to say...I am not sure...I suppose that these *qigong* practices came from a school of ancient Daoism, and although I did practice according to their conditions—having the cerebrum rest, settling down, being tranquil, but the state I achieved was the state without thought, that is, the zone in which there was no conscious thought. I think the phenomenon and practice are like the Buddhist meditation skill that I spoke of before. Isn't it what we used to call "an old monk enters a trance" (very calm and without worldly passions)? One can be completely without any ratiocination. It's very good. When one has had this experience, it feels so great, so [when] going to do it again, one has expectations, waiting for it to come, hoping for it. Then it won't work. If you expect and hope for it to come, it won't come. You have to let go. You mustn't think "that was so wonderful yesterday; I still want it to happen again today"; it won't work. You have to set it aside, set it aside, set it aside. Only if you don't look forward to it will it happen. If you want it to come, it won't. I achieved this, I think it's very good; it seems it's a trance, it's Buddhist, different from their *qigong*. Later I returned to Beijing, and went to live in a temple in the Western Hills for two months.

...I didn't continue the exercise. This is one aspect. Another aspect is that my life has always been quite flat, mild flavored, with no excitement, which seems to have benefited my life. It's as though I don't have any great demands on life. I don't have any great joys or pleasures derived from the satisfaction of some desire. At the same time, I have no unhappiness, no anger or frustration from unsatisfied desires or demands. I simply don't really have any great desire.

● Why I have an interest in Traditional Chinese Medicine

Alitto: As for medicine, you mentioned in *Eastern and Western Cultures and Their Philosophies*, upon an analysis of Chinese and Western medicines, that these two entities symbolize a difference between Eastern and Western cultures. Later you continued to study medicine? Even at present do you still...

Liang: One could say that I am mindful of it, mindful of medicine.

Alitto: Yes, this is because you are really interested in it. Why do you have this interest? I know that long ago you had this interest. Why did you, after all?

可我去呢，我是睡眠的问题，也很见好。这个见好呢，当然也还是靠大脑静下来了，不用大脑了。可是我没有像气功疗养院所指点给我的，好像路子不是那样，可能像是佛家的。我附带说一句话，我不敢……我猜想吧，我的看法，他们这个气功是中国古时道家那一派的，而我呢，虽然按照它的条件去做功夫，要大脑休息下来，要清净，可是我就达到了一种境地，这种境地呢，就是一念不起，一个念头也不起，好像是佛家的定功。这个是不是一种从前说的“老僧入定”，可以一念不起，很好……有过这个经验之后，觉得很好啊，所以再去做的时候，就有点期待心，等着它来，盼着它来，不行了。你期待它、盼着它，它不来了。就是，你还是要放下，你不要说是“昨天的那个过得很美，我今天还愿意再来一回”，不行，你还是得放下，放下，放下，不要有一个期待心，那么才会出现。我所得的这个，我认为很好的这个，好像是“入定”吧，是佛家的，跟他们的气功不很一样。我后来回到北京，到西山上庙里头去住过两个月。

……我没有继续深入、继续去做这个功夫，这是一方面。再一方面，好像在自己生活上有好处的，就是无论什么事情，我总是很平淡。我很平淡呢，就是好像没有多大要求，也不用满足要求而高兴啊、喜欢啊，因为不满足而生气、不高兴啊，两面都没有，两面都是放得很平，平平淡淡，平平淡淡。

- **我为什么对中医感兴趣**

艾：就是医学，您在《东西文化及其哲学》也是提到了，中医、西医啊做了一个分析，可以说是象征着东方文化和西方文化的一个分别了，那您以后也是继续研究医学吗？就是到现在还是在……

梁：可以说是很留心，很留心对医学。

艾：是，那是因为您对这个很感兴趣。为什么感兴趣呢？我知道很早以前，您感兴趣，就是到底为什么？

Liang: Because life is the object of this study. This is especially true of Chinese medicine. Transmitted down from ancient times, the most important method of treatment is not herbal medicine, but acupuncture and moxibustion. Even earlier back, the latter was termed "stone probe" (*zhenbian*). This character ***bian*** has a stone radical. The ancients used very acuate rock for the purpose of treating sickness. At that time there were no metal needles, so very hard stones were used on your body, somewhere you didn't know...

This represents Chinese culture, Chinese learning, and Daoist thought. The Chinese medical tradition derives from the Daoist tradition. What was the Daoist tradition like? I often say that Westerners are outward looking, looking at the externals, while the Chinese focus on life itself, and turn their vision inward to the life experience itself. Turning inward onto their own bodies, the Chinese knew about energy channels. Chinese doctors call blood vessels energy channels. These are channels for vital forces and blood. In traditional Chinese parlance, these were called the vital forces and blood circulation. They are circulated along the energy channels.

How were the Daoists able to determine the circulatory system? The reason is Daoist thought. I'll explain. This is because the Daoists focus their discipline precisely upon this circulatory system. In a man's life, the blood/vital force is in the midst of circulation, an unceasing continuous circulation, but we don't know how it circulates and flows. We are not conscious of it. We use our brains and thoughts to deal with the external, to look after the external. Daoism does the opposite; it turns the direction of observation from outward to inward, and makes one a bit self-conscious of the unconscious. There was an element of autonomy in the Daoist effort. They not only wanted to understand the unconscious, but also to influence it, to alter it.

The Daoists wanted to change the circulation of the vital force and blood from something unconscious to something conscious, to change it from something out of one's control to something within one's control. Once one was able to control and influence the unconscious, one could become an immortal. An immortal was different from an ordinary human being like us.

He can do things that we cannot do. When the temperature is hot, an ordinary person perspires. When the temperature is too cold, an ordinary person becomes numb. But an immortal would not. In ancient times, very early, this kind of skill or discipline existed. In *The Zhuangzi*, it was already there. He was able to achieve longevity. He had a very powerful control of the life force, of life.

梁： 它是以生命为研究对象，特别是中国的医学，从很古的时候传下来的，主要不是用药，是用针灸，更早的时候它叫针砭，更早的时候。那个“砭”呢，它是石字旁，石头啊，石字旁，一个“乏”字。很早的时候中国古人治病啊，他就是用那个尖的石头，那时还没有针，拿很坚硬的石头来，在你的不知道什么地方给你……

这个是代表中国文化，代表中国学问，代表道教。中国的医学是出于道教。那么道家是怎么样呢？就是我常常说：西洋人呢总是向外看，这个中国人呢，是回到自己生命上。回到自己身体上。回到自己身体上他就知道经络，中医叫做经络、经脉，经络、经脉在人身上。中国笼统的话说，气血，气跟血，气血循环流转，经络或者经脉就是气血循环的路了，道路了。

这个怎么能够认出来，特别怎么能够很清楚地懂得这个经络呢？是道教。底下就可以讲明一下，说明一下，就是这个气血在人身上的流通，因为道家做的功夫就是在气血流通上。我们一个人生活，气血本来都是在流通中，是不停止地流通，不停地流通，可是我们不知道它怎么流通，不自觉，因为我们的头脑、心思都用到外边，照顾到外面。道家呢，相反，它把那个向外的、总是在观察外边的，它回来，转回头来，把不自觉的变成自觉，有一分的自觉，它就有一分的自主性，它自己一方面知道了，一方面就能够左右变动它。

道家就是这个，对自己的身体的气血的流行啊，从不自觉变到自觉、不自主变到自主，……这个能够自主啊，能够自主之后，就是成仙了。仙人嘛，就跟我们普通人不同了，我们做不到的事情，他就能做到。比如我们普通人平时，平时我们要出汗，天太冷了之后，冻了，太冻了，冻僵了，他们都没有，没有这个问题。大概很早，在中国古代就有这种功夫吧。《庄子》这本书里……他可以长寿，在他的生命生活上，有很高的自主的能力。

● I am not a sage.

Alitto: The third question is more difficult to answer. I have been reading the written materials. Concerning my views of your beliefs and your personality, it is the same as with a lot of other historical personages. That is, a person who Westerners would say is sacred. In English it is "holy." No matter whether Buddhist or Confucian, in this concept of a sage there are areas of similarity. That is, someone going into a realm that transcends everything, and giving the folks the knowledge of that transcendent realm. (Liang: Right.) I say that in your innermost soul, not necessarily on the conscious level, possibly on the unconscious level, you felt that as a sage you would save humanity. I do not mean by any means that you have consciously anywhere said, "I am a sage." But this interpretation I came to is not made casually, but only after having read your works for a long time. Do you have any reaction to this?

Liang: To which question?

Alitto: The sage question. Can you be considered a sage?

Liang: From what I understand and what I think in my mind, a sage is not an ordinary person. The words and actions of a sage and those of others do not appear to be that different, but in reality the sage, his life-being and personality go far beyond ordinary people. His life-being is different. His life-being completely tops that of an ordinary person. Before, in ancient times, it was Confucius; later I should recognize Wang Yangming. His life-being was thoroughly and completely higher than ours.

Alitto: You share many things with Wang Yangming. Like you, he first delved deeply into Buddhism, and then later left it. He also was, like you, a man of action who carried his ideas into practice in the real world. He wasn't a closeted scholar who just wrote and taught. So I think that you and he have a lot in common.

Liang: But Wang Yangming's life-being—his life was not that of an ordinary mortal's. He had already reached that stage whereby he was not an ordinary person. But I am still just an ordinary person.

Alitto: So you feel that you are still just an ordinary person?

Liang: An ordinary person. I'm possibly an ordinary person who is a bit different from other ordinary people. That is, it's as though I have seen something from afar. What do I get to see? I catch a glimpse from afar of Wang

• 我不是个圣人

艾： 那第三个问题是比较难说的，我自己是看书面的资料，我自己关于您的信仰、您的性格的看法就是跟对历史上很多别的人物一样，就是一种好像西方人说是神圣的一个人，英文是说 holy。那么，您无论是佛学或是儒学，圣人这个观念呀，有一些类似的地方，就是说要到一个超脱一切的一个领域，到那个领域以后还是会到民间、人间，给他们解释那个超脱一切的领域的知识。（梁：对，对。）我说您灵魂深处——也不一定是有意识的那一层——可能是无意识的那一层，是在觉得您是来救人类，就是圣人了。我的意思也并不是说，您是有意识地处处都说"我是圣人"，我不是这个意思了。不过我的这个说法呢，我想了很久，看了您的著作，看了很久，才想出来的，也不是随便的。您对这个问题有没有反应？

梁： 哪个问题？

艾： 就是说圣人，您算一个圣人吗？

梁： 我所懂得的、我心里所想得的，圣人不是平常人。圣人他说话行事可以说跟其他人不大两样，可是实际上他那个人、他那个生命、他那个人格，已经完全超过普通人了。生命不同了，生命完全高过普通人。在从前，古时候就是孔子，后来我应当承认王阳明，他对生命已经透彻，完全高过我们。

艾： 您自己和王阳明也有很多类似的地方。他也是好像先深入佛学，以后出来。他也是一个活动者，在社会上实行、实践，也不是专门写东西、讲学问的。所以我自己觉得您和他有很多类似的地方。

梁： 可是就阳明的生命说，他不是普通人了，已经不是普通人了。可是我现在还是一个普通人。

艾： 您觉得您还是一个普通人吗？

梁： 普通人。我可能比其他的普通人不同的一点的，就是我好像望见了，远远地看到了，看到了什么呢？看到了王阳明，看到了

Yangming, and Confucius. Besides, I cannot see very clearly; its as though I'm looking through a mist, and from a great distance in the mist I see what Confucius is all about, what Wang Yangming is all about. Viewing them at a great distance—my level [of understanding] is only to such a degree as this.

Alitto: But suppose Wang Yangming was right in front of us, and we asked him "Your honor Shouren, are you a sage?" He wouldn't...

Liang: He would not admit to it.

● My own understanding of the cosmos

Alitto: This question involves philosophy. In this ever-changing world, what is eternal truth?[67] That is, is a universal, eternal truth possible? Do you think that an intellectual should...

Liang: In general, a particular body of knowledge explores and pursues truth. That body of knowledge seeks to become universal, to be fundamental [to human understanding]. I think that any scientific discipline pursues the profound. The more it pursues the profound, the more it will pass into the realm of philosophy. So, paying attention to philosophy is helpful in doing science. This is an idea of mine.

Alitto: That is to say, each society has its own ideology. Each era has its own ideology. Even science is an ideology produced in a particular era. Some say that it cannot transcend, that even science cannot transcend its temporality or its locality. Is an eternal truth possible?

Liang: I'm afraid that this is a relative term. I can't understand Einstein sufficiently well, because the basis of his scholarship is in the natural sciences, in mathematics and in mechanics. But his worldview, his Theory of Relativity touches upon philosophy; it slips into the realm of philosophy. I very much like his Theory of Relativity and feel that it corroborates my own understanding of the cosmos. To be more specific, it is commonly thought that space is horizontal, while time is vertical. But I think this is just a vulgar view, and does not get to the cosmological truth.

The horizontal is space, and the vertical is time. It's really not this way. Space and time are joined together. Moreover, there is space within time. The cosmos is in flux, infinitely varying, and is endless. Anyone who has any

孔子。我是望到，远远地望到，并且还不能很清楚地看见，好像天有雾，在雾中远远地看见了孔子是怎么回事、王阳明是怎么回事，远远地看见。我的程度只是这么一个程度。

艾：不过假设王阳明就在我们面前，我们问他："守仁公，您是不是一个圣人？"那他也不会……

梁：他也不会承认。

- **我的宇宙观**

艾：这个问题牵扯到哲学。在这个多变的世界上，什么才是永恒的真理？就是获得一些普遍的、永恒真理是可能的吗？您认为作为一个知识分子应该……

梁：大概一种学问往深里去探讨、去追究，它都要走入普遍性，走入根本。我以为任何一门科学，往深里追求，越追求，越追求，它就会到哲学里头去，所以留心一下哲学，是对搞科学有帮助的。我有这么一个意思。

艾：就是说，每一个社会有每一个社会的意识形态，每一个时代有每一个时代的意识形态，连科学也是在一个时代里发生的一种意识形态。有的人说，不能超越，连科学也不能超脱它的时代性、地方性。永恒的真理到底可能吗？

梁：恐怕是一个相对比较的话吧。我不大能够懂这个爱因斯坦的学问，因为他的学问基础是在自然科学——在数学、在力学。可是他的宇宙观，他讲相对论也就谈到了哲学了，跑到了哲学里头去了。他那个相对论我倒是很喜欢，觉得我所对宇宙的了解，可以从他那里找到一种印证。更具体地说，说得明白一点，对宇宙的认识或看法，普通总是觉得横的是空间，纵的是上下古今，普通都是这样分开来说。可是我觉得这是一个世俗之见，没有得到宇宙的真理。

横的是空间，纵的一个是时间——不是这样的，时空是合起来的，而且是空在时之内，空间在时间内。宇宙就是一个

understanding of human life would feel that the cosmos is infinitely in constant flux, that one is in the mist of this flux, and that one cannot be separated from it. From heaven above to the earth below, all things in nature are one—in the old Chinese phrase, "the myriad things of nature are one body." This one thing is in flux; it varies infinitely. That is to say, time and space cannot be separated. Space is part of time. Space and time are not two entities.

Aren't there a lot of sayings from Confucius in *The Analects*? In one section: "The master was on the river bank"—Confucius was on a riverbank—and he said, "It passes on just like this, never ceasing day or night!"[68] It was referring to the flow of the water. He saw the water flowing and said, "It passes on just like this, never ceasing day or night!" Unceasing flowing like this day and night. This was a sigh. This sigh was not in reference to the water flowing before him, but rather it referred to the entirety of the cosmos, the entirety of human life, the entirety of human history. This statement has profound significance, but people are fully occupied with the affairs of the moment, busy with the affairs of life. They have no time; they are too busy, they are busy the entire day dealing with their environments and thus lack a deep understanding [of this which I have just outlined].

My meaning, my informal interpretation is: I feel that Einstein, through the discipline of physics, gained an insight, an understanding of the broader cosmos. He did not separate time and space; he held that they were the same thing and that there was space in time. The entirety of the cosmos is in flux like this; we ourselves are also in flux.[69] We don't want to take too narrow or too close a view of the world. We should take the broad view of things. Taking the broad view enables us to be broad-minded, and see that anxiety about things is of no use; the broad view tells us not to always get confused amidst the gamut of human emotions. The ancients had this saying, "Head upwards looking beyond the farthest heavens, taking the broad view..." I forget what follows. Yesterday didn't I write the eight characters: *kuorandagong, wulaishunying* (with an all-encompassing, empty and impartial mind, taking things as they come)?

I feel that we should be that way, not be tossed and confused by the gamut of emotions, but transcend these; we should also not hold on to the illusions [of existence of self and the world].

● My views on death

Alitto: Mr. Liang, you are very old and wise. Do you have any views on death?

变化流行，一点也不能停住，凡是对人生、对生命真有体会，他就会感觉到宇宙是一个变化流行，自己也是在变化流行之中，自己跟这个变化流行不可分。天地上下，天地万物——按中国老话说，天地万物一体，是一回事。这个一回事呢，它是一个变化流行的，也就是刚才说的不要把空间跟时间分开，空间是在时间之内，空间、时间不是两回事。

《论语》那个书不是记载着孔子的很多话吗？《论语》上有那么一章："子在川上"——孔子在河边上，说"逝者如斯夫，不舍昼夜"——逝就是水流，他看见水流，"逝者如斯夫，不舍昼夜"，昼夜不停地这么样流，这样一个叹息。这个叹息不是就是说他眼前看见的水，而是说整个的宇宙，整个的人生，整个的人类历史。这个话意义很深，可是人都忙于眼前的事情，忙于生活上的事情，没有时间啊，太忙啦，终日忙着应付，应付环境，缺乏深的体会。

我的意思、我的随便的一个看法吧，我觉得爱因斯坦他从物理，他对广大的宇宙还是有所悟、有所了解，他不把时空分开，空、时是一回事，空在时中。整个宇宙的变化是如此，我们自己一个人也是在变化中，不要看得太短，不要看得太近，要放眼来看，放眼来看心胸就可以开大，什么事情不用着急，不要常常颠倒在喜怒哀乐之中。好像古人有那么一句话，叫做"昂首天外，放眼……"，什么东西我忘记了。昨天不是我写了八个字："廓然大公，物来顺应"，我觉得是要那个样子，不要颠倒于喜怒哀乐之中，超过这些，不要执着。

• 我怎么看待死亡

艾： 梁先生是年纪很大了，而且具有智慧的人，您现在对人的死亡有没有见解？

Liang: I have already said, death does not mean complete extinction. It is not what most people think, that death is the end of everything. Didn't I use the eight-character phrase: *xiangsixiangxu, feiduanfeichang*?—Life, divided into endless instants, is at best similar and continuous; the meaning of life is neither interrupted nor persistent. Life is basically like this. The ego or me of today is similar to the ego or me of yesterday. The me of right now and the me of one minute ago are also similar. And that's all there is to it. They are not the same. But there is no break, no discontinuity. It's not permanent. It's not the same thing. All humans are like this; all sentient beings are like this. So, this is my view of death.

Alitto: People nevertheless always fear death. People always fear...

Liang: They don't want to die. Actually there is no need for fear. There is no need to hope for immortality.

Alitto: No hope for immortality?

Liang: No hope for long life. It is best to follow the natural course. Let nature take its course. That is having "an all-encompassing, empty and impartial mind."

● Looking back on my life: the plainer, the better

Alitto: When I came here in 1973, I didn't have the opportunity to see you. I did go look at Jishuitan. The last sentence of my book is, "Under these circumstances, what would be his thoughts?" That is to say, you are of great age, your friends from the old days have passed away, but you still retain your self-respect, and you have grandchildren. If you took a walk by Jishuitan, what would you think of?... What reflections do you have looking back on your whole life?

Liang: I wouldn't have any. Let me tell you this. You understand me. I am a Buddhist. Buddhists view everything very flatly. There are no important problems, nothing is of consequence. In my case, I have always made my mood as flat and plain as possible; the plainer, the better. My life was also like this. For example, I drink plain water, not tea. I feel that tea is a bit of a stimulant and so I feel that it is better not to drink tea. Just plain boiled water is fine. My diet is light. I don't eat meat and things that people regard as delicious; moreover, I eat very little. I pay no attention to taste and flavor. A state in which all aspects of life are dull and flat is best for me. So, if you ask me what reflections I have, I have nothing.

梁：我曾经说过，死亡不会断灭，不像有些个人就以为死了就完了，没有这个事情。我不是说了八个字："相似相续，非断非常"？生命本来就是今天的我跟昨天的我相似就是了，前一分钟的我跟后一分钟的我相似就是了，早已不是一回事，这就叫"相似相续"，连续下来，不会断——非断，非常——常是恒常，不是一回事，早已不是一回事。人都是如此，生命都是如此，那我也还是如此。

艾：人总是怕死嘛，人总是怕……

梁：不愿意死。其实不需要怕，不需要希望长生。

艾：也不需要希望长生?

梁：不需要希望长生，任其自然，因为任其自然才是"廓然大公"。

- **回顾一生：越平淡越好**

艾：1973 年我来的时候，没有机会看见您，积水潭我是去看了——在我那本书中最后一句话就是："在这种情形之下，梁先生会在想什么？"就是说您年纪很大了，当您的朋友都去世了，可是您还有以前的自尊心，有孙子，您假如是在积水潭那边散散步，会想到什么？……回想过去的一切，您会有什么感想啊?

梁：也没有什么。我要说的一句话，你了解我，我是一个佛教徒，佛教徒他把什么事情都看得很轻，没有什么重大的问题，什么都没有什么。再说到我自己，我总是把我的心情放得平平淡淡，越平淡越好。我的生活也就是如此。比如我喝白水，不大喝茶。我觉得茶，它有点兴奋性，我觉得不要喝茶好，给我白开水的好。我吃饮食，我要吃清淡的，一切肉类，人家认为好吃的东西我都不要吃，并且我吃得还很少，不注意滋味、口味。生活里无论哪一个方面，都是平平淡淡最好。所以你问我有什么感想，我没有什么。

Notes

1 Here Liang says outright what I suggested in my first article on him, that he saw himself as acting in a messianic role of Bodhisattva. Like many of the first generation of radical reformers—Kang Youwei, Liang Qichao, Tan Sitong and, to some degree, Zhang Taiyan, all of whom had a deep and abiding interest in Buddhism—he saw his activist role in society and politics as Bodhisattva-like.

2 Throughout these interviews, Mr. Liang maintained that he is simultaneously a Buddhist, Confucian, Daoist, Marxist, Vitalist (à la Bergson), and who also has a great respect for Christianity. In my view, this is part of a long tradition of eclecticism in Chinese thought, one of the first more important examples being the Han Dynasty "National Doctrine" (国教), which was Dong Zhongshu's eclectic mixture of Confucian teachings, Legalist teachings, Daoism, and cosmologies derived from the *Book of Changes* and folk religion. At the end of the Han, the earliest folk religious text we have, the *Taipingjing* (《太平经》) is similarly eclectic in composition, even including Moist (墨子) elements. In my view, this is a traditional attitude of Chinese intellectuals, even into the twentieth century. Liang's friend, Li Dazhao, for instance, was simultaneously a French-style Vitalist and a nationalist while he was embracing Communist internationalism. Often Westerners do not understand this attitude, and take it to be self-contradictory.

3 In the West, "Chan" (禅) is almost universally known in the Japanese reading of the word "Zen," because the Japanese version made the biggest impact in Western popular culture, especially in the 1950s.

4 *Daśabhūmi*—the "ten stages" in the fifty-two sections of the development of a Bodhisattva into a Buddha. The first of these is worldly wisdom, which has not been "fertilized" by Truth, and so is called the "dry" wisdom stage (干慧地). Each of the ten stages is connected with each of the ten "*pāramitās*," which Mr. Liang proceeds to discuss next.

5 *Pratyeka*-Buddhahood (辟支佛), by which only the "dead ashes" of the past is left. At this stage, one understands the twelve *nidānas*, or chain of causation, and so attains complete wisdom.

6 佛地。The point at which the Bodhisattva has arrived at highest enlightenment and is just about to become a Buddha.

7 Throughout his life and in all that he said and wrote, Mr. Liang stressed practice (praxis) and practicality (effectiveness). This central strand of his thought is obvious even in his discussion of Buddhism, which most people have nothing to do with either. Mr. Liang's personality, as exemplified by his actions throughout his life to the very end, was itself a manifestation of these points of emphasis. He himself used the Chinese phrase "表里如一" (unity of inner feelings and outer

action) to describe himself later in this day's interview. That is, he would translate any idea he had into action in the real world. His personal actions were always like this (as shown by the episode of his conduct during the "Criticize Lin Biao and Criticize Confucius" Campaign discussed below), and his public actions, such as the way in which the entire Rural Reconstruction Movement was designed specifically to express his cultural philosophy.

8 *The Analects* 7.21: The master did not speak of extraordinary things, feats of strength, disorder, and spiritual beings. (《论语·述而篇第七》，二十一章：子不语怪、力、乱、神。)

9 I asked Mr. Liang this question several times during these interviews as well as those conducted later in 1984. The only mistake he admitted to, in his vast production of writings over many decades, is this confusion of "intuition" and "instinct."

10 In many respects, Mr. Liang's Rural Reconstruction Movement was a twentieth century version of the Taizhou school, of which Wang Xinzhai (Wang Gen) was the leader. Liang hoped that through education, the masses would all become enthusiastic in seeking Sagehood. This was precisely what Wang Gen and the Taizhou school was all about. Wang Yangming, after all, was a high-ranking official. His student Wang Gen was a commoner who, like Liang, had a sense of mission to lead a social movement, not a political one. And like Wang Gen, Liang again and again refused to serve as an official.

11 This is Cheng Hao's (程颢) phrase that appears in his "Letter on Fixing One's Nature" (《定性书》). It appears in the writings of other important Neo-Confucians, such as Zhu Xi and Wang Yangming. The original passage is: A general rule of the cosmos is that its mind permeates all things, even though it itself has no mind. It is a rule of the Sage that his emotions are in accord with all things in the universe, even though he himself has no emotions. Therefore, the Superior Man has an all-encompassing, empty and impartial mind, taking things as they come. (夫天地之常，以其心普万物而无心；圣人之常，以其情顺万物而无情。故君子之学，莫若廓然而大公，物来而顺应。) I have used the more colloquial English phrase "take things as they come" rather than the more accurate but stilted possibilities of "react appropriately to the various phenomena as they present themselves," or "harmoniously react to things as they come." Mr. Liang thought highly of the phrase, and used it often. He also assessed Cheng Hao as the only Song Dynasty thinker who really understood Confucianism.

12 Throughout his life, Mr. Liang refused to accept the designation "scholar." Ironically, the word "scholar" (学者) appears in almost everything published about him in Chinese. I think that he did this, not out of modesty. On the other hand, the title "thinker" he always readily accepted (along with "Confucian," "Buddhist," "Marxist," and so on). In English, of course, there is no comparison between the two designations. Only one scholar or academic in perhaps hundreds of

thousands would merit the title "thinker." To me, though, even the term "thinker" does not begin to do him justice. Perhaps alone in the twentieth century, he had two exceedingly rare qualities. He was both a genuine thinker and a man of action, and his actions were always determined by what he thought.

[13] I think that previously it had been widely speculated that Yuan Shikai's agents had assassinated him. In fact, the affair turns out to be a farcical tragedy. As Huang had indeed written an ambiguous article backing Yuan Shikai's imperial plans, he was somehow considered by Sun Yat-sen's Revolutionary Party to be on Yuan's side. So, Huang fled to San Francisco to escape from Yuan's wrath, and was shot to death by the Revolutionary Party assassin because he was considered Yuan's backer. The order, carried out on Christmas night, came down from Sun himself.

[14] Astonishing as it seems today, it was solely on the basis of this essay that Cai appointed Liang as professor at Peking University. Liang, of course, had never even attended the university, much less had specialized academic training in Indian thought.

[15] One of Gu Hongming's granddaughters taught at the International Chinese Language Program in Taipei (国际华语研习所, colloquially known as the Stanford Center), and I got to know her very well. Later she went to California to teach Chinese, where she remained. I had asked her if there were any family records, papers or artifacts left from Mr. Gu, but she said that it had all been lost. He was born, raised and educated outside of China. The great irony is that, although he held a position for a time in Zhang Zhidong's (张之洞) staff, he had mastered several European languages before learning Chinese. His important writings were in English. Mr. Gu was unique among Chinese intellectuals in the twentieth century in that he was far more thoroughly and completely culturally conservative than any other. W. Somerset Maugham's sketch of Gu ("The Philosopher") forms the center of his book *On a Chinese Screen* (1922).

[16] Liang was referring, very vaguely, to the original Anhui clique general Zheng Shiqi (郑士奇) who had been appointed by the Zhili clique in 1923 to rule Shandong. In 1925, as a result of the Second Zhili-Fengtian War in late 1924, the Fengtian clique general Zhang Zongchang (张宗昌) became the ruler of Shandong. Curiously, Liang does not mention the Fengtian clique in this statement, even though it was the victory of Fengtian over Zhili that was responsible for the changed political situation in Shandong and for the end of Liang's school there. The Anhui clique was not involved, as it was the Zhili clique that had appointed Zheng Shiqi.

[17] The goal of these schools cum government agencies was nothing less than the complete transformation of the nature of government, a very profound goal indeed. The institutions of local school and local government were to meld into one, with the local government administrators relating to the populace in a teacher-student relationship. In Chinese society, education always carried with it

a certain moral content. So, the local school teachers were to serve as quasi-clergy as well. The ideal was the "schoolification of society" (社会学校化). What could be more profound a goal for local government than that!

[18] The Heze area was "wilder" than Zouping, with more bandits and crimes. Sun's first task (which he made his primary task) was to establish law and order, and so he concentrated his efforts on training militia.

[19] Mr. Liang's major goals in rural reconstruction were indeed to "organize" the countryside and diffuse modern technology there. Practically every political figure during the Republic did indeed complain that China was, as Sun Yat-sen put it, "a sheet of loose sand." Sun, and many others, complained that Chinese society was suffering not from a lack of "liberty," but from a surfeit of it. Everyone, then, hoped to transform the sand into cement, but the question was how. In the late Qing, moreover, a completely new concept appeared—mobilization. It appeared simultaneously with the idea of a modern nation to which its citizens owe loyalty. Therefore, underneath the organization question was the perceived need for mobilization. All figures were also interested in diffusing modern technologies throughout rural society. Liang's Rural Reconstruction Movement, however, had one other goal that these other leaders and movements did not include and, by their nature, could not include. It was a cultural revival that was to preserve Chinese cultural values—epitomized in his term "reason" (理性). Liang emphasized the idea that rural reconstruction must not be a political movement, but rather a grass-roots cultural movement. He had concluded by the late 1920s that governmental power was inherently like "an iron hook," and society was like a bean curd. No matter what good intentions the iron hook might possess, as soon as it goes to "help" the bean curd, it destroys it. "As soon as you take power, you are separated from society... No matter if even a sage took power, it would not work." *Theory of Rural Reconstruction* (《乡村建设理论》), 1937, p. 319. He never mentioned this special goal of rural reconstruction during these interviews.

[20] Liang Peishu (梁培恕).

[21] Intellectually, Liang seemed to have been on the same wave length as Tao. Tao's famous reversing of the order of the characters of his name (from Zhixing to Xingzhi) is the meaning necessary here. It was quite in line with Liang's own emphasis on practice and "life-changing" knowledge. Aside from Liang's own rural work style having commonalities with Tao's, Liang also admired his self-sacrificing personal character. Of course, they also shared an antipathy to Chiang Kai-shek.

[22] This is in reference to the Fujian Incident (闽变) of November 1933. As they were his close friends, Liang states that Chen Mingshu and Li Jishen founded this government (actually a revolt against the Nanjing National Government). Other leaders in the 19th Route army, such as Cai Tingkai (蔡廷锴) and Jiang Guangnai (蒋光鼐) were also in volved. The major motivation of the revolt was antipathy

toward Chiang Kai-shek, especially toward his policy of appeasement toward Japan. The promised aid from the Jiangxi Soviet was not forthcoming and this led to the collapse of the enterprise, which began in January of 1934. Xu Minghong played a crucial role in this incident.

[23] I was completely amazed at Mr. Liang's capacity to summarize these meetings with Mao with such accuracy. This description and analysis was exactly the same as he had recorded just a few months after the event. I myself had observed that he must have made his point very well, because shortly after this, Mao began stressing "the special, distinctive features of Chinese society," history, and culture.

[24] This is indeed true. Liang had always argued that until the customs, habits and attitudes of the masses changed, constitutional government would be a mere superficial copy of a foreign institution that would definitely fail. "China has not Reached a Stage where It can Have a Successful Constitution." (《中国此刻尚不到有宪法成功的时候》) Jan. 4, 1934, *Dagongbao* (《大公报》). He continued this argument after the war as well. It is not a little ironic that Liang, who created and, for a time, led the only truly liberal democratic political force in that period in China, the last incarnation being the Democratic League (民主同盟), had little faith that liberal democracy could work in China.

[25] At Mao's request (order?) Liang returned to Beijing from Beibei, Sichuan, in January, 1950.

[26] These two events were separated by several years. Zhang was Fu Zuoyi's secret representative in the surrender negotiations in 1948. He wasn't accused of "having illicit relations with a foreign country" until 1951. He was arrested in January of 1968 (relatively late), sent to the famed Qincheng (秦城) prison for high level political prisoners, where he died in 1973.

[27] It was almost certainly 1974, as the campaign started in the latter part of 1973. Criticism of Confucius was, of course, meant to be criticism of Premier Zhou Enlai, and so the Confucian hero, the Duke of Zhou, was added to the list, a clear pun on the surname Zhou.

[28] Newspaper reports outside of China included Liang's quotation of this *Confucian Analects*.

[29] Despite Liang's founding of the non-Nationalist non-Communist democratic political group during the war, and despite his leading it precisely during its most significant period, 1947, he is mentioned less than Zhang Junmai or even Luo Longji in the Western language historical scholarship of the period. Obviously, these latter figures promoted themselves more into the limelight than Liang did. It is also often forgotten how active Liang was as the intermediary not only between the two major Chinese political parties, but also between them and George Marshall. For his part, Marshall greatly admired Liang and the group

of liberal democratic intellectuals he led. Indeed, in Marshall's mind, the ideal solution to the conflict between the Nationalists and the Communists was to have Liang's group, which he described as "a fine group of men," emerge as an important political force that might lead China to democracy.

30 Mr. Liang's point here is that he was out of communication with Li Jishen in Guangzhou. This would explain why Mr. Li didn't contact him before reporting to the Nanjing National Government that Mr. Liang was a part of the Guangdong Provincial Government.

31 Never having held an official post was something of which Mr. Liang was extremely proud. He mentioned it several times in his writing, and mentioned it to me during these interviews and those a few years later.

32 Actually, Liang had devoted himself to national affairs, at least part-time, for his entire adult life. His first employment in 1917 was a critically important post in a national ministry. The next year he published a quasi-political pamphlet, "If We do not Take Action, What will Happen to the People?" (吾曹不出，如苍生何？) Even during the 1920s and 1930s, Liang continued to have contact with political power-holders, and sought to influence their conduct and national affairs. During the war and after, of course, he devoted himself to political tasks, stopping only after he retired as leader of the Democratic League in late 1946.

33 This is one of many remarks that Liang made to me about Christianity. He tended to think highly of it because pious Christians tended to be honest, decent people who were altruistic.

34 Referring to *Confucius as a Reformer* (《孔子改制考》), 1898.

35 Lin Zaiping was a colleague of Liang's at Peking University with whom, along with Xiong Shili, he often engaged in philosophical discussion. Xiong also seems to have been influenced by Lin. Liang's assessment of Lin, as was often the case when he assessed historical figures, focused more on personal character than on intellectual prowess. Foreign historians have ignored Lin, so not much is known about him abroad.

36 Liang always seemed to be seeking total control over the self, and he admired anyone who seemed to have achieved it. Both of these men, Lin and Wu, were able to fall asleep at will. As sleep was always one aspect of his life over which he never had control, he was exceedingly impressed by those who had this "talent." Probably because Mr. Liang's mind was always hyperactive, he had difficulty with sleep throughout his life, beginning at a young age. As I reminded him a few minutes after this, he had been greatly impressed by a Hypnotism performance he saw in 1912. He took the performance as further evidence of the power of the mind over the body. It obviously made a powerful impression, as he recalled it decades later and mentioned it in his writings.

[37] Alone among the various people Liang admired, Mr. Wu Yongbo (Wu Guanqi) seems to be the only one who apparently left no mark on history and historical scholarship. I suspect that the biography Mr. Liang wrote for him is the only thing published about him.

[38] *The Analects* 15.6 (《论语・卫灵公篇第十五》, 六章).

[39] Once again, it appears that every one of Liang's early friends, acquaintances, family, family friends—as well as everyone he admired—were anti-Yuan Shikai. He mentions this kind of opposition to Yuan again and again as a manifestation of integrity and nobility. At the time of Yuan's attempt to reestablish the monarchy (with himself as the monarch), Liang was just twenty years old, in Beijing, and had just become an active member of society. After the Republican Revolution itself, the Monarchist Movement was the first major political crisis he encountered. It seemed to have left a lasting impression.

[40] Ma Yifu (1883-1967) was educated in Europe, America, and Japan, and in fact authored works on the history of European literature. He was known primarily, however, as a master of Chinese, especially Confucian philosophy. Mr. Ma was also a noted seal and woodblock carver. As Mr. Ma was a cloistered academic, one assumes that it was his scholarship, not his social or political activities, that Liang admired so much.

[41] Before I published my biography of Liang, *The Last Confucian*, most foreign scholars who had even heard of him, considered him to be the very epitome of a "conservative" in all senses of the word.

[42] It was at the time of the interviews that all things Western acquired a certain panache among the young, who highly prizes things like American jeans. (Ironically, almost all "American jeans" are now made in China, along with most other "American" products.) There was, for instance, a fad of wearing Hong Kong-made sunglasses with the brand sticker still on the lenses to prove they were an "authentic" foreign product.

[43] From *Eastern and Western Cultures and Their Philosophies* onward, Liang's attitude toward preservation of Chinese culture was different from most other cultural conservatives in that he did not argue or try to persuade others of Chinese culture's merits. Throughout his life, he seemed to have an unflappable self-confidence that, even though some of the outer accoutrements of traditional culture might be lost, there was no possibility that the core would disappear. He always stressed that the future world culture that would be a form of Chinese culture was going to come about, not because the world's people were going to be "persuaded" of the superiority of Chinese culture, but because the "objective realities" in the evolving world would bring about an emergence of it by a process not dissimilar to biological evolution. Depending upon how one interprets *The Analects* 9.5 (《论语・子罕篇第九》, 五章), there might or might not be an irony

in this. Liang had made allusion to this passage after he had escaped from the Japanese in Hong Kong at the end of 1941. In this passage, there is no question that Confucius expresses a cool self-confidence in the continuity of Chinese culture, and yet he (Confucius) might have a crucial role in this continuity: When Confucius was in jeopardy in Kuang, he said: "Since King Wen of the Zhou is now dead, doesn't the mission of culture fall upon me? If Heaven were going to destroy this culture, a mortal like myself would not have been allowed to know about [this culture]. So, if Heaven is not going to destroy this culture, what can these Kuang men do to it?" (子畏于匡，曰："文王既没，文不在兹乎？天之将丧斯文也，后死者不得与于斯文也；天之未丧斯文也，匡人其如予何?") When the Japanese invaded Hong Kong on December 25, 1941, Liang was there running the public organ of the predecessor to the Democratic League, the newspaper *Guangmingbao* (《光明报》).

[44] *The Mencius*, Lilou II, 19. (《孟子・离娄章句下》，十九章). The original sentence: Mencius said, "That whereby man differs from the lower animals is but small. The mass of people cast it away, while superior men preserve it. Shun clearly understood the multitude of things, and closely observed the relations of humanity. He walked along the path of benevolence and righteousness; he did not need to pursue benevolence and righteousness." 孟子曰："人之所以异于禽兽者几希，庶民去之，君子存之。舜明于庶物，察于人伦，由仁义行，非行仁义也。"

[45] Referring to *The Mencius*, Gaozi I, 8 (《孟子・告子章句上》，八章).

[46] From the context, it is clear that "Trend toward Diversification," or "The Pluralism Trend," or "Trend toward Pluralism" (多元化趋势) is the name of a publication by Russell, because "published" follows the reference. I, however, could find no publications by Russell with a title that resembles this. Perhaps Mr. Liang read a Chinese translation with such a title, or misremembered the title, but I do not know to which publication this title refers.

[47] This is a reference to *The Mencius*: "Men's mouths agree in having the same relishes; their ears agree in enjoying the same sounds; their eyes agree in recognizing the same beauty—shall their minds alone be without that which they similarly approve? What is it then of which they similarly approve? It is, I say, the principles of our nature, and the determinations of righteousness. The sages only apprehended beforehand that of which my mind approves along with other men. Therefore the principles of our nature and the determinations of righteousness are agreeable to my mind, just as the flesh of grass and grain-fed animals is agreeable to my mouth." (口之于味也，有同耆焉；耳之于声也，有同听焉；目之于色也，有同美焉。至于心，独无所同然乎？ 心之所同然者何也？谓理也，义也。圣人先得我心之所同然耳。故理义之悦我心，犹刍豢之悦我口。) In the end, Liang's insistence of the existence of a universal morality comes back to this argument by Mencius. As I noted above, it is not dissimilar to his first pronouncement on the

subject in *Eastern and Western Cultures and Their Philosophies*, in which he claims a universal moral sense rooted in human biology (à la Kropotkin).

48 Of course, the opposite argument might be made as well: The closer to the corporeal, the less chance of individuation. Animals' corporeally based likes and dislikes are far more similar to each other than humans' likes and dislikes are to each other. Likes and dislikes more deeply rooted in physiology (simple pleasure and pain) can be argued to be more similar. Liang argues that those common properties that are rooted in the corporeal provide for more individuation. He says that likes and dislikes arising from intellect, ratiocination and calculation are more likely to be similar. Of course, if he is locating the source of universal morality in human biology (as he did much earlier in *Eastern and Western Cultures and Their Philosophies*), this argument makes some sense. It was why the Anarchist Kropotkin appealed to him so much, and why in the same book he equated instinct with intuition.

49 This is one of the many times I tried to have Mr. Liang speak to the question of universal values and the source of morality. In each case, he proceeds from Mencius' argument that values are inherent in human biology.

50 In English, of course, "reason" or "rationality" does not connote anything like what Liang is suggesting. As I note later, some culturally conservative Western intellectuals referred to this "moral sense" that Liang speaks of by other terms. For example, Cardinal Henry Newman, a prominent nineteenth century thinker, used the term "illative sense." It means what Liang's "rationality" (理性) means. One such Western intellectual did indeed use the English term "rationality" exactly the way Liang did. That was Samuel Taylor Coleridge.

51 What follows is a summary of Liang's argument in *Eastern and Western Cultures and Their Philosophies*. He does not alter the original argument at all, but insists still that human societies by their very nature will evolve a kind of Chinese culture. He said the same thing about the inevitability of socialism for all human societies, so in his mind, there is a parallel between the two entities—Chinese culture and socialism.

52 I refer here, in a very general way, to Max Weber's use of the term "rationalization" or "intellectualization" (exactly as in the Chinese 理智化). In Weber's theory, intellectualization produced modern scientific and technological knowledge; in his book *Eastern and Western Cultures and Their Philosophies*, Liang states precisely this same theory. That is, one of the two strongly developed aspects of Western civilization is "intellect" (理智), while Chinese civilization developed "intuition." Western intellect produces modern science and technology. Along with intellectualization/rationalization, Weber's vision of the process of modernization was centered on "calculation." (Modern capitalism and bureaucracy are based on the assumption that all things can be mastered by calculation, i.e., the intellect.) Weber's implied definition of modernization, at least in my reading, was that it entailed a process whereby all social and economic institutions and processes

were made more efficient for the overall end of world mastery. Value-oriented organizations and processes transform into goal-oriented institutions and actions. Thus, the supreme value becomes efficiency, that is, "means." I agree with certain postmodern critics of modernization who see this process as the heart of the modern problem. Lyotard, for example, terms efficiency (maximum output for minimum input) "performativity," and ascribes to it much of the evil in human life. All this efficiency and calculability in political, social, and economic spheres was not possible without a change of values in ethics, religion, psychology, and culture. The ethos of efficiency (rationality) penetrates into every aspect of life. Each area of human activity has different values and ultimate ends, the overall result being that there are a plurality of values and of metanarratives that all seek to answer the same perennial human questions that religion and ethical systems once focused on. The ultimate irony (among many ironies) of the process is that the "means" become universal, while "ends" are fragmented and relativised. This situation itself, then, destroys all ultimate ends and goals. It might be described as the "slow death of God." The only universal values are those biologically based, having to do with survival. Needless to say, I myself do not subscribe to the "Eurocentric" and teleological elements in Weber's theory, which sees Western civilization's unique achievement as modern rationality, a rationality that was destined to spread around the world. Some of his disciples, such as Talcot Parsons, later developed the teleological aspect of his theory to an absurd degree. Weber himself insisted that he was merely describing a situation he observed. He is "guilty," however, of extreme Eurocentrism, in that he saw the process of rationalization/modernization as a unique Western product that would eventually be imported by every society on earth. I myself view the process itself as one that is universally human, not necessarily tied to the geographic area where it first occurred. One hundred years ago, however, it was indeed universally held, most certainly by almost all Chinese intellectuals, to have come about because of certain features of Western civilization, and which endowed Europe with its huge capacity for ruthless world mastery.

[53] That is, for reasons of national pride, certain aspects of the culture are preserved, even though those aspects are no longer part of the mainstream of daily society. Another phenomenon related to this is the commercialization of culture. The Noh drama of Japan is something that almost no one can appreciate, but the Japanese state protected it from the market forces that would have destroyed it. In Europe, a major object of museumification is Christianity, in that the people and governments take great pride in the magnificent churches, and also profit from the tourism these structures attract, but the churches no longer have a central place in the daily life of the people as they once did.

[54] Such a statement does very much separate Liang from mainstream contemporary thought in China and abroad. Foreign academics would take this opinion of women are concerned to be the very epitome of male chauvinism.

[55] By this logic, of course, socialism in China was even more so. In the two decades before World War I, Russia was industrializing very rapidly. Not so in the case of the two decades before 1949 in China. This has now been changed by China's thirty years of rapid economic development and "Socialism with Chinese Characteristics."

[56] This is not the opinion of the majority of historians of modern Russia.

[57] I must say that Liang's picture of the Soviet Union probably came partly from his second son, who was a researcher at the Soviet Union Research Institute attached to the Party Central Committee. The implications of some of these statements, such as this one, are alarming. If, for instance, the U.S.S.R. cannot be considered a socialist country, "from Khrushchev to Brezhnev," then, the Stalinist U.S.S.R. was a socialist country.

[58] Liang was remarkably perceptive, in that this is precisely what happened a few years after he predicted it.

[59] I was struck at how much Liang's views on such matters had been affected by general popular views, and, as such, shockingly naive. He admitted as much. Naturally he knew nothing of international affairs that had not presented by the Chinese media.

[60] Yu Qingtang (1897-1949) was a Columbia University, Teacher's College Ph.D. who had a successful career in academia, and for a time was also involved in the penal system in Jiangsu. She worked in social education, women's education and adult education. Professor Yu also published on rural education, which is probably why she and Mr. Liang were friends. She was the director of the Social Education Bureau in the Department of Education in 1949, but died that year.

[61] This is the second of the first two lines of the poem "A Short Poem Written at the Moment When a Rising River Looked like a Rolling Ocean" (《江上值水如海势聊短述》), which go "I was stubborn by nature and addicted to perfect lines, fought to the death to find words that startle." (为人性僻耽佳句，语不惊人死不休。) Indeed, this would be an accurate assessment of Liang, one which he himself makes. He was "stubborn by nature" by his own admission.

[62] It is this "fault" of Liang's that was partly responsible for his stubborn adherence on his own views, no matter what the cost.

[63] It would appear that Mr. Liang did read some of the various classic colloquial language novels, including those at the end of the Qing Dynasty, but he certainly didn't read much fiction. For the most part, he maintained the orthodox Confucian attitude toward works of fiction—that such things were not quite worthy of the attention of a proper gentleman. Mr. Liang seldom saw films or plays, and seemed to have little patience with them. Mr. Hu Yinghan told me of

an incident that took place in the Zouping County town in the 1930s. An acting troupe performed a contemporary drama. Such an event was exceedingly rare in rural Zouping so apparently most of the rural reconstruction institute students attended. Mr. Liang, however, left early in the play.

64 Kawakami Hajime (1879-1946) was an early member of the Japanese Communist Party, and Marxist scholar. His autobiography (*Jijoden*《自叙传》) was published after his death in 1946. In it, he refers often to Confucius and Chinese Confucian texts, which is perhaps why Liang sought out the book. Although he was a pioneer Marxist scholar in Japan, he still proclaimed throughout the book that his major life priority was spirituality. He had, moreover, an exceedingly eclectic concept of spirituality. It is easy to see why Liang was attracted to him.

65 When he invited me out to a vegetarian restaurant the week after this, Mr. Liang did respond to my toasts in beer with taking a few sips himself. As he said, one eats to satisfy oneself, but one drinks to satisfy others. This is perfectly consistent with his interpretation of the spirit of Chinese culture, which stresses respect for the "other" in a relationship.

66 Mr. Liang had something of a hobby in medicine, as did his father, Liang Ji, who often brewed the medicine for members of the family.

67 This is, of course, the central epistemological question of modern times. I asked this question in several forms throughout these interviews, trying to get Mr. Liang to articulate his view on the question. He answered in several ways, but none sufficient to satisfy me. By 1980, postmodernism began to make itself felt in American academia, and by 1990 it was dominating it. The answer to this question from postmodern or postmodern-like "theory" is relatively direct: "No." As Jean Baudrillard (1929-2007) put it, "The secret of theory is, indeed, that truth doesn't exist."

68 *The Analects* 9.17 (《论语・子罕篇第九》，十七章).

69 Liang had very early seen Einstein as reinforcing ancient truths. In *Eastern and Western Cultures and Their Philosophies*, he claimed that the Theory of Relativity confirmed scientifically the Consciousness-Only Buddhist view of a world in which fundamental reality is manifest in the changing phenomena of successive events acting according to the Law of Cause and Effect (因明). Master Taixu (太虚大师) argued the same thing after Liang did. They were not alone among May Fourth era Chinese intellectuals in claiming that Einstein had proved scientifically their own cosmologies.

编后记

《这个世界会好吗？—— 梁漱溟晚年口述》（双语精选本）以北京“一耽学堂图书室”整理的录音资料和 *Has Man a Future?—Dialogues with the Last Confucian*（外语教学与研究出版社，2010 年 3 月）为底本，精选最能体现梁漱溟先生思想与经历的谈话内容，将原来按时间顺序整理的访谈文本按主题与逻辑顺序重新调整结构，划分为梁漱溟的“思想”、“历史经历与社会交往”以及“品评当年人事”三大部分，并选书中精彩语句作为小标题。编者核实并订正了书中绝大部分人名、地名、事件，为表区分，整理者与编者添加的说明文字用楷体标注。

梁漱溟先生长子梁培宽先生与“一耽学堂图书室”在整理录音、帮助核实文本内容、提供图片资料等方面花费了大量时间与精力，在此特表诚挚谢意！

本书编者

2010 年 9 月

On Nov. 7, 1918, Liang Shuming's father, Liang Ji, encountered his son on his way out. The two spoke of a news report on the war in Europe.

"Has man a future?" asked Liang Ji.

"I believe that the world is going to be better by the day." Shuming responded.

"I hope that will be so," said Liang Ji, and left the house.

Three days later, Liang Ji drowned himself in Jingye Lake.